The Middle of Nowhere

The Middle of Nowhere

Rediscovering Saskatchewan

....

SELECTED AND WITH AN INTRODUCTION BY
DENNIS GRUENDING

FIFTH
HOUSE
PUBLISHERS

SASKATOON & CALGARY

Front cover painting: *How Often at Night*, by William Kurelek, reproduced with permission from The Isaacs Gallery, Toronto, and the Estate of William Kurelek
Map by Brian Smith/Articulate Eye
Cover design by NEXT Communications Inc.

The publisher gratefully acknowledges the support received from the Saskatchewan Arts Board, The Canada Council, and Heritage Canada.

Printed and bound in Canada by Friesens, Altona, MB
96 97 98 99 00 / 5 4 3 2 1

CANADIAN CATALOGUING IN PUBLICATION DATA

Main entry under title:
The middle of nowhere
ISBN 1-895618-68-1

1. Saskatchewan - History. 2. Saskatchewan - Description and travel. I. Gruending, Dennis, 1948–

FC3511.M53 1996   971.24   C95-920195-5
F1072.M53 1996

FIFTH HOUSE LTD.
#201-165-3rd Avenue S   #9-6125-11th Street SE
Saskatoon SK Canada   Calgary AB Canada
S7K 1L8   T2H 2L6

Contents

𝒯HE ℛIVER

Contents

The Promised Land

Contents

The Dry Land

Contents

THE NEW JERUSALEM?

Acknowledgements

THIS PROJECT involved much reading and research. While the task was mostly mine, I wish to thank Heather Wood for diligently locating material in Saskatchewan. My daughters, Maria (12) and Anna (10), also helped in Ottawa. Maria spent numerous Saturdays with me in libraries, helping to find many of the stories chosen for this book. Anna stuffed and addressed envelopes containing letters to potential contributors. My wife and dear companion, Martha Wiebe, supported me unfailingly in this project as she has in all others. It was a pleasure to work with Charlene Dobmeier and her colleagues at Fifth House Publishers.

Map created by Brian Smith/Articulate Eye

To Martha, Maria, and Anna

But when a Saskatchewan man
shakes the dust of the province from his person
and departs for far-off places where the air is warm and the wind
is quiet and there are hills and trees and water on every side,
he finds himself, more often than not, still bound in spirit
to that great and strange and savage land that shaped him . . .

EDWARD McCOURT
Saskatchewan

———————

Introduction

ORBERT WELSH was eighty-six years old and blind when he met Mary Weekes in 1931. Welsh, a Metis, born in 1845, had spent his life as a trader and buffalo hunter, roaming the prairies and parklands. Friends had invited Weekes along to pay a birthday visit to the old man, who lived in Lebret. She found the stories Welsh and his pals told so intriguing that in the following months she returned to sit with him every day, recording on a dictaphone. Her book, *The Last Buffalo Hunter*, was published in 1939, and was soon out of print.

"I found it interesting," Weekes wrote, "to hear these men of the old North-West who spoke, first English, then French, Cree and Sioux, re-live their colourful experiences of long ago." She described Welsh as an uneducated man by contemporary standards, but indicated with respect that he spoke seven languages.

Welsh lived during exciting times, but he was also witness to profound and disturbing change, including the destruction of the once-mighty buffalo herds and the increasingly desperate plight of aboriginal people who had inhabited the plains for over twelve thousand years.

Reading from *The Last Buffalo Hunter*, as you will in this book, you experience these changes through Welsh's eyes. He provides an arresting account of daily life in the old North-West based on his experience as a hunter, trader, and freighter.

Events are described very differently in the writing of Lieutenant William Francis Butler, a man with rank and a formal education. A British military officer, Butler had been involved in the campaign against Louis Riel and the Metis in Manitoba in 1870. Later, he became a kind of one-man royal commission, asked to report on conditions in the western interior, and to do so he completed a demanding six-thousand-kilometre trip from Fort Garry through Fort Carlton, to Rocky Mountain House, then back again. Butler's recommendations to the Canadian government included organizing a police force and placing Indians on reserves. He wrote a book about his journey and called it *The Great Lone Land*, in which he compared the prairies and their "vast expanses of grass," with the "great ocean itself."

While Butler's prose is accomplished and poetic, it is interesting that he describes the western interior as a "lone" land. In the fur-trade era, Europeans frequently depicted the region as an empty, dangerous, and forbidding place. This idea of a lone land is the first of the great mythologies about the western interior of Canada.

Europeans believed they had discovered it, that it was an empty and lonely place before they arrived bringing civilization and order. Butler may have been enamoured with the land and its aboriginal inhabitants, but he had an unquestioned belief in the British Empire, in progress, and what he perceived as a great civilizing project.

In fact, the North-West was alive with people, languages, and interests, a place big enough for everyone. But it would not last. Butler's recommendation for a police force came to pass with the organizing of the North-West Mounted Police in 1873. By that time the process of treaty making with the Indians had begun as well. Alexander Morris, backed by members of the new force, negotiated Treaty Four at Fort Qu'Appelle in 1874, and Treaty Six at Fort Carlton in 1876.

Some chiefs, notably Big Bear and Poundmaker, held out as long as possible. They saw the future more clearly than most and understood that treaties spelled the end of their freedom and their way of life. Eventually, starving and dispirited, those bands selected reserves as well.

After the treaties and the defeat of the Metis, Butler's lone land became the mythological promised land. Calgary-based historian Douglas Owram describes how "the image of the west was transformed in Canadian writings from a semi-Arctic wilderness to a fertile garden well adapted to agricultural pursuits."

Hundreds of thousands of settlers poured into the region in the late 1800s and early 1900s. This period lies at the heart of the Saskatchewan myth for a great number of people. Our grandparents or great-grandparents came here as homesteaders, and for many, this is Saskatchewan's golden age, a time of hardship and courage, hope and community.

Most often the story of agricultural settlement is portrayed as a victory over nature and the elements. It is also a tale told almost exclusively from the male perspective. But there are notable exceptions.

Georgina Binnie-Clarke was a feminist and activist who came to the Fort Qu'Appelle area early in the century to prove that a woman could manage a farm on her own. Her experiences are recounted in *Wheat and Woman*, excerpted here. Binnie-Clarke and other farm women lobbied, without success, to have legislation changed to enable women as well as men access to virtually free land for homesteads. The pioneering story, although central to our mythology, must be approached with caution. Many homesteads failed, and a good number of settlers lost everything and left, penniless and disillusioned. The 1930s demonstrated that the image of the province as a green and fertile garden could not be sustained. A good deal of the land should never have been ploughed and broken; Saskatoon failed to outstrip Chicago in population and importance as some local boosters had predicted.

The Depression is an event central to Saskatchewan character and mythology. The myth of the promised land, which had lured settlers to the area, was succeeded by the dry land of the dirty thirties. It was an unsettling time. Hardship, disenchantment, and a sense that the destiny of the province was being decided in Ottawa and in boardrooms far away led to ferment and agitation, first the farm movement, then protest politics, finally the Social Credit and CCF.

Tommy Douglas, elected in 1944, led the first socialist government in North America, a development that stunned the political establishment. Douglas, of course, was a Baptist minister and was fond of quoting from scripture about "building Jerusalem in this green and pleasant land."

This image of the new Jerusalem, of agrarian radicals building progressive movements, undertaking daring social experiments and using cooperation as a tool, is the last great Saskatchewan myth, one filled with the resonance of the Social Gospel. The New Jerusalem, like the promised land and the dry land, is an agrarian myth. In it, the farmer remains central, a noble character besieged by the weather, the bankers, the grain trade, and the railroads.

Ironically, considering all of the hardships endured, the new Jerusalem is also a myth about progress. The Second World War and the years that followed were generally good ones for farmers, and there was a level of prosperity, at least for the white community. But on the farms, machines and technology came to replace people and labour. The depopulation of rural Saskatchewan, which began in earnest during the Depression, continued unabated following the war. My parents had two quarter-sections of land when they married in 1946. They thought this would provide them with a living for the rest of their lives, but they grew poorer with each passing year. It was the same for many others, and one of our central community events became the farm auction sale, as people sold out and moved to the city, or Alberta or British Columbia.

The loss of all of these people and the disaster their leaving spelled for the rural community has coexisted with the powerful mythology and rhetoric of progress. The flip side of this belief in progress is a sentimentality about the past and a way of life that has been lost. This occurs to me when I see the many community histories being written in Saskatchewan. I contributed to one some years ago for my hometown of St. Benedict. The central message in most of these histories is that the past was a much more comfortable place than the present. The future rarely intrudes, perhaps because many people fear there is no future for their communities, under seige by economic forces over which they appear to have little control.

The belief in progress was being questioned as early as the 1950s. These doubts and observations were stated lucidly by writer Wallace Stegner. His family had a homestead near Eastend, Saskatchewan, from 1914 to 1920, but the farm failed, and the Stegners returned to the U.S., where Wallace became an accomplished author, winning the Pulitzer prize.

In the early 1950s Stegner returned briefly to Eastend, which he disguised thinly as the town of Whitemud. He wrote a series of magazine articles later collected in the classic *Wolf Willow*, excerpted here. Stegner wrote that "it is impossible not to believe in progress in a frontier town . . . everybody is there for the new start."

But thirty years after leaving it, Stegner asked some hard questions about Whitemud, and by extension about life in Saskatchewan. "Has Whitemud," he asked, "anything by now that would recommend it as a human habitat?" Stegner was fond of Whitemud, and gentle, but ultimately pessimistic about its future. He looked at his home with an unblinking eye and asked, "Who would want to live here now?"

Stegner was talking about more than Eastend; he was describing the decline of the whole rural mythology. In Saskatchewan, by some time in the 1960s or 1970s, the sustaining myth of the new Jerusalem had lost much of its resonance. Chastened by years in power, the CCF had been transformed from social movement to reigning government. The appeal of the Social Gospel had diminished amid an increasingly secular society. Federally, the prairie populism represented by John Diefenbaker was defeated along with him. There have been attempts by Saskatchewan politicians like Ross Thatcher and Grant Devine to create a new mythology, and a Saskatchewan where the ethic of competition would replace that of cooperation. But the scope and importance of politics itself appears to have declined. There is no shortage of controversy in Saskatchewan—we are defined by the intensity and intelligence of our politics. They remain important, but no longer define us in broader, mythological terms.

While researching this book I have read hundreds of writers and thousands of pages about Saskatchewan. It is difficult to discern a contemporary mythology as great and encompassing as the lone land, the dry land, or the new Jerusalem. Perhaps this is because it often takes time and distance to place events and trends into context. Some of the best writing about agricultural settlement or the Depression, for example, did not occur until well after those events. We await descriptions that will render Saskatchewan's present and future as compelling as its past.

It's worth observing that while ever more of Saskatchewan's people are living in the province's cities, we have created little in the way of an urban mythology. Fiction writer Guy Vanderhaeghe says that prairie writers exhibit an inferiority complex about their cities as places where nothing interesting or important happens. In fact, the term, "the middle of nowhere," seems to rank second only to bad jokes about Moose Jaw when it comes to describing Saskatchewan from beyond the province's borders.

Saskatchewan, of course, is not the middle of nowhere, as the selections in this book attest. As one who has left the province, I am struck by the insight of Edward McCourt when he says that the Saskatchewan person who departs for far-off places is most often "still bound in spirit to that great and strange and savage land that shaped him . . . "

I am grateful to those who, over a period of three hundred years, have left a record of their lives and experiences on our library shelves: fur trader Anthony Henday, Cree chief Thunderchild, the great map maker and travel writer David Thompson, William Butler, Norbert Welsh, James Gray, Wallace Stegner, Maria Campbell, Maggie Siggins, and Sharon Butala, to mention only a few. You will find all of them represented in the pages that follow.

To describe the spirit of a place is an elusive matter, but the essence of the Saskatchewan experience and spirit can be retrieved if one is patient and digs deeply enough. This book is my attempt to do just that, to delve and to dig, and to probe for the heart and soul of Saskatchewan.

The River

This country lasted long with only Indians here,
and then the white man came, and they came with might . . .
In the days that I remember, an Indian would prepare himself
to go on a long and difficult journey.
So must all be ready for this road of life.

CHIEF THUNDERCHILD
Voices of the Plains Cree

The Saskatchewan

MARJORIE WILKINS CAMPBELL

THE INDIANS CALLED IT "KISISKATCHEWAN," the river that flows rapidly. For many years they talked about it to the white men who came in ships to Hudson Bay and by canoe up the rivers and lakes to the east. Down its swift waters they brought peltries to barter for tobacco and brandy or rum, bright beads, and the iron that shoots fire. It was the highway to the great Manitoba, the water of the prairies, and the lake the merry singing Frenchmen called "Ouinniping," the way that led from the plains of the buffalo and the land of many fur-bearing animals. The Indians talked of vast mountains toward the setting sun and a far-off blue water.

Not every white man's ears were open to the sayings of the red men. But some listened. Some, coming to the New World from the Old, dreamed day and night of finding a passage to the Western Sea. Some, also coming to the new land from the old, dreamed of a more immediate and a more personal reward, a fortune from furs. A few combined business with altruism and sought to make the fortune while they were searching for the Pacific Ocean.

Originally it was the French who came up the rivers and lakes by canoe. The English arrived in great white-sailed ships chartered by the group of London traders known since 1670 as the Company of Adventurers Trading into Hudson's Bay, anchoring at their new forts of York, Prince of Wales (now Churchill) and Albany. It was not by accident that the French strung their posts along the routes used by the Indians when bringing furs to the English. The trade was a lucrative one.

Characteristically the English didn't go to seek the Indians and their rich cargoes. They adopted the attitude that "with civility and good usage" the Indians would come to them. The French, on the other hand, troubled themselves to win the loyalty and friendship of the red men. They provided feasts and entertained at the long ceremonial gatherings the Indians loved.

They gave them gifts. To a large extent they lived their kind of life, and they got most of the furs.

With a big investment in the land some Englishmen began to realize that more than civility and fair play was required. Also, some of them saw that the life the French were living close to the Indians was greatly to be preferred to the austere English relationship of master and servant. One such was Henry Kelsey, who may have been more Irish than English from his scant records.

Henry Kelsey had entered the employ of the Hudson's Bay Company as a mere boy, back in 1684. He had seen service along the forts of the bay with the French des Groseilliers and Radisson. According to old company records, he was "a very active lad, delighting much in Indians' company, being never better pleased than when he is travelling with them," a man rare among the Englishmen of his day. He learned to speak the Cree language fluently, and could make his way in Assiniboin, the tongue of the people "who cook on stones." In common with many a Frenchman before him and later, he liked Cree women. To Kelsey it was perfectly natural to travel with the Indians, to go inland with them and persuade them to "work beaver."

The trip from York Factory led along the accustomed route of wide rivers and narrow lakes well known to the Indians who brought furs to the white traders. After many days of travel Kelsey came with them to a wide river with many white rapids, a river which the Indians called Kisiskatchewan. They paddled out into the wide, swift-flowing river and Kelsey made a base camp, calling it Dering's Point, after the then deputy governor of the Hudson's Bay Company. He was the first white man to visit the Saskatchewan. The year was 1691.

Kelsey's canoes were heavily laden and the Indians told him of fine hunting grounds to the south, down toward the land of the Assiniboin (or Sioux). Kelsey, with more wisdom than foresight, decided not to paddle against that mighty current, and cached his heavy cargo, to return for it later. Apparently he spent a pleasant enough year with the Indians. They took him out to the prairies where the men hunted buffalo and the women made pemmican for the winter's food supply. Emulating the French, Kelsey gave the natives gifts with much ceremony. The first trip of a white man to the Saskatchewan, even though it is not certain that he actually travelled on the river, seems to have been mutually satisfactory. He returned to the fort in the spring with a good fleet of Indians, the desired furs, and the news, which must have reached French ears, that the Saskatchewan was indeed a vast river, so vast that it might reach the Western Sea. The English may have heard but they did not heed his news. Much later someone named a lake in his memory.

Pierre Gaultier de Varennes, Sieur de La Vérendrye was a Frenchman with very good ears. La Vérendrye had served France well in New England, and later in Europe where he was wounded at the Battle of Malplaquet in 1709. Because of these services and because he was profoundly interested in the search for the Western Sea he was granted the monopoly of the fur trade in the Northwest and set out from Montreal in June of 1731. Unfortunately for him, however, his government did not see fit to finance his projected explorations and he had to pay his own way, largely from the fur trade with the Indians. His position was far from easy. The two projects, exploration and the development and maintenance of a paying fur trade, did not combine well. La Vérendrye was continually forced to show that he was not neglecting the one for the other. In Montreal the businessmen who had backed the venture were bitter in their accusations, while the good will of the government cooled as the western passage failed to materialize. Truly, his precarious position could not fail to sharpen his ears.

Broadly, the English had established their fur posts to the north along Hudson Bay, while the French strung theirs like beads along the rivers and from Lakes Superior to Winnipeg. Perhaps the trip of young Kelsey was having some effect. Perhaps there were other considerations. But La Vérendrye began to be a little more aware of those English forts which were also fur posts. Spurred, on the one hand, by necessity for curtailing the activities of the English so as to retain his own fur trade and, on the other, by the sharp goading from Montreal and Quebec, La Vérendrye still had his own great desire to discover that western passage. When, after many long and successful exploration trips, he had to return to Montreal to defend his position he left his youngest son, Louis-Joseph, called the Chevalier, in command.

Louis-Joseph was educated to command under such circumstances as prevailed around Lake Winnipeg in the seventeen-forties. As a boy he had been trained in mathematics and drawing so that he could make maps of the country he explored. With his older brother he had made a trip of incredible hardship and daring up the Missouri to where they thought they were within sight of the Rocky Mountains. He had survived a massacre at Fort St. Charles. He had his father's happy faculty for winning the affection of the Indians, and he spoke Cree well. In fact he was an adopted son of the Crees and had wintered with some of them at the lower part of Lake Winnipeg. He knew the land of white water at the mouth of the great river sometimes known as the White Water, sometimes as the Pascoyac, the Saskatchewan.

Winnipeg is a very large lake, the largest in any of the provinces of Canada.

Young La Vérendrye spent much time exploring its low shoreline, especially in the vicinity of those beckoning rapids above the mouth of the river that leads to the west. He explored the rivers and smooth lakes so as to avoid the rapids and founded a fort at the confluence of a small, less-turbulent stream with the Saskatchewan, calling it Fort Bourbon. It was there, in the spring of 1749, that he prepared for the voyage that his father could not then take, but which he, Chevalier Louis-Joseph, would gladly undertake for the honour of the name of La Vérendrye and on behalf of King Louis XV. He had the assurance of the Indians that, with comparatively light loads, they could travel it for many moons' paddling. With high excitement he embarked on his great adventure.

This trip was to be the culmination of all the voyages his father and he and his brothers had taken and had talked about, ever since Louis-Joseph was a child. It was the one voyage, above all others, most likely to bring to the family of La Vérendrye the distinction that their intricate fortunes demanded. The young man thought of the delight with which he should journey east to Montreal, of the scene when he should tell his father of this vast highway to the west.

The river was very wide, the current strong and fast. Paddling against it was slow and laborious work. One must think of the ease with which heavily laden canoes could make their return. One must think, too, of the vast lands to be explored, lands rich with beaver, those darkened with buffalo, of the places where the tribes rode fleet-footed horses and never used canoes. So Louis-Joseph told himself as his men dug paddles into the strong current. He knew now why some Indians called it white water. Like lace it swirled against its low-wooded banks, no dream under the clear summer sky but probably the reality for which he had been born.

The men sang with the strong, digging rhythm of canoe-men pulling against the stream. What a country! What a river! The Crees had brought back copper when they travelled north to the land of the Dogribs. There was game aplenty, moose and fine deer, and fish in the river. Louis-Joseph de La Vérendrye was making the observations which Governor-General La Jonquière would shortly use in his report on the discovery of the Pascoyac, 1749.

"The river [Pascoyac] is the most convenient route by which to pursue the discovery of the western sea from the ease with which you can transfer your effects thither by canoe, get guides there easily and have always the same tribe, Cree, to deal with as far as the height of land, which is not the case by the prairie road. There you encounter different tribes, all enemies, and different languages, causes of hindrance and difficulty which occasioned considerable expense formerly."

If only his father were with him on this route! But he would be next year, or the year after, the son hoped.

Day after day the canoes struggled up the river, their progress not fast because the current was so strong, yet every day a little nearer their objective. La Vérendrye made careful notes and drew his maps. He chose a possible site for a fort on the waterway where the Indians could be prevented from taking their furs to the English at Forts York and Prince of Wales. It was called Pascoyac. Travelling many leagues he finally came upon a great disturbance of the waters where the river divided into two, one branch apparently coming from the west, the other from the southwest. It was the Forks, the spring rendezvous of the Crees, the place where they went to deliberate whether to trade with the English or the French.

With a La Vérendrye on the river, the first white man to voyage even to the Forks, there was no doubt which country would get the bulk of the fur that year.

Louis-Joseph did not go beyond the Forks. Joyfully he headed his canoes downstream, east to Montreal to tell his father the great news of the Saskatchewan.

Henday's Journal

ANTHONY HENDAY

In 1754, five years after Louis-Joseph de La Vérendrye's trip to the forks of the Saskatchewan, the Hudson's Bay Company (HBC), alarmed at losing trade to the French, sent Anthony Henday out with a band of Cree Indians who were returning to the prairies after trading at Fort York. The party initially followed the river systems, but later left the Saskatchewan, travelling through parklands near the current sites of Melfort and Humboldt, crossing the South Saskatchewan River north of Saskatoon, passing through the Eagle Hills, and finally reaching the foothills of the Rocky Mountains.

JULY 21 [1754]. Sunday. Paddled two miles up the River, and then came to Keiskatchewan River, on which the French have two houses, one of which we expect to see to-morrow; paddled up it 8 miles West; passed a large lake, which helps to supply the River.

22. MONDAY. The Musketoes are now intolerable, giving us neither peace day nor night; paddled 14 miles up the River West, when we came to a French house. On our arrival two Frenchmen came to the water-side, and in a very genteel manner, invited me into their house,—which I readily accepted. One of them asked me if I had any Letter from my Master, and where, and on what design I was going inland. I answered I had no letter, and that I was sent to view the Country, and intended to return in the Spring. He told me the Master and men were gone down to Montreal with the furs; and that they must detain me till their return. However they were very kind; and at night I went to my tent, and told Attickashish, or Little Deer, my Leader, that had the charge of me, who smiled and said they dared not. I sent them two feet of tobacco, which was very acceptable to them.

23. TUESDAY. Invited to Breakfast and Dinner; thanked me for the tobacco, and presented to me some moose flesh.

24. WEDNESDAY. Took my departure from the French Settlement, and paddled up Keiskatchewan River 6 miles; the Course West. Then left it and paddled 16 miles W.b.S. across a Lake; then came to Peatago [Carrot] River; here are the largest Birch trees I have yet seen.

25. THURSDAY. Paddled up Peatago River 27 miles S.W.b.W. Large Birch trees on both sides the River. We still live on fish and are all heartily wishing for a change of food. This river is small, but good water as yet. To-morrow we shall leave our canoes and travel . . .

AUGUST 1. THURSDAY. Travelled 12 miles S.W.b.S., fine level land and tall woods; passed three small creeks of sweet water. The Indians killed two moose; I am now entering a pleasant and plentiful country.

2. FRIDAY. Travelled 10 miles S.W.b.S. Hills and Dales with little woods. Indians killed 6 Waskesew.

3. SATURDAY. Travelled 10 miles S.W.b.S. Level land with cherry trees, on which are plenty of fruit, plenty of Filberts. Indians killed 2 moose.

4. SUNDAY. Travelled 10 miles N.W. Land and Woods as yesterday. Met with 7 tents of Asinepoet Indians. I smoaked with them,—but have no hopes of getting them to the Fort,—as what cloth &c. they had were French, and, by their behaviour, I perceived they were strongly attached to the French interest, Indians killed 2 Moose.

5. MONDAY. Travelled 11 miles W.S.W. Level land and poor Woods; killed four Waskesew, or Red Deer, a stately animal, but the flesh coarse, and no manner equal to Moose flesh; however all is welcome to us.

6. TUESDAY. Travelled 11 miles W.S.W. Level lands, and tall ledges of woods;

crossed several small creeks of good water, which is acceptable; not having seen any these three days past.

7. WEDNESDAY. Travelled none. Indians killed 3 Waskesew and 2 Moose.

8. THURSDAY. Travelled none. All hands feasting, smoking, drinking, dancing and conjuring.

9. FRIDAY. Level land; poplars and Willows. Passed two Salt Lakes, large lumps of Salt candid (sic) laying round the edges. Indians killed 2 Moose.

10. SATURDAY. Travelled 4 miles W.b.N.; then put up to feast &c.

11. SUNDAY. Travelled 11 Miles S.W.b.W. Level lands, short grass; no woods; and no water but what is salt.

12. MONDAY. Travelled 7 Miles W.S.W. Level land, with small black Cherry trees, yielding plenty of fruit. Nothing but salt lakes.

13. TUESDAY. Travelled 7 Miles W.S.W. Level land, short Grass, Dry-woods, and several salt water lakes. We are now entered Muscuty plains, and shall soon see plenty of Buffalo, and the Archithinue [Blackfeet] Indians hunting them on Horse-back . . .

19. MONDAY. Travelled 10 Miles W.S.W. in Muscuty plains; fine land, no woods; several salt-water Lakes; have passed but 4 places of fresh water, these five days past.

20. TUESDAY. Travelled 15 Miles North; then came to Wapesekcopet [South Saskatchewan] River. It is large; the banks are high; on which grow Birch, Poplar, Hazle, Elder, Fir, etc.; killed 5 Waskesew.

21. WEDNESDAY. The Indian Men made temporary Canoes of Willows, covered with parchment Moose skins. The Women gathered plenty of excellent berries, and cherries. I angled a few small Trout; and in the evening we crossed the River in our Slender Canoes, without any accident happening . . .

SEPTEMBER 5. THURSDAY. Travelled 12 Miles West. Level land, with plenty of fruit trees; plenty of Moose, Waskesew, Swans, Cranes, White & Grey Geese, also a few Ducks. We are yet in Muscuty plains. Here are a great many Asinepoet Indians. The Buffalo has taken the route upwards, and is the reason we have not yet met with Archithinue Natives.

6. FRIDAY. Travelled W.S.W. 10 Miles. Hillocks and Dales & all ledges of woods all burnt. Indians killed 5 Moose & 2 Waskesew; met with five tents of Mekesue, or Eagle Indians. I gave their leader half a foot of Brazile tobacco, and smoked with them; they were very kind, and made me a present of some tongues, & a bladder full of fat. I could perceive no difference between them and the Asinepoet Natives with regard to the language; but one circumstance

surprised me much, and that is, the men do not cover their nakedness; which are the only natives that do not attend to decency. The women are cloathed the same as the other Asinepoet Indians. The Natives inform me that they are a tribe of that brave Nation; and take their name from Eagles being plenty in the district they inhabit. The Leader promised to collect furs, and go down with me to the Fort. They never had traded with any European or Canadian. My Guides & Companions seemed afraid of them.

The Nahathaway and Chipewyan

DAVID THOMPSON

Thompson arrived on the Saskatchewan in the winter of 1785–86 as a teenager employed by the HBC. He spent the next thirty-five years in the western interior, trading for furs, and, more important, making astronomical sightings and mathematical calculations. He became an accomplished map maker and was a keen observer of aboriginal people and their customs. His diaries rank among the world's great travel literature. He spent several years with the Nahathaway (Cree) in what is now northern Saskatchewan and Manitoba.

The Nahathaway Indians

HAVING PASSED SIX YEARS in different parts of this region [the Muskrat Country], exploring and surveying it, I may be allowed to know something of the natives: its inhabitants are two distinct races of Indians. North of the latitude of fifty-six degrees, the country is occupied by a people who call themselves "Dinnie", [but] by the Hudson's Bay traders [they are called] "Northern Indians" and by their southern neighbours "Chee-pa-wy-ans" . . .

Southward of the above latitude the country is in the possession of the Na-hath-a-way Indians, their native name . . . The French Canadians . . . call them "Krees", a name which none of the Indians can pronounce; this name appears to be taken from "Keethisteno", so called by one of their tribes and which the French pronounce "Kristeno", and by contraction Krees ("r", rough cannot be pronounced by any native). These people are separated into many tribes or extended families, under different names, but all speaking dialects of the same language, which extends over this stony region and along the Atlantic coasts southward to the Delaware River in the United States . . . and by the Saskatchewan River westward to the Rocky Mountains . . . It is easy of pronunciation and is readily acquired by the white people for the purposes of trade and common conversation.

The appearance of these people depends much on the climate and ease of subsistence. Around Hudson's Bay and near the sea coasts, where the climate is very severe, and game scarce, they are seldom above the middle size. [They are] of spare make, the features round, or slightly oval, hair black, strong and lank, eyes black and of full size, cheekbones rather high, mouth and teeth good, the chin round, the countenance grave yet with a tendency to cheerful. And the mild countenances of the women make many, while young, appear lovely, but, like the labouring classes, the softness of youth soon passes away.

In the interior, where the climate is not so severe, and hunting more successful, the men attain to the stature of six feet, well proportioned, the face more oval, and the features good, giving them a manly appearance; the complexion is of a light olive, and their colour much the same as a native of the south of Spain, the skin soft and smooth.

They bear cold and exposure to the weather better than we do, and the natural heat of their bodies is greater than ours, probably from living wholly on animal food, for they have no vegetables during winter, and only berries during the open season, yet suffer no inconvenience for want of vegetable food. They can bear great fatigue but not hard labour. They would rather walk six hours over rough ground than work one hour with the pick axe and spade, and the labour they perform is mostly in an erect posture, as working with the ice chisel piercing holes through the ice or through a beaver house, and naturally they are not industrious. They do not work from choice, but necessity, yet the industrious of both sexes are praised and admired; the civilized man has many things to tempt him to an active life; the Indian has none, and is happy sitting still and smoking his pipe . . .

The natives in their manners are mild and decent, treat each other with kindness and respect, and very rarely interrupt each other in conversation. After a long separation the nearest relations meet each other with the same seeming indifference as if they had constantly lived in the same tent, but they have not the less affection for each other, for they hold all show of joy or sorrow to be unmanly. On the death of a relation, or friend, the women accompany their tears for the dead with piercing shrieks, but the men sorrow in silence, and when the sad pang of recollection becomes too strong to be borne, retire into the forest to give free vent to their grief.

Those acts that pass between man and man for generous charity and kind compassion in civilized society are no more than what is every day practised by these savages, as acts of common duty. [If] anyone [is] unsuccessful in the chase [or] has lost his little all by some accident, he is sure to be relieved by the others to the utmost of their powers; in sickness they carefully attend each other to the latest breath . . .

The Chipewyans

Their physiognomy is of an oval form, the skull convex, the chin pointed, the cheek bones raised, the nose prominent and sharp, the eyes black and small, forehead high, mouth and teeth good, hair black, long, and lank, and of the men coarse; the countenance, though not handsome, is manly; tall in stature, of spare make, but capable of great fatigue. They are a peaceable people, abhorring bloodshed; the Nahathaways look on them with a sort of contempt; being themselves too much inclined to war, they consider the hunter to be naturally a warrior. The Dinnae themselves give some occasion for this, in imitating what ceremonies they learn from them, yet treating their women like slaves, a conduct which the Nahathaways detest. When quarrelling, the Dinnae never resort to arms but settle the affair by wrestling, pulling hair, and twisting each other's necks.

Although to their neighbours they are open to ridicule, yet not so to the white people, who encourage their peaceable habits, and [they] themselves justly remark that a fine country and plenty to eat may encourage people to go to war on each other, but the fatigue they go through in hunting makes them glad to rest at night. Although they often suffer hunger, yet the steady frugality they strictly observe never allows distress to come on their families. Their country has very large and many lesser lakes. When the land is scarce of deer, or long calms come on, they take to the lakes to angle trout or pike, at which they are very expert, and although they use our hooks, for large fish [they] prefer their own, which are of bone, and a fish caught with their bone hooks does not get loose as sometimes happens to our hooks.

Whether fish or meat, whatever is not required is carefully put by for [the] next meal. They carefully collect every article that can be of use to them; and when they remove, which they very often do, from place to place, the women are very heavily loaded; the men with little else [to carry] than their gun and their fishing tackle; even a girl of eight years will have her share to carry, while the boys have some trifle or only their bows and arrows. This hard usage makes women scarce among them, and by the time a girl is twelve years of age, for the young men cannot readily obtain a wife, she is given as a wife to a man of twice her age, and on this account polygamy is rare among them.

The hardships the women suffer induces them too often to let the female infants die as soon as born, and [they] look upon it as an act of kindness to them, and when any of us spoke to a woman who had thus acted, the common answer was, she "wished her mother had done the same to herself".

Upon reasoning with the men, on the severe laborious life of the women, and the early deaths it occasioned, and that it was a disgrace to them, and how very different the Nahathaways treated their women, they always intimated [women] were an inferior order of mankind, made for the use and service of the men; the Nahathaways were a different people from [them], and they were not guided by them; and I found [women] were too often regarded as the property of the strongest man, until they have one or more children. I have been alone with them for months, and always found them a kind good people, but their treatment of the women always made me regard them as an unmanly race of men.

Whether in distress, or in plenty, or in whatever state they may be, I never saw any act of a religious tendency; they make no feasts, have no dances, nor thanksgivings; they appear to think everything depends on their own abilities and industry, and have no belief in the greater part of the religious opinions of the Nahathaways. From the regular migrations of the water fowl and the reindeer, they infer something of a manito takes care of them, but neither does, nor can, prevent their killing them. They believe in a future state, and that it is much the same as in this life; they appear to have no high ideas of it, but [think it] somewhat better than the present; they dread death as a great evil, but meet it with calmness and fortitude. The wife of the deceased must mourn his loss for a year; her hair, which is cut off and placed beside him when dead, is now allowed to grow and she may become a wife, but there is no restraint on the men at the death of their wives; they take a wife as soon as they can, and seldom allow a widow woman to pass a year of mourning. They do not bury their dead, but leave them to be devoured; this they might easily prevent by covering them with wood or stones, which is sometimes done, and sometimes the dead is placed on a scaffold, but these instances are very rare. Some of them have an ancient tradition that a great spirit descended on a rock, took a dog, tore it to small pieces and scattered it, that these pieces each became a man, or a woman, and that these men and women are their original parents, from whom they have all come, and thus the dog is their common origin. On this account they have very few dogs; frequently several tents have not a dog among them, and they abhor the dog feasts of the Nahathaways and the French Canadians; the latter regard a fat dog as a luxury, equal to a fat pig.

Their morals are as good as can be expected, they exact chastity from their wives and seem to practise it themselves; they are strictly honest; and detest a thief; and are as charitable and humane to those in want, as circumstances will allow them.

When the martial tribes [Blackfeet, Piegans, &c.], by right of conquest over the Snake Indians, took possession of the great plains, the Nahathaways occupied the lands thus left, and from the rigorous clime of sixty-one degrees north went southward to fifty-six degrees north. The Dinnae, or Chipewyans, in like manner occupied the country down to the last-named latitude, and westward by the Peace River to the Rocky Mountains; and have thus quietly extended themselves from the Arctic regions to their present boundary, and will continue to press to the southward as far as the Nahathaways will permit.

Fur Trade and Empire

Sir George Simpson

Simpson was governor of the HBC, and as such virtual emperor of the western interior. He was calculating and imperious, but an able administrator and an untiring traveller in the territory he ruled. Letters to his employers in London were lucid and blunt in their assessments of the company's employees, its competitors, and the aboriginal people who lived in Rupert's Land.

Governor Simpson to A. Colvile

FT. GARRY 20 MAY 1822

MR. MCTAVISH JOINED ME AT YORK about the middle of Octr. and with him I was busily occupied in making various arrangements for the business of the ensuing season, until the Rivers and Lakes set fast early in December, when I took my departure for the interior, making a circuitous journey of about 1500 miles by Norway House, Cumberland, Swan River, Qu'Appelle and Brandon House and arrived at this place early in March, much gratified by my trip as it gave me a thorough knowledge of the Country and Trade, and introduced me to the acquaintance of some of our fresh allies, who received me with much politeness and attention.

I am sorry to say that the prospects of Trade in the Districts through which I passed, were by no means flattering; the late arrangements have given mortal offence to the Indians, a settled and sullen melancholy seems to have arrested their exertions, and altho' the Factors and Traders have used the most conciliatory measures to cheer them, they are as yet unsuccessful. Their immediate wants have been fully supplied, but of course the scenes of extravagance are at an end, and it will be a work of time to reconcile them to the new order of things. I have made it my study to examine the nature and character of the Indians and however repugnant it may be to our feelings, I am convinced they must be ruled with a rod of iron, to bring, and keep them in a proper state of subordination, and the most certain way to effect this is by letting them feel their dependence upon us. In the Woods and Northern barren grounds this measure ought to be pursued rigidly next year if they do not improve, and no credit, not so much as a load of ammunition given them until they exhibit an inclination to renew their habits of industry. In the plains however this system will not do, as they can live independent of us, and by withholding ammunition, tobacco and spirits, the staple articles of trade, for one year they will recover the use of their Bows and spears and lose sight of their smoking and Drinking habits; it will therefore be necessary to bring those Tribes round by mild and cautious measures which may soon be effected . . .

Little or no provision has been made for them [Swiss emigrants to Red River Colony] here, indeed the crops were so unproductive, and the Provision Trade during the Summer so triffling, that nothing of consequence could be collected, and the unprecedented and almost total failure of the Buffalo with the encreased population, has made this Colony the most distressing scene of starvation that can well be conceived. I have not heard that any persons connected with the Settlement, have actually perished through hunger, but soul and body have been kept together on next to nothing, chiefly by a little musty Grain which Mr. McDonell served out with great economy and an esculent root called "Indian Potatoes" resembling a horse raddish in appearance but very insipid; this root which is plentiful here they eat either raw or boiled, but possesses little nourishment . . .

Mr. West has some idea that through the interest and exertions of Mr. Harrison a fund may be raised or got from some of the Charities to open

Schools for the instruction and maintenance of Native Indian Children; he takes a very sanguine view of this scheme which is to diffuse Xtian Knowledge among the natives from the shores of the Pacific to those of the Bay and will no doubt on paper draw a very fine representation of the advantages to be derived therefrom, which may attract the attention of Philanthropists, but in my humble opinion will be attended with little other good than filling the pockets and bellies of some hungry missionaries and schoolmasters and rearing the Indians in habits of indolence; they are already too much enlightened by the late opposition and more of it would in my opinion do harm instead of good to the Fur Trade. I have always remarked that an enlightened Indian is good for nothing; there are several of them about the Bay side and totally useless, even the half Breeds of the Country who have been educated in Canada are blackguards of the very worst description, they not only pick up the vices of the Whites upon which they improve but retain those of the Indian in their utmost extent. The Indians of this Country are certainly quick of apprehension and have a thirst for knowledge; they would gladly be relieved of the burthen of maintaining their children, but I suspect the plan would not be productive of any real good. I give my ideas thus freely for your private information in case the subject should come before the Committee, if they were known by the very pious I might be looked upon as a true North Wester. The Committee I understand are desirous that Mr. West should attend at York Factory during the business months, this visit will not only interfere with our operations, but may be injurious in other respects, the Transport Season is so very limited that the best use must be made of our time, our Stores, Shops, Counting Houses etc must be open on Sundays as on Week days; from the Governor downwards we must closely attend from 4 A.M. till 10 P.M, otherways things will revert to their former irregularity; the men of each District must have their two or three Days Drinking bout, and Brigades must start as they can be dispatched without respect to Days; the Parson will be the only idle man about the place, and he will have an opportunity of seeing the whole routine of our business which may be converted to an improper use at some future period, or he may feel it a point of Duty to give information of our immoral conduct (according to his doctrine) to people who might afterwards make a handle of it to the injury of the concern. Mr. West I believe to be a very good well meaning man and strictly correct in his conduct, but as the Hudsons Bay Compys Chaplain or Servant, inclined to deal too freely in politicks.

Many Tender Ties

Sylvia Van Kirk

C ONTRARY TO WHAT MIGHT BE ANTICIPATED, the Canadian trader did not conform to the image of the "womanless frontiersman". Fundamental to the growth of a fur-trade society was widespread intermarriage between the traders and Indian women . . . [T]he norm for sexual relationships in fur-trade society was not casual, promiscuous encounters but the development of marital unions which gave rise to distinct family units. There were differences in attitude and practice between the men of the two companies; yet fur-trade society developed its own marriage rite, marriage à la façon du pays, which combined both Indian and European marriage customs. In this, the fur-trade society of Western Canada appears to have been exceptional. In most other areas of the world, sexual contact between European men and native women has usually been illicit in nature and essentially peripheral to the white man's trading or colonizing ventures. In the Canadian West, however, alliances with Indian women were the central social aspect of the fur traders' progress across the country.

An explanation for this phenomenon can be found in the nature of the fur trade itself. Both the attitudes of the Indians and the needs of the traders dictated an important social and economic role for the native woman that militated against her being simply an object of sexual exploitation. Fur-trade society, as in both Indian and pre-industrial European societies, allowed women an integral socio-economic role because there was little division between the "public" and "private" spheres, between the spheres of work and home. The marriage of a fur trader and an Indian woman was not just a "private" affair; the bond thus created helped to advance trade relations with a new tribe, placing the Indian wife in the role of cultural liaison between the traders and her kin. In Indian societies, the division of labour was such that the women had an essential economic role to play. This role, although somewhat modified, was carried over into the fur trade where the work of native women constituted an important contribution to the functioning of the trade.

An analysis of the evolution in the choice of marriage partners among the traders provides insights into the changing nature of fur-trade society. Indian wives were "the vogue" during the initial stages of the fur trade when the traders were dependent upon the Indians for survival. The important economic role of the Indian wife reflected the extent to which the traders adopted a native way of life. Nevertheless, fur-trade society was not Indian; rather it combined both European and Indian elements to produce a distinctive, self-perpetuating community. This process was symbolized by the emergence of a large number of mixed-blood children. The replacement of the Indian wife by the mixed-blood wife resulted in a widespread and complex pattern of inter-marriage among fur-trade families. It produced a close-knit society in which family life was highly valued. James Douglas echoed the sentiments of many of his colleagues when he declared that without "the many tender ties" of family, the monotonous life of a fur trader would be unbearable. Fur-trade society was not static and the shifting influence of its dual cultural roots was mirrored in the experience of successive generations of mixed-blood girls. Initially Indian influences were strong, but there was a noticeable tendency, particularly on the part of Company officers, to wean their daughters away from their Indian heritage and to encourage them to emulate the style of European ladies. After an absence of over a century, the actual appearance of white women in the Canadian West was to have serious repercussions, particularly upon the fur-trade elite. Their coming underscored the increasing class and racial distinctions which characterized fur-trade society in the nineteenth century. In the Rupert's Land of the 1830s, a genteel British wife was a conspicuous status symbol for a Hudson's Bay Company officer, but, ironically, the white wife also presaged the ultimate decline of the fur trade. Her presence was most visible in the Red River Settlement, where, like the missionary, she symbolized the coming of a settled, agrarian order. This would be a world in which native women would have little role to play . . .

In reconstructing the role of women in the fur trade, the paucity of sources, in particular those written by native women, presents a difficult challenge. One is forced to piece together snippets of information from the extensive collections of traders' journals, letters and wills which have survived. Although a substantial body of evidence can be amassed in this way, it is understandably coloured by the male perspective. As is often the case in the history of women, an analysis of this material reveals that there is a significant disparity between the traders' perception of the women's position and the reality of their actual lives . . . With regard to Indian women, most of the fur traders believed that women occupied a degraded position within western Indian societies; the Indian woman in their view had everything to gain by becoming the wife of the "superior" trader. In reality the Indian woman may have enjoyed an easier existence at the fur-trade post, but she sacrificed considerable personal autonomy, being forced to adjust to the traders' patriarchal views on the ordering of home and family. In the final analysis, it is debatable whether the lot of an Indian woman in marrying a European was improved to the extent that the fur traders claimed.

Recollections of an Assiniboine Chief

DAN KENNEDY (OCHANKUGAHE)

I T IS SAID the Assiniboines were thirty thousand strong before the advent of the whiteman. Our hunting territory extended from the White Earth and Missouri Rivers in Montana, due north to the junction of the Assiniboine and the Red Rivers, then westward to the Saskatchewan River, from there south to the Cypress Hills, ending at the Bear Paw Mountains in Montana.

Visualize yourself gazing down on one of our encampments—the tall conical buffalo skin teepees, arranged in a wide circle; men riding up laden with buffalo meat; young men patrolling troops of horses on the outskirts of the camp; the elders sitting around in groups or in council, smoking the long-stemmed stone pipes; boys at target practice with their bows and arrows; the women processing meat for pemmican; others stretching hides on rectangular pole frames; and still others busy at porcupine-quill embroidery of exquisite geometric design . . .

To the Plains Indians, the buffalo was the staff of life. After a hunt the women kept themselves busy cutting the meat into long thin slices, which they hung on horizontal poles to dry. The sliced meat was turned over each day until it dried into jerk meat and was then packed away in parfleches. These parfleches were made from flint hides with the hair scraped off. They were decorated with colours in geometric designs.

Our favourite relishes from the buffalo were the tongue, liver, kidneys and rennet. The tongue was cooked before it was eaten but the liver, kidneys and rennet were eaten raw.

Buffalo bladders were washed, inflated and dried in the sun, then used as containers for rendered buffalo fat. The rind of the buffalo stomach was peeled off and made into water bags. The horns were boiled until they were soft enough and were then carved with a knife into ladles, spoons and combs.

Before the white traders brought the thread, the Indian women had only the buffalo sinew for sewing purposes. This fibrous tissue was taken from the back of the buffalo. The sinew was found on either side of the spine from the shoulder blade to the rump. Moccasins were sewn from smoked buffalo hides. During cold winter months the hunters wore fur jackets, leggings, caps and mitts from the buffalo hides. During the sore-eye moon (March) when the snow started to melt, the smoked buffalo moccasins were worn with the hair on the outside to keep the feet dry.

Indian lodges were made from the tanned buffalo hides. It usually took nine to fourteen hides, depending on the size of lodge required.

In our teepees we had copper and brass pails and other utensils, which were procured from traders in exchange for furs and buffalo robes.

We also had perfumes concocted from scented herbs and barks of trees and varied according to individual tastes. In our toilet accessories we used a red powder to paint our faces. Our toilet was incomplete without a liberal application of this red powder on our faces. Our young men and maidens were just as fastidious in these matters as the young people of today.

We had no matches in those days, but we had an ingenious way of lighting our fires. We sliced a fungus that is native to the plains into thin slices and then into tiny cubes. We sprinkled gun powder on these and allowed them to dry in the sun. The cubes were carefully preserved in a pouch, and when we had occasion to light the fire, we placed one of them in dry grass or any combustible material, and struck the flint on a piece of steel, producing a spark that ignited the powder, which in turn produced the flame and the fire.

When hunting the buffalo in the old days, before the Assiniboines had horses, the warriors would cleverly camouflage themselves from the beasts. A hunter weaved sage brush into a wreath and inserted ten- or twelve-inch sage vertically half way round the crown. When the wreath was worn as head gear it made the wearer invisible.

Another camouflage was the snow crust used by the still hunters. A large snow crust from the snow bank was pierced with a stick and held by the hunter in front of him. With this camouflage he crawled cautiously towards the buffalo until he reached the striking distance, then fired at the unsuspecting buffalo and thus made his kill.

The animals are born with the inherent instinct of scents and tracking is no problem with them, but man has only the eyesight and mental faculties with which to diagnose and find the answer to the riddle of footprints. It takes five years of intensive training to master this riddle of prairie craft.

Tracking requires aptitude and resourcefulness. Take, for instance, the footprints of a man in the snow. If the footprints are long and the steps far apart, the tracks were made by a tall man, but if the footprints are short and the steps close to each other it is a short man, and so forth. Take a stick and poke at the tracks and you will find out how old they are. The harder the crust, the older the tracks. Obviously, tracking is more difficult in summer.

The Assiniboines had an ingenious way of trapping and capturing eagles. They dug a pit and roofed it with poles, which they carpeted with moss and scattered grass. Then they placed a jack rabbit on the roof of the pit and the hunter descended into the pit and remained there until an eagle landed to eat the rabbit. While the eagle was preoccupied with the rabbit, the hunter grabbed the eagle by its legs and killed it. Eagle catchers wore frost-cured flint hide gauntlets so that the sharp talons of the eagle would not penetrate to the hands.

The Saulteaux also had a unique way of snaring eagles. They built a circular enclosure with shrubbery. Inside this shrubbery they staked a long pole to the ground.

They then placed a jack rabbit in life-like posture between the pole and the enclosure. Lastly, they made an aperture in the shrubbery fence to fit the eagle and set the sinew snare in the opening. When an eagle saw the decoy (the jack rabbit) it alighted on the pole and looked at the rabbit to make sure that it was a rabbit. Being satisfied, it flew down and landed outside the shrubbery fence, circled around until it saw the aperture, then entered and snared itself.

The approach of spring promised a release to my people from their long confinement in winter quarters, from depleted food supplies and limited hunting range, and gave them visions of renewed buffalo hunts, the warpaths and other activities.

At the first sound of the rumbling of thunder, the symbols of sacrifice, the red shroud and other fabrics were taken out from sacred packages and presented as offerings to the benevolent Manitou, the Thunderbird. Sweet grass was burned on coals taken from the fireplace and, over the burning incense, the worshippers proffered their pipes, calling on the Great Manitou to bless nature with abundance, so the tribe would grow and prosper.

Some of our more venturesome braves were unable to resist the urge of the warpath and had departed on their perilous adventures to seek new laurels. Who knew? Would the Manitou of the warpath smile on their venture, would some amongst them win the much-coveted honour to adorn their heads with the eagle feather?

A Winter of Hardship

$\mathcal{E}$DWARD $\mathcal{A}$HENAKEW

This is an account rendered by the elderly Cree chief Thunderchild and written down by Rev. Edward Ahenakew, also a Cree, who lived for a time on Thunderchild's Reserve near the current site of Turtleford.

HEN I WAS STILL YOUNG and my father was alive, we came through a winter of great hardship. My brother took me with him on many long hunts, but the buffalo were scarce that year, and there was hardly any food. Everyone looked for old bones to make grease, but it was rancid.

At first there were plenty of foxes. We caught many in deadfall traps, and traded their skins for tobacco, shot, tea, and sugar, when traders came to our camps; but when we tried to buy pemmican, they would not sell us any.

We had travelled far out onto the plains, and there were no more trees to make traps. We were told that there was food at Fort Pitt, and we started in hope towards that post. We still had five horses and many dogs, but wolves followed us, and when we camped our dogs would chase them. Sometimes the dogs killed a wolf, but every day wolves killed some of our dogs. We had to kill dogs too, for we had nothing else to eat; then, we had to kill our horses for food.

One day *Na-pa-ke-kun* (Night Scout) came to our camp. He told us that the people we had left at the encampment had also tried to reach Fort Pitt when they learned that there was food there, and they had died along the way. He and his wives were the only ones left. They had five horses, and they killed one for food, but would give us none. We took the skin, and we boiled that and ate it, but we were too weak to follow *Na-pa-ke-kun* north when he went on with his wives and the other horses. We could go no farther.

The winter was ending. Our women seemed to be stronger than the men. Though they were not eating, they kept moving, if it was only to make fires to keep us warm. The three little children with us were only skin and bones, and their mothers cried over them. We found it hard even to breathe.

One night I dreamed that someone came to me and said, "You can save yourself. Look to the south!" And looking south, I saw that the country was green, but to the north there was only darkness. I tried to flee to the south. The dream was vivid, and when I awoke it was almost morning. I lay thinking about the dream, and then I told it to my father. "Maybe it is only hunger that made me dream," I said. But my father told me, "Dreams count, my son. Try to go south, all of you; and if I cannot follow, leave me. I will do my best."

The thaw had begun. The women went ahead of us, carrying all they could. I had a gun and I tried to hunt, but I had to rest often. Gophers were appearing, and we killed some and made fires with buffalo chips to cook them. We camped four times before we came to any bush. Then early one morning, my aunt suddenly cried out that she had seen an "old man buffalo." We thought that she had gone crazy but we looked where she pointed and there stood a buffalo, about two hundred yards away. "A-a-hay-a-ay. It is going to be hard. Who can go?"

My brother took his loaded gun and moved slowly down the valley, resting often, for he was very weak. We stayed and watched. Sometimes he was out of sight, and then we would see him again, crawling towards where the buffalo had been, but it had moved on and we could not see it.

After a long time, we heard the sound of my brother's gun, and I went to meet him. He told me that he had hit the buffalo, and it would surely die, but we would have to move our camp and follow its trail. It took us a long time to pull down the tent and move slowly after the buffalo. It was not far, but we were weak. My aunt took the gun. "I will follow the trail," she said, "and I will kill the buffalo if it is still alive." The other women went with her, all except my mother.

Night came, and it was bright moonlight when we heard the women returning, dragging great loads of meat. They were able to bring most of it back to where we had camped. The buffalo was old and its meat was tough. The women boiled it to make soup, and that was easier for us to eat, but after long hunger my mother and my brother almost died. A-a-hay, we were poor, but now we could fatten ourselves a bit, and we began to feel life in our bones once more.

When I was stronger, I wandered through the bushes where we had pitched our tent, and I saw an old camp, with the tracks of foxes and wolves around it. There was a mound of melting snow, and when I kicked it I saw a corpse, a man dead from hunger. I went back to our camp and we moved to the river, hoping that we might meet some Stoneys, my aunt's people.

Each day, we were able to walk a little more, and the snow was almost gone when we reached the river. Away to the west, we could see people moving in single file. We knew they might be Blackfoot and so we loaded our guns in readiness, but when they saw us they turned towards us, moving slowly, for they had no horses and were carrying heavy loads. They were Stoneys, and they greeted my aunt affectionately as a daughter.

There were eleven families, and everything they had was in the loads on their backs, for they had killed and eaten their horses. But they had buffalo meat, and they fed us grease and dried meat. When we had eaten they wanted to go on, though my father asked them to camp with us by the river, at the old Sun Dance place. We gave them tobacco and tea, and they gave us meat; but the next day they crossed the river. We were sorry to see them go.

We camped at the old Sun Dance place, where there was plenty of wood. The women found a buffalo head and neck in the snow, and they made a fire to boil it. I climbed the bank of the river, and as I sat there I saw something that moved and disappeared again with the wind. I went to find out what it was, and I came to a big snowdrift with a pole at the top, from which a bit of cloth blew in the wind. It marked a cache.

I took off my coat and began to dig through the hard crust of snow. Down inside the drift I found hides that covered the meat of two buffalo, cut in pieces. I had to sit down then, for I remembered my dream and was overcome with feeling and with thankfulness to the spirits who had guided us.

I tied the meat into one of the hides and pulled it down the bank as far as I could, and then I left it and went on to our camp. I found the others eating the head that the women had boiled, and my sister-in-law called to me to come and eat. I ate, and when I was finished I said to my father, "We will have another meal, a good one," and I told him what I had found. "Dreams count, my son," he said to me. "The spirits have pitied us and guided us."

The women hurried to bring the meat to our camp, and we stayed at the Sun Dance place until they had dried much of it and made pemmican, and had scraped and tanned the hides. When all that was done, we moved on. It was spring, and we went to where there were maple trees, and made sugar. Truly a change had come, for now we had sugar; and the hunting was good, with a kill every day. It was pleasant in that valley, just to be alive and well, all of us; and yet we felt ashamed to be so poor, without any horses. It was lonely too.

I had begun to feel that I must have things of my own, and I was restless. I said that I would go to see if I could find some of our people, and I had not gone far when I saw a rider, a Stoney whose name was Chō-ka-se. I told him all that had happened to us, and he said, "Come with me and I will lend you horses and carts." He came back to our camp with me. My father was surprised that I had come back so soon, and he was pleased that Chō-ka-se would lend us horses and carts; but that is the Indian way.

Then Chō-ka-se took us to his camp and he gave us what we needed to travel. Scouts who had gone ahead had found the women who had been with *Na-pa-ke-kun*. He had died of starvation and yet they still had the horses that they had refused to share with us. The scouts came on Big Bear's band too, those with horses helping to carry the others. All through the country north of the Saskatchewan River there had been many deaths from starvation, and the Crees were moving west along the river, hoping to make a truce with the Blackfoot. The scouts said that the Blackfoot had not starved, for they had many horses and could follow the buffalo herds.

We travelled west until we came to a Blackfoot camp. They knew of the hardship we had suffered and we were invited into a big tent. At first we could use only signs, and then one of the Crees came who could interpret. My brother made the Blackfoot his namesake; the old man gave him a fine horse and cart. He gave me a two-year-old to ride, but I made up my mind after all the troubles of that winter that I would never again be dependent upon others.

The Last Buffalo Hunter

MARY WEEKES

These descriptions of buffalo hunts were told to Mary Weekes by Norbert Welsh when he was eighty-six years old and blind. Welsh, a Metis, had been a buffalo hunter and a trader on the plains and in the valleys of the Saskatchewan and Qu'Appelle Rivers since the 1860s.

ON A SECOND HUNT THAT WINTER, a lot of us, twenty or thirty men, crossed the river. We travelled for two days, but saw no sign of buffalo. Our rations were getting low. Our chief, Ak-a-pow, Gabriel Dumont's father, called a meeting. He asked us what we thought we should do. There was no sign of buffalo and we were nearly out of fresh meat. One man got up and asked Dumont to propose what we should do.

Dumont appointed four men to get up early in the morning and go scouting for buffalo. One was named to go to the east—more north than east; one to the south-east; one to the south-west; and the other to the north-west. I was named the first, and directed to go to the south-west. That would be in the direction of where Calgary is now, but on the west side of the south branch of the Saskatchewan River . . .

I could see buffalo all over. There were thousands and thousands of them travelling in the direction in which I had seen the bull. There was not one herd, but many. Our Chief decided that we would have breakfast before we did anything. He went from tent to tent and gathered up all the food. We had a good breakfast, and by ten o'clock were ready to chase the buffalo.

Two or three men took a herd. That afternoon twenty-five men shot three hundred buffalo. Buffalo never came very close to camp. They would smell us, bunch together, and move away. They seldom came nearer than two or three miles.

The next day we went after the buffalo again and killed four hundred. All around us, as far as we could see, the plains were black with buffalo. The prairie seemed to be moving.

There was one thing that I did not like about that hunt. I saw hundreds of buffalo, during that week, slaughtered for their hides. The whole carcass was left to rot on the plains. One time I saw three fine fat buffalo cows lying dead, side by side. I jumped off my horse, cut out their tongues, tied them to my saddle, and took them home. Buffalo tongue was very choice.

There were many bands of hunters on the plains beside ours. In all my years of buffalo hunting, I never destroyed buffalo for their pelts alone. I always took the whole carcass, except the head, home.

My wife had once said that since we were going to make a living hunting buffalo, she did not want me to kill more than we could dry and pack. She told me that if I brought in an extra hide without the carcass, she would not dress it. One day my brother-in-law and I were travelling on the prairie, and we sighted a little herd of buffalo. I let fly and killed a cow. We skinned it, and took a little of the fattest part of the animal. When we reached our tent, I threw the hide and saddle down. My wife smiled, and lightly kicked the hide away. She meant what she said. I gave the hide to my mother-in-law . . .

After the second day of this particular hunt there were a great many buffalo shot for their hides. Too many. But I can say that very few of the hunters in our brigade wanted to kill buffalo just for the hides.

We camped there for a week. We had a hundred people in our brigade, and they were all loaded—the carts followed the hunters. It took us four days to get home. All around us the buffalo travelled. When we got back to Round Plain [near Dundurn], we found the buffalo there, too. We had a good time that winter. Plenty of buffalo.

The Yankees shot more buffalo for their hides than all the Indian and half-breed hunters put together. The Indians knew better. They did not want to see the buffalo gone forever. Parties of Yankees used to come up to the North-West to shoot for sport. They would sit on a hill and shoot. Once Buffalo Bill came on a shooting trip, and shot five hundred buffalo—just for fun.

Colonel Cody was known as "Buffalo Bill," because he contracted with the Kansas Pacific Railway to supply its laborers with buffalo meat. In eighteen months he killed four thousand two hundred and eighty buffalo. In 1883 he organized the "Wild West Show," an exhibition designed to represent life on the frontier.

The Palliser Expedition

IRENE M. SPRY

A British military officer and adventurer, Captain John Palliser led a scientific and surveying expedition from 1857 to 1860 across the southern prairies and on through passes of the Rocky Mountains on behalf of the Royal Geographical Society. A campaign promoting agricultural settlement in the western interior had begun, but little was known in detail about the land and resources of the southern plains. Fur traders stayed mainly on the northern river systems, and both traders and explorers were fearful of the plains Indians. Palliser is best remembered for his conclusion that the southern prairies were unfit for human habitation. Prominent among the members of his team was Dr. James Hector, a geologist and naturalist. In this following excerpt from Irene Spry's book, the expedition is moving west across what is now the Regina Plains, guided by a Cree named the Peacemaker.

NOW THEY WERE READY TO START OFF into the trackless wilderness they had come so far to see. Here, at last, as Palliser stood looking to the west, he could say, 'westward of this . . . is unknown, and the whole country in this latitude is untravelled by the white man.'

The first night out they camped in the Squirrel Hills, where they had good wood, water, and grass, but there were signs that they were getting into arid country again with poor, stony soil, where there would be difficulty in finding pasture. The next day the Peacemaker counselled them to load the carts with wood; there would be no more wood, except in the valleys of the rivers. Their course lay due west; as far as the eye could reach, nothing but desolate plains met the view. These 'desolate plains' are the Regina Plains, where now so much first-class wheat is grown. They came to a little creek called the Creek-before-where-the-Bones-lie and, in the evening, to another creek, the Creek-where-the-Bones-lie. The Indian name was Wascana creek; on it the city of Regina stands today, with its fine buildings, beautiful lake, and tall trees. Then, a hundred years ago, there was little water and very little grass; some small willows, but no wood fit for fuel. The nearest inhabitants were an old man and some women and children, in two Indian lodges on the first of the two creeks. The young men were all away hunting buffalo.

The next camping-place of the expedition was on Moose Jaw Creek. Here they found a number of Indian tents, among which, right in the middle, stood a large medicine lodge covered with hierographic characters, birds, and animals of various designs. Again there were only women and children. The women asked leave to come and see the wives of the men of the party, and expressed considerable surprise when they told them they had none. No Indian could survive for long without his wife, who did so much of the work that was essential for survival. Only war-parties travelled without women.

On Moose Jaw Creek there was wood, water, and grass, but once again the Peacemaker told them to load the carts with enough wood to last for five days. There was no more to be had east of the Elbow.

The next day they had great difficulty in getting over Moose Jaw Creek. The steep banks of what seemed an insignificant stream made it impossible to get the carts and wagons across, and they had to make a long detour to the south before they could find a possible crossing-place. They got to 'Thunder Mountain Creek' (Thunder Creek), where there was no wood at all; so they cooked their supper with buffalo dung and some of the wood they had brought with them.

They were now near the Missouri Coteau, the long, low hill that is the edge of the next upward prairie 'steppe'. Hector and McKay, who had gone off to explore to the south, did not catch up with the main party when it made camp. Palliser delayed the start next morning, hoping the doctor's party would come up with them. He was disappointed. When his party stopped for dinner they could see Indian tents; before they had finished their meal they were surrounded by Crees, who had at first thought they were a herd of buffalo. The Crees had seen nothing of the doctor. He still did not arrive next morning.

Palliser waited; he was worried. Perhaps Hector and McKay had got ahead of the main party, not knowing of the delay caused by the trouble over crossing Moose Jaw Creek. At last they set off again. Twenty-five of the Indians went with them.

There was still no sign of Hector and McKay the next night, and again Palliser delayed the start of the main party in the morning; but at long last they arrived, with a large contingent of Crees. They had slept the night before in one of the Cree lodges and were very hospitably treated, having received many invitations to the festivities in various tents. In the tent in which the doctor slept, a Blackfoot scalp was hanging. The women danced around it, forcing the captured wife of the dead brave to join them in the dance. Hector's party had had to spend the night previous out on the open plain without food, fire, or blankets, after riding over seventy miles.

They had met an Indian travelling on foot, returning from burying his relatives who had died of smallpox the year before. According to Indian custom he had thrown away all his clothes to celebrate the event and as a sort of sacrifice to the Manitou of the prairies. The doctor gave him their only blanket.

This was the party's first encounter with the dreaded smallpox, a disease of almost yearly occurrence and fearfully fatal among the Indians. McKay told them that half the Indians tenting round Fort Ellice the year before had died from it. They had heard rumours there that there was an epidemic of it at Fort Carlton, where they were to spend the winter. It looked as though sick Indians might be a more serious danger than Indians who were fighting fit! . . .

At last the expedition had reached the great, mysterious river that had for so long been its object. Open plains sweep up to the high banks of the South Saskatchewan; lofty, sandy cliffs fall steeply to the river-bed. From the top of the river-bank, the explorers could see ten miles up the deep valley, with all the windings of the river laid out below them. In spring and early summer, when mountain snows are melting, its waters come down in spate; when Palliser first saw it, at the end of summer, there were still deep channels and a strong current, but very noticeable, also, were sand-bars, with a heavy growth of young willows, and, projecting into the stream, points of land on which grew woods of willow, birch, and poplar.

Sixteen miles above the Elbow, where the Coteau crosses the river, the valley is wide and the banks are very high. Below the Elbow the valley narrows . . .

Summer was drawing to a close. The flowers were all dead, killed by the frosts at night, so Monsieur Bourgeau had now only the seeds to collect. A violent gale blew their tents down twice in one night, for the tent-pegs had a bad hold in the loose sand. (This was not the only problem caused by the sand: it blew uncomfortably into their blankets, and, on the march, the carts sank into it up to the axles.) The next day was fine. A large grizzly bear came out of a clump of willows and lay sunning himself on the side of a hill on the opposite side of the river, just near enough for them to be able to see that it was a bear and not a buffalo. As they had no means of getting quickly across the river, they had to content themselves with viewing him through a telescope.

The grizzly was calm, but the men from Red River were not. They were getting more and more excited and worried as the expedition went deeper into Blackfoot country. When they learned that Palliser hoped to push on still farther, up the South Saskatchewan to where the Red Deer joined it, they were horrified. They had not forgotten that thirty-odd years earlier the Hudson's Bay Company had abandoned its post at the Forks of the Red Deer and South Saskatchewan as being too dangerous and too costly; this had given that part of the country a bad reputation. The men tried hard to persuade Palliser that the party was not sufficiently numerous and that to proceed any further into Blackfoot territory with such a small party was too dangerous. They thought they had done wonders already in having gone as far as they had. Wisely, Palliser discussed the matter with McKay, who knew the country and the men. He had a pretty shrewd idea of the risks involved. He was, besides, a man of undoubted courage and strength of character. He replied: 'Captain, if you say the word go, I will say, hurrah, let's go; but if you ask my advice, I will tell you plainly that I think it is too dangerous, and more than this, if you press it, your men will break up, and beyond Beads, John Foulds, and old Hallet I could not say who would stick to you.'

Palliser took his advice. Most unwillingly, and unconvinced, he abandoned the project of pressing on farther west. He prepared to cross the Saskatchewan and make tracks for winter quarters at Fort Carlton. It turned out to be a wise decision. The horses very nearly gave out as it was, before they reached the Fort. Even another few days' work might have been disastrous.

The Great Lone Land

WILLIAM FRANCIS BUTLER

*Lieutenant Butler, like Palliser, was a native of Ireland and a
British military officer. In 1870 he was commissioned to report on
conditions in the Saskatchewan country, and to do so he made a
difficult six-thousand-kilometre round trip from Fort Garry to Fort
Carlton and on to the Rocky Mountains. His subsequent recommendations to the Canadian government included the organizing
of a police force. He wrote a book of eloquent, poetic prose
describing his journey. The Great Lone Land is an enduring
classic of travel literature.*

THE OLD, OLD MAPS which the navigators of the sixteenth century
framed from the discoveries of Cabot and Castier, of Varrazanno and
Hudson, played strange pranks with the geography of the New World.
The coast-line, with the estuaries of large rivers, was tolerably accurate; but the
centre of America was represented as a vast inland sea whose shores stretched
far into the Polar North; a sea through which lay the much-coveted passage to
the long-sought treasures of the old realms of Cathay. Well, the geographers of
that period erred only in the description of ocean which they placed in the
central continent, for an ocean there is, and an ocean through which men seek
the treasures of Cathay, even in our own times. But the ocean is one of grass,
and the shores are the crests of mountain ranges, and the dark pine forests of
sub-Arctic regions. The great ocean itself does not present more infinite variety
than does this prairie-ocean of which we speak. In winter, a dazzling surface of
purest snow; in early summer, a vast expanse of grass and pale pink roses; in
autumn too often a wild sea of raging fire. No ocean of water in the world can
vie with its gorgeous sunsets; no solitude can equal the loneliness of a
night-shadowed prairie: one feels the stillness, and hears the silence, the wail
of the prowling wolf makes the voice of solitude audible, the stars look down
through infinite silence upon a silence almost as intense. This ocean has no
past—time has been nought to it; and men have come and gone, leaving behind
them no track, no vestige, of their presence. Some French writer, speaking of

these prairies, has said that the sense of this utter negation of life, this complete absence of history, has struck him with a loneliness oppressive and sometimes terrible in its intensity. Perhaps so; but, for my part, the prairies had nothing terrible in their aspect, nothing oppressive in their loneliness. One saw here the world as it had taken shape and form from the hands of the Creator. Nor did the scene look less beautiful because nature alone tilled the earth, and the unaided sun brought forth the flowers . . .

At the "forks" of the Saskatchewan the traveller to the east enters the Great Sub-Arctic Forest. Let us look for a moment at this region where the earth dwells in the perpetual gloom of the pine-trees. Travelling north from the Saskatchewan River at any portion of its course from Carlton to Edmonton, one enters on the second day's journey this region of the Great Pine Forest. We have before compared it to the shore of an ocean, and like a shore it has its capes and promontories which stretch far into the sea-like prairie, the indentations caused by the fires sometimes forming large bays and open spaces won from the domain of the forest by the fierce flames which beat against it in the dry days of autumn. Some 500 or 600 miles to the north this forest ends, giving place to that most desolate region of the earth, the barren grounds of the extreme north, the lasting home of the musk-ox and the summer haunt of the reindeer; but along the valley of the Mackenzie River the wooded tract is continued close to the Arctic Sea, and on the shores of the great Bear Lake a slow growth of four centuries scarce brings a circumference of thirty inches to the trunks of the white spruce. Swamp and lake, muskeg and river rocks of the earliest formations, wild wooded tracks of impenetrable wilderness combine to make this region the great preserve of the rich fur-bearing animals whose skins are rated in the marts of Europe at four times their weight in gold. Here the darkest mink, the silkiest sable, the blackest otter are trapped and traded; here are bred these rich furs whose possession women prize as second only to precious stones. Into the extreme north of this region only the fur trader and the missionary have as yet penetrated. The sullen Chipwayan, the feeble Dogrib, and the fierce and warlike Kutchin dwell along the systems which carry the waters of this vast forest into Hudson Bay and the Arctic Ocean.

This place, the "forks" of the Saskatchewan, is destined at some time or other to be an important centre of commerce and civilization. When men shall have cast down the barriers which now intervene between the shores of Lake Winnipeg and Lake Superior, what a highway will not these two great river systems of the St. Lawrence and the Saskatchewan offer to the trader! Less than 100 miles of canal through low alluvial soil have only to be built to carry a boat from the foot of the Rocky Mountains to the head of Rainy Lake, within 100 miles of Lake Superior. With inexhaustible supplies of water held at a level high above the current surface of the height of land, it is not too much to say, that before many years have rolled by, boats will float from the base of the Rocky Mountains to the harbour of Quebec. But long before that time the Saskatchewan must have risen to importance from its fertility, its beauty, and its mineral wealth. Long before the period shall arrive when the Saskatchewan will ship its products to the ocean, another period will have come, when the mining population of Montana and Idaho will seek in the fertile glades of the middle Saskatchewan a supply of those necessaries of life which the arid soil of the central States is powerless to yield. It is impossible that the wave of life which rolls so unceasingly into America can leave unoccupied this great fertile tract; as the river valleys farther east have all been peopled long before settlers found their way into the countries lying at the back, so must this great valley of the Saskatchewan, when once brought within the reach of the emigrant, become the scene of numerous settlements. As I stood in twilight looking down on the silent rivers merging into the great single stream which here enters the forest region, the mind had little difficulty in seeing another picture, when the river forks would be a busy scene of commerce, and man's labour would waken echoes now answering only to the wild things of plain and forest. At this point, as I have said, we leave the plains and the park-like country. The land of the prairie Indian and the buffalo-hunter lies behind us—of the thick-wood Indian and moose-hunter before us.

March to the Wilderness

SAM STEELE

Steele had been a private in the Red River Expedition against the Metis in Manitoba. When the North-West Mounted Police force was established in 1872 he joined and participated in the force's long march west from Fort Garry.

MANY EXAGGERATED REPORTS of the state of affairs in the north west reached the ears of the government at Ottawa, and no doubt caused them to put off doing what should have been done as soon as Lieutenant Butler's report had been submitted. However, on May 3, 1873, Sir John Macdonald introduced a Bill for the establishment of a police force in the North West Territories. This body was not to exceed 300 men, "who should be mounted as the government should from time to time direct," the commissioner and superintendents to be *ex-officio* justices of the peace. The salaries were small when considered in relation to the hardships of the service and the banishment from the advantages of civilization; but the government probably relied on the spirit of adventure regardless of compensation which is innate in every Anglo-Saxon in his early manhood . . .

At Short Creek, on the banks of the Souris, by La Roche Percée, "A" division under Inspector Jarvis left the rest of the train, to proceed to Fort Edmonton via Forts Ellice and Carlton, a distance of 875 miles by trail. The commissioner was compelled to transfer the majority of the men and all of our horses except the officers' chargers to other divisions, and Jarvis received in their stead the quartermaster and several of the youngest and weakest men, 55 sick and almost played-out horses recovering from a severe attack of epizootic, 24 waggons, 55 ox-carts with 12 drivers, 62 oxen, 50 cows and 50 calves to help us on to Fort Ellice.

The commissioner with the main force left La Roche Percée on July 29. We were a disconsolate lot when we saw the force depart on their long trek, but we had a much harder time before us than any experienced that year. There were no oats for the horses, although they had never before done work on grass alone. Erroneous reports of travellers in the northern part of the prairie region had been made to the effect that horses could do 40 miles a day on grass. The people forgot to say that they had ridden and driven on horseback and in buck-boards with a herd of acclimatized native ponies driven behind them, and none of them were obliged to be under saddle or in harness for more than a couple of hours in the day at most.

We remained in camp getting everything put in shipshape order until August 3, when we started for Fort Ellice. Every man, including the sick, was employed. The latter drove teams, and as we went on improved in health. We had a bad time of it for several days after we left La Roche Percée, the horses being so weak that they had to be changed twice both forenoon and afternoon to enable our little force to make 8 miles a day, and the cows and the calves became so footsore that they would lie down every few yards unless a goad were constantly applied. The guide was able to keep ahead of the transport at a slow walk, leading his little pony and cart. The cart train and the yoke oxen followed, while we drove the herd of cows and calves before us. The country over which we passed, now covered with fine farms and comfortable homes, was gently undulating and luxuriant with grass, which caused our horses and cattle to show signs of returning vigour.

We reached Fort Ellice on August 14. It was a large fenced enclosure, with the usual style of dwellings and stores, and stood on the bank of the Assiniboine about 300 feet above the river, surrounded by bluffs of aspen and poplar. The valley, which is more than a mile wide, was very pretty, partly timbered, and there were occasional grassy bottoms on which large herds of ponies, many of them pintos (piebald), and numbers of cattle were grazing. Our horses and cattle were turned out on the flats, and as there were quicksands in different places we had a good deal of practice hauling them out of those death traps, which the Indian ponies knew enough to avoid.

On August 18 we pulled out from Fort Ellice towards the west, leaving behind us the quartermaster, the sick men, half of the cows and calves, a large quantity of provisions and stores and several horses, which were not in good enough condition to be brought with us . . .

On the Salt Plain we met several brigades of carts driven by hunters, freighters and traders with packs of buffalo robes, dried meat and pemmican. Inspector Jarvis bought a supply of pemmican, which is the best food in the world for the traveller, soldier and sailor, either on the plains of America or in the Arctic regions. It was cooked in two ways in the west; one a stew of pemmican, water, flour and, if they could be secured, wild onions or preserved potatoes. This was called "rubaboo"; the other was called by the plain hunters a "rechaud." It was cooked in a frying-pan with onions and potatoes or alone. Some persons ate pemmican raw, but I must say that I never had a taste for it that way.

After eight long weeks of weary days we reached Fort Carlton. Here perfect discipline existed. The offices and stores were neat, and over each door was painted in French and English the name of the store and office, together with the class of goods in the buildings. After a week's rest we pulled out of Carlton. As we left we were informed that the Blackfeet and Crees were again on the warpath. The country through which we went was a good stock country, but we found the cart trail very rough with roots and stones, and the horses were now beginning to show signs of the long march without grain. Game was very plentiful, and the cranes, white wild geese or wavies were in profusion, with considerable numbers of the grey Canadian goose. Our guns and rifles were kept busy during each halt, Corporal Carr on one occasion shooting even wild geese with one barrel . . .

From now on the trouble with our tired horses and oxen increased. Heavy rains had fallen, reducing the trails to a deplorable state, and the poor horses in the waggons staggered along with marvellous pluck. They suffered much more than the oxen and, as the nights became colder, when they lay down to rest the unfortunate brutes became so stiff that they could not rise without help, and I had to call the men up many times during the night to lift them by main force and rub their stiffened limbs to restore the circulation. This occurred so often that the men themselves became exhausted from fatigue and want of sleep.

To add to our troubles, some of the teams would be hours behind the leaders, and we who were in the rear with the cattle and worn-out horses had to stay and help them along. Axes and spades were in constant demand to repair the numerous bad spots on the trail, long stretches of which were under water, often for hundreds of yards. There is a saying that Canadians are born with an axe in their hands, and the way everyone used his on this trek proved to me its truth. In the rear our party were obliged to walk all the time; our horses could carry us no longer. The loose ones we were driving would sometimes fall, and be unable to rise. Carr and I, with a pole under the brisket, had to lift the wretched brutes to their feet while the shoeingsmith assisted to steady them.

At last, however, we reached Victoria, a Company's post with a palisaded enclosure, situated on a narrow ridge along the Saskatchewan. There was a mission founded by the Rev. George McDougall, one of the pioneers of the Methodist church, and round the fort and on the river bank clustered the thatched log houses of the Scotch and English half-breeds who had followed him to the place. These people made a living by hunting buffalo, fishing and freighting. They sowed their crops in the spring, and never saw them again until harvest. If the crops failed it did not matter, for the distance to the herds of buffalo was not far, and the numerous lakes of white fish were near at hand, Whitefish Lake Mission being located about 60 miles north of Victoria.

We enjoyed the halt here among the good people of the settlement. The Cree Indians who had recently come in to trade at the fort came to see and wonder at us. One of them was known by the breathless title of "Sky-Blue-Horn-Sitting-Down-Turning-Round-On-A-Chair"! Before we left Victoria the O.C. made arrangements to leave the cows, calves and weak oxen there for the winter months, under a contract with one of the settlers at 15 dollars a head for oxen and cows and 10 dollars each for calves.

Our progress from here to Edmonton was slow and the going very difficult . . .

Big Bear

HUGH DEMPSEY

Big Bear was a Cree chief and political leader. His was one of the largest Indian bands to roam the parkland and plains in pursuit of the buffalo. Big Bear understood better than most how completely life would change with the coming of white settlers. He resisted signing a treaty, holding out for better conditions, until he and his band were starved into submission.

BIG BEAR, THE SON OF A CHIEF, was in a favoured position as he grew up. People recognized in him the quality of leadership, though he was less flamboyant than his father. He had a ready wit, was highly intelligent and made friends easily. "When he was a boy," said a Cree elder, "people noticed him because he was smart right away. Even then they knew he would be a leader because he got to know so many things when he was still young. He was wise even then."

Having an Ojibwa father also made him different from the Cree boys in camp. The two tribes were closely allied, yet the Ojibwa were recognized for certain differences. Most important of these was their relationship with the supernatural. The Ojibwa were the ones who most often went away to seek visions. They were the ones who made powerful medicines, which could strike down an enemy or help a friend. They made the hunting amulets so prized by the Cree hunters and could foretell the success or failure of a war party. Of course, the Cree had medicine men, too, but their reputations paled in comparison to the power of the Ojibwa.

Immediately after the smallpox epidemic, Big Bear had a vision. It was the first of several visions he was to experience during his lifetime, but it was one with far-reaching implications. In this vision he saw "the coming of the white man, his purchase of the land, the bounteous presents from the Great Mother," and as it was sarcastically described in later years, "the generosity of the new-coming race to his."

The Cree knew that the smallpox had come from the white men, so when Big Bear caught the disfiguring disease, it was his first real "gift" from them.

The dream was a warning that sickness would not be the only tragedy, because all the omens of the vision were bad. In 1838 no one could imagine the white man's presence consisting of any more than a few forts along the rivers and a large settlement at Red River. True, they were responsible for the growing half-breed population, but there was no reason to think that the white man would ever be anything more than a small, necessary evil in their lives. Certainly, no Cree had even thought of selling his hunting grounds to the white man. Who in his right mind would give up the millions of buffalo on the plains, the lakes teeming with fish, and the forest with its game and fur animals? Besides, what would the white man ever do with the land? And what would he do with the Indians?

Yet Big Bear's vision was there, to be recalled and retold whenever significant events occurred in the years to come . . .

In 1866, an event occurred that was the first step in a series of incidents to shatter the complacent life of Big Bear and other Cree leaders along the Saskatchewan River. That summer, they learned that the Iron Stone was missing from its hill near the Battle River. Of all the monuments dedicated to Old Man Buffalo, the Iron Stone was the greatest and most venerated. It was a meteorite composed almost entirely of iron so soft it could be cut with a knife. A total of 386 pounds (176 kg) in weight, it was believed by the Indians to have been placed there after the flood by *Nanebozo*, the great spirit of the Ojibwa. Not only did the stone have protective powers, but the holy men said it grew in size as the years passed. At one time, a person could lift this sacred stone, but now it had grown so that even if someone wrapped his arms around it, he could not raise it from the ground. The Iron Stone was not just a protector of the buffalo; it was the guardian of all the Indians in the region. Offerings were left beside it when the Cree went to seek the buffalo, for they knew that as long as the stone stayed in their hunting grounds, there would be food. Now it was gone.

"The medicine men," observed a visitor several years later, "with unbroken faith in the creed of their fathers, prophesied dire evils to follow the removal of the stone which Manitou had placed on the hill. The buffalo would disappear, there would be a pestilence and fierce war. At the time the prophecy was made, I am told, the plains were black with buffalo, 'whose ponderous tramping made the prairie quiver'; there were no indications of disease; war, though not unknown, was infrequent."

Where had the Iron Stone gone? The Indians soon discovered that Methodist missionaries had loaded it on a cart and taken it a hundred miles (160 km) north to Victoria mission, where it sat in the churchyard. Later, it was shipped to a Methodist college in Ontario, far from the land it had once protected. Missionary George McDougall knew what he had done by taking the stone, for he commented that "for ages the tribes of Blackfeet and Crees have gathered their clans to pay homage to this wonderful manitoo." He also noted that the taking of the idol had "roused the ire of the conjurors. They declared that sickness, war, and decrease of buffalo would follow this sacrilege."

Big Bear, the vision seeker, and holder of the bear bundle and a sacred medicine pipe, often hunted in the area of the Iron Stone, as did his fellow chiefs Little Pine and Sweet Grass. Until that year, the missionaries had been little more than a divisive element, causing some Indians to turn their backs on the old ways and to separate themselves from those the missionaries called pagans. But in taking the Iron Stone, the white medicine men showed themselves to be a threat and a danger to the traditional life of the Indians.

Leaders like Big Bear had heard how white men and half-breeds at Red River were killing all the buffalo, so that the Ojibwa and Cree in the district had to travel for days before finding any game. Other white men were breaking the land and living from the soil without ever going on a hunt. Were missionaries the advance scouts for these people? In war, scouts went ahead to find if it was safe to travel, and the others followed behind. Perhaps the white man was doing the same.

Three years earlier, Broken Arm and Little Hunter had gone to a missionary, complaining that they were poor and hungry. He had told them to give up buffalo hunting and to use their horses for farming. "How can I get my young men to take a hoe and dig up the new sod?" protested one of the chiefs. "I cannot get the young men to work at new ground while the good buffalo meat is so near." So now, as though in answer to the chief's question, the missionaries had taken the stone that protected the herds. This action sowed the first serious doubts in the minds of Big Bear and other chiefs about the intentions of the white man. Until then, neither fur trader nor missionary had done anything to upset the daily lives of the Indians. Now, their motives were in question.

Parsons on the Plains

$\mathcal{J}$OHN $\mathcal{M}$c$\mathcal{D}$OUGALL

McDougall's father, Rev. George McDougall, was a well-known Methodist missionary in the West. In his youth, John frequently accompanied his father, and later became a missionary as well. Henry Steinhauer, an Ojibwa from Ontario, was a Methodist missionary. Maskepetoon was a Cree chief who converted to Christianity.

OUR GUIDE SAID we might strike the Indians very soon, for now the whole country gave signs that large herds had recently been roaming and feeding all around. Next day we came to a large trail, indeed to many large trails paralleling each other. A large company in a compact mass had travelled this way. As our party was small, we were constantly on the watch against surprise.

Notwithstanding all our watchfulness, we were surprised in the early afternoon by a troop of Indian cavalry dashing at us from out of the bluff on one side, and another from the other side. With whoops and yells and fine horsemanship they bore down upon us. I did not know what to think. Peter did not seem to mind them. He sat his horse straighter than before. Soon I knew these were friends sent out to escort us into camp. Presently we saw a flag, and coming up over the hill a small body of riders, and in the centre a "kingly-looking man."

"That is Maskepetoon," said Mr. Woolsey.

We dismounted as we met. The chief thanked Father for coming and invoked a blessing on our meeting. They all shook hands and in company with the chief and escort we continued on our way to the camp.

I took stock of the Indians around us and of their horses. The men were fine specimens generally, a large percentage very good-looking. All were armed with either bow and quiver or flint-lock guns. Nearly all were painted—red, yellow, and blue being the chief colours—red predominating. Their costumes varied from a breech-cloth to perforated leather shirts and leggings. Fancy-coloured calico was common for little shirts which were not more than waists and the sleeves of which came a little past the elbow.

Most of the young men had their hair "banged," and I believe that fashion originally came from the plains. Most of them had brass pendants hanging from the hair and ears, as well as brass collars and armlets. Some wore scalp-locks dangling from arm or leg, which not many moons since were the pride of the original owners on whose head they had grown.

Horses were of all colours and sizes—some very smart and frisky, many exceedingly handsome. The saddles were home-made—some with a bone and wood frame covered with rawhide, others a pad of dressed leather stuffed with moose or deer hair. Stirrups were wood covered with rawhide; stirrup leathers and girths were softened rawhide. Saddle-cloths were home-made too, consisting of the skins of bear, wolf, dog, or buffalo trimmed with strips of red and blue Hudson's Bay strouds—a strong cloth made for this trade.

Many more men had ridden out to meet us, and crowds of boys, two and three on one pony, were joining our *cortège* all the while. The ponies were as full of fun as the boys, many of whom were naked, except for the paint and brass ornaments and beads with which they were bedecked.

We ascended a ridge and saw the large camp before us. There were rings within rings of white tents, varying in size but all of one shape. All were made from the buffalo's hide and many of them were covered with hieroglyphics and paintings indicative either of supernatural power or of martial achievement. Their projecting ventilators, tasselled with buffalo hair, flapped gently in the breeze.

In and out among their tents and beyond them for a mile all around, hundreds of horses were feeding. On almost every knoll groups of guards could be seen whose duty it was to watch over these herds of horses, and the camp also. Everywhere among the tents were stagings made of peeled poles on which was spread the meat of recent hunts in various phases of curing. Here meat was cured without either sugar or salt, but only by the sun and the wind. And either as dried meat, or pemmican, or pounded meat and grease, it will keep for many years.

Women were dressing skins, scraping hides, rendering tallow, pounding meat, making pemmican, slicing up the fresh meat and hanging it on the stages. Some were cooking. Some were sewing with awl for needle and sinew for thread. Scores of naked children were playing and eating and crying in every direction. Hundreds of dogs, half wolf, were fighting and stealing and barking as we rode through the circle of lodges on into the centre of the camp. Here stood a small cluster of large tents.

We alighted. Again the chief welcomed the strangers to his country and camp, once more invoked Heaven's blessings upon the meeting, and then invited us to enter a large tent which was to be our home while in the camp.

Here we found Mr. Steinhauer and his people. This was the first time in the history of the country that three Protestant missionaries had met on the plains. This was the first time in the history of the Methodist Church that a Chairman of a District had visited the Saskatchewan country.

Soon a steaming repast was served of buffalo tongues and "boss." This is the third set or back ribs, unique to the buffalo on this continent. To us this nice, fresh, delicious meat was a feast indeed. We had fed on comparatively nothing, then surfeited on fat bear meat, and made our jaws weary with tough bull meat. But this—no epicure could ask for more or better in the way of meat. Our table was the ground, our mats buffalo robes, our dishes tin. Had we not brought a little salt and tea there would have been none, for the western Indian had not as yet acquired the taste for either. But the kindly manner and princely hospitality, and the delicious quality and large quantity of the meat our hosts served us with, more than made up for anything we might have thought necessary or lacking.

In due time, after our meal was over, the chief asked Father when he would be ready to address his people. Father said that as soon as the camp could be gathered he was ready.

Then the chief summoned two men and said to them, "Ride forth on either side and shout to my people and say, 'Our friends, the praying men, have arrived. One of them is from afar. He is now about to speak to us words of truth and wisdom. All who can be spared from care of camp and guard of horses, come and listen.'" And the criers went forth and shouted as they rode.

Presently, from the whole circumference of the big camp, throngs of men and women and children gathered to where we were with the chief. The Christians were intensely interested, but the pagans were intensely curious. All were reverent and respectful, for all were religious in their way. Our little company, with the native Christian following, sang some hymns while the crowd gathered. Then the Rev. Mr. Steinhauer prayed.

After that Father began his address. He told of the coming of Jesus, how He had found the world in darkness, and men worshipping idols. He told of the commission given to man to preach the Gospel to every creature and what this Gospel had done for the nations who had accepted it. He showed that true civilization originated in and was caused by Christianity. He said that it was because of the command of Jesus that eastern Christians sent missionaries to the Saskatchewan.

He congratulated them on their country. He foretold the extinction of the buffalo, and the suppression of tribal war, and the necessity of this people's preparing for a great change in their mode and manner of life. It was the business of himself and brethren to teach and prepare them for the change which was bound to come.

He prophesied the ultimate settling of this country. He assured them that the government would do the fair and just thing by them. This had been the history of the British government in her dealings with the Indians, always to do justly and rightly by them.

He congratulated them on having a chief like Maskepetoon, who, while brave and strong, was a lover of peace and earnestly desirous of helping his people in every way. He urged them to listen to him and obey him.

He told them that if God spared his life his purpose was to come and dwell with them and become one with them in this great country God had given them. He assured them of the profound interest all Christian people had in them, and urged them to have faith in the Great Spirit and in His Son Jesus.

Treaty Six

ALEXANDER MORRIS

Morris was lieutenant-governor of the North-West Territories from 1872 to 1876 and during that time negotiated four treaties with Indian tribes in what is now Manitoba and Saskatchewan. As white settlement and commerce pushed westward, the government wanted the Indians out of the way. Morris was accompanied by a guard of North-West Mounted Police during the treaty negotiations with the Cree chiefs at Fort Carlton in August 1876.

I THEN PROCEEDED TO THE INDIAN CAMP, together with my fellow Commissioners, and was escorted by Captain Walker and his troop. On my arrival I found that the ground had been most judiciously chosen, being elevated, with abundance of trees, hay marshes and small lakes. The spot which the Indians had left for my council tent overlooked the whole.

The view was very beautiful: the hills and the trees in the distance, and in the foreground, the meadow land being dotted with clumps of wood, with the Indian tents clustered here and there to the number of two hundred.

On my arrival, the Union Jack was hoisted, and the Indians at once began to assemble, beating drums, discharging fire-arms, singing and dancing. In about half an hour they were ready to advance and meet me. This they did in a semicircle, having men on horseback galloping in circles, shouting, singing and discharging fire-arms.

They then performed the dance of the "pipe stem," the stem was elevated to the north, south, west and east, a ceremonial dance was then performed by the Chiefs and head men, the Indian men and women shouting the while.

They then slowly advanced, the horsemen again preceding them on their approach to my tent. I advanced to meet them, accompanied by Messrs. Christie and McKay, when the pipe was presented to us and stroked by our hands.

After the stroking had been completed, the Indians sat down in front of the council tent, satisfied that in accordance with their custom we had accepted the friendship of the Cree nation.

I then addressed the Indians in suitable terms, explaining that I had been sent by the Queen, in compliance with their own wishes and the written promise I had given them last year, that a messenger would be sent to them.

I had ascertained that the Indian mind was oppressed with vague fears; they dreaded the treaty; they had been made to believe that they would be compelled to live on the reserves wholly, and abandon their hunting, and that in time of war, they would be placed in the front and made to fight.

I accordingly shaped my address, so as to give them confidence in the intentions of the Government, and to quiet their apprehensions. I impressed strongly on them the necessity of changing their present mode of life, and commencing to make homes and gardens for themselves, so as to be prepared for the diminution of the buffalo and other large animals, which is going on so rapidly.

The Indians listened with great attention to my address, and at its close asked an adjournment that they might meet in council to consider my words, which was of course granted.

The Rev. C. Scollen, a Roman Catholic Missionary amongst the Blackfeet, arrived soon after from Bow River, and informed me that on the way he had learned that Sweet Grass, the principal Chief of the Plain Crees, was out hunting and would not be at Fort Pitt, and that he was of opinion that his absence would be a great obstruction to a treaty.

After consulting with my colleagues, I decided on sending a messenger to him, requesting his presence, and succeeded in obtaining, for the occasion, the services of Mr. John McKay, of Prince Albert, who had accompanied the Rev. George McDougall on his mission last year.

In the evening, Lieut.-Col. Jarvis arrived with a reinforcement of the Mounted Police, and an excellent band, which has been established at the private cost of one of the troops.

On the 19th, the Commissioners, escorted by the Mounted Police, headed by the band, proceeded to the Indian encampment.

The Indians again assembled, following Mist-ow-as-is and Ah-tuk-uk-koop, the recognized leading Chiefs.

I asked them to present their Chiefs; they then presented the two head Chiefs, and the minor ones.

At this juncture, a messenger arrived from the Duck Lake Indians, asking that I should tell them the terms of the Treaty. I replied that if the Chiefs and people had joined the others they would have heard what I had to say, and that I would not tell the terms in advance, but that the messenger could remain and hear what I had to say. He expressed himself satisfied and took his seat with the others. I then fully explained to them the proposals I had to make, that we did not wish to interfere with their present mode of living, but would assign them reserves and assist them as was being done elsewhere, in commencing to farm, and that what was done would hold good for those that were away.

The Indians listened most attentively, and on the close of my remarks Mist-ow-as-is arose, took me by the hand, and said that "when a thing was thought of quietly, it was the best way," and asked "this much, that we go and think of his words."

I acquiesced at once, and expressed my hope that the Chiefs would act wisely, and thus closed the second day.

The 20th being Sunday, the Rev. Mr. John McKay, of the Church of England, conducted divine service at the fort, which was largely attended; the Rev. Mr. Scollen also conducted service.

At noon a messenger came from the Indian camp, asking that there should be a service held at their camp, which Mr. McKay agreed to do; this service was attended by about two hundred adult Crees.

On Monday, 21st, the head Chiefs sent word that, as the previous day was Sunday, they had not met in council, and wished to have the day for consultation, and if ready would meet me on Tuesday morning. I cheerfully granted the delay from the reasonableness of the request; but I was also aware that the head Chiefs were in a position of great difficulty.

The attitude of the Duck Lake Indians and of the few discontented Saulteaux embarrassed them, while a section of their own people were either averse to make a treaty or desirous of making extravagant demands. The head Chiefs were men of intelligence, and anxious that the people should act unitedly and reasonably.

We, therefore, decided to give them all the time they might ask, a policy which they fully appreciated.

On the 22nd the Commissioners met the Indians, when I told them that we had not hurried them, but wished now to hear their Chiefs.

A spokesman, The Pond Maker, then addressed me, and asked assistance when they settled on the land, and further help as they advanced in civilization.

I replied that they had their own means of living, and that we could not feed the Indians, but only assist them to settle down. The Badger, Soh-ah-moos, and several other Indians all asked help when they settled, and also in case of troubles unforeseen in the future. I explained that we could not assume the charge of their every-day life, but in a time of a great national calamity they could trust to the generosity of the Queen.

The Honourable James McKay also addressed them, saying that their demands would be understood by a white man as asking for daily food, and could not be granted, and explained our objects, speaking with effect in the Cree tongue.

At length the Indians informed me that they did not wish to be fed every day, but to be helped when they commenced to settle, because of their ignorance how to commence, and also in case of general famine; Ah-tuk-uk-koop winding up the debate by stating that they wanted food in the spring when they commenced to farm, and proportionate help as they advanced in civilization, and then asking for a further adjournment to consider our offers.

The Commissioners granted this, but I warned them not to be unreasonable, and to be ready next day with their decision, while we on our part would consider what they had said.

The whole day was occupied with this discussion on the food question, and it was the turning point with regard to the treaty.

The Indians were, as they had been for some time past, full of uneasiness.

They saw the buffalo, the only means of their support, passing away. They were anxious to learn to support themselves by agriculture, but felt too ignorant to do so, and they dreaded that during the transition period they would be swept off by disease or famine—already they have suffered terribly from the ravages of measles, scarlet fever and small-pox.

It was impossible to listen to them without interest, they were not exacting, but they were very apprehensive of their future, and thankful, as one of them put it, "a new life was dawning upon them."

On the 23rd the conference was resumed, an Indian addressed the people, telling them to listen and the interpreter, Peter Erasmus, would read what changes they desired in the terms of our offer. They asked for an ox and a cow each family; an increase in the agricultural implements; provisions for the poor, unfortunate, blind and lame; to be provided with missionaries and school teachers; the exclusion of fire water in the whole Saskatchewan; a further increase in agricultural implements as the band advanced in civilization; freedom to cut timber on Crown lands; liberty to change the site of the reserves before the survey; free passages over Government bridges or scows; other animals, a horse, harness and waggon, and cooking stove for each chief; a free supply of medicines; a hand mill to each band; and lastly, that in case of war they should not be liable to serve.

Two spokesmen then addressed us in support of these modifications of the terms of the Treaty.

I replied to them that they had asked many things some of which had been promised, and that the Commissioners would consult together about what they had asked that day and the day before, and would reply, but before doing so wished to know if that was the voice of the whole people, to which the Indians all assented.

After an interval we again met them, and I replied, going over their demands and reiterating my statements as to our inability to grant food, and again explaining that only in a national famine did the Crown ever intervene, and agreeing to make some additions to the number of cattle and implements, as we felt it would be desirable to encourage their desire to settle.

I closed by stating that, after they settled on the reserves, we would give them provisions to aid them while cultivating, to the extent of one thousand dollars per annum, but for three years only, as after that time they should be able to support themselves.

I told them that we could not give them missionaries, though I was pleased with their request, but that they must look to the churches, and that they saw Catholic and Protestant missionaries present at the conference. We told them that they must help their own poor, and that if they prospered they could do so. With regard to war, they would not be asked to fight unless they desired to do so, but if the Queen did call on them to protect their wives and children, I believed they would not be backward.

I then asked if they were willing to accept our modified proposals.

Ah-tuk-uk-koop then addressed me, and concluded by calling on the people, if they were in favour of our offers, to say so. This they all did by shouting assent and holding up their hands.

The Pond Maker then rose and said he did not differ from his people, but he did not see how they could feed and clothe their children with what was promised. He expected to have received that; he did not know how to build a house nor to cultivate the ground.

Joseph Toma, a Saulteaux, said he spoke for the Red Pheasant, Chief of the Battle River Crees, and made demands as follows: Men to build houses for them, increased salaries to the Chiefs and head men, etc. He said what was offered was too little; he wanted enough to cover the skin of the people, guns, and also ten miles of land round the reserves in a belt.

I asked the Red Pheasant how it was that he was party to the requests of his people, and how, when I asked if that was their unanimous voice he had assented, and yet had now put forward new and large demands.

I said it was not good faith, and that I would not accede to the requests now made; that what was offered was a gift as they had still their old mode of living.

The principal Chiefs then rose and said that they accepted our offers, and the Red Pheasant repudiated the demands and remarks of Toma, and stated that he had not authorized him to speak for him.

Mist-ow-as-is then asked to speak for the Half-breeds, who wish to live on the reserves.

I explained the distinction between the Half-breed people and the Indian Half-breeds who lived amongst the Indians as Indians, and said the Commissioners would consider the case of each of these last on its merits.

The treaty was then signed by myself, Messrs. Christie and McKay, Mist-ow-as-is and Ah-tuk-uk-koop, the head Chiefs, and by the other Chiefs and Councillors, those signing, though many Indians were absent, yet representing all the bands of any importance in the Carlton regions, except the Willow Indians . . .

And now I close. Let us have Christianity and civilization to leaven the mass of heathenism and paganism among the Indian tribes; let us have a wise and paternal Government faithfully carrying out the provisions of our treaties, and doing its utmost to help and elevate the Indian population, who have been cast upon our care, and we will have peace, progress, and concord among them in the North-West; and instead of the Indian melting away, as one of them in older Canada, tersely put it, "as snow before the sun," we will see our Indian population, loyal subjects of the Crown, happy, prosperous and self-sustaining, and Canada will be enabled to feel, that in a truly patriotic spirit, our country has done its duty by the red men of the North-West, and thereby to herself. So may it be.

Thunderchild's Conclusion

Edward Ahenakew

I T SEEMS TO ME that since we have been fenced into reserves, the Cree nation has shrunk, that there are fewer of us. The white men have offered us two forms of their religion—the Roman Catholic and the Protestant—but we in our Indian lands had our own religion. Why is that not accepted too? It is the worship of one God, and it was the strength of our people for centuries.

I do not want to fight the white man's religion. I believe in freedom of worship, and though I am not a Christian, I have never forgotten God. What is it that has helped me and will help my grandchildren but belief in God?

He looks upon the wrong that is done on earth, and knows what would correct it. But we ourselves must find the way and do it.

I remember old Indians who were afraid of guns, even of metal knives.

In the days before my father, the Hudson's Bay Company had a wintering post at Battleford, but there was too much fighting there between the Crees and the Blackfoot, and so the Company went down the river and built Fort Carlton. They gave the Indians one boatload of goods for the use of the Saskatchewan River. That was soon past and forgotten.

This country lasted long with only Indians here, and then the white man came, and they came with might. That was permitted by God. Yet see how they treat the nation that is weaker. Surely our nation is not to be wiped out. In the days that I remember, an Indian would prepare himself to go on a long and difficult journey. So must all be ready for this road of life.

The Promised Land

As far as he could see there was neither tree nor bush—
nothing to clear away before you start to plough, my father reflected.
He was already plotting out his farm.
A little cluster of low hills suggested a site for house and barn,
if only because it was good for nothing else.

JAMES M. MINIFIE
Homesteader

The Queen City

$\mathcal{E}$ARL $\mathcal{G}$. $\mathcal{D}$RAKE

Regina was founded in 1882 and named capital of the North-West Territories the following year. The town was named for Queen Victoria.

THE GOVERNMENT OF CANADA and the Canadian Pacific Railway were responsible for choosing the site of Regina. However, there was one man who influenced the choice more than any other—Lieutenant-Governor Edgar Dewdney. As early as May 10, 1882, Dewdney wrote: "From what I can gather the crossing of Pile of Bones Creek appears to me to be the most favourable point and the country around it is magnificent." During that spring the Governor made inspection trips along the railway route as far west as Rush Lake, in order to choose a site. He was scheduled to be accompanied by General Manager Van Horne of the C.P.R., but it seems unlikely that this busy executive actually did make the trip at this time. At any rate, the Railway concurred in the choice and its president, George Stephen, telegraphed to the Prime Minister from Winnipeg on August 12, "Dewdney here. Have agreed on location of capital new province on Pile of Bones Creek." Acting primarily on Dewdney's advice, the Government also made Regina the headquarters of the North West Mounted Police.

Thus was made the extraordinary decision to establish the capital of the North West on a site which had no notable natural features to commend it for urban settlement. Indeed, the site offered insufficient water, poor drainage, no sheltering hills, and no timber for fuel, lumber or shade. Dewdney's professed reasons for rejecting Indian Head, Qu'Appelle, Fort Qu'Appelle and Moose Jaw in favour of Regina were that it "was as good a point as any and more central and that it was surrounded by a very large area of the best wheat land in the Territories . . . " A further consideration was that there were fewer speculative squatters at the Wascana than at the other sites. In truth there were no very choice townsites in the area, except at Fort Qu'Appelle. This historic and beautiful centre, nestling in the broad wooded valley between Mission and Echo lakes, was a suitable capital location, but it seems not to have been seriously considered because it was sixteen miles north of the all-important rail line. The Railway's decision not to lay steel into this established community and the Government's failure to press it to do so were probably due as much to the desire to reap profits from a new townsite as to the professed engineering reasons against entering the valley.

The only really strong point in Regina's favour was its central position in relation to the provisional district of Assiniboia and to a large area of rich agricultural land. When the fertile areas of the North West Territories had been divided, on May 8, 1882, into the districts of Saskatchewan, Alberta and Assiniboia, these districts had been envisioned as eventually developing into three distinct provinces . . . According to this scheme Regina would ultimately become the capital of the province of Assiniboia. As Sir John A. Macdonald put it, "I believe Regina will make a very creditable and respectable capital for Assiniboia. The other provinces, Saskatchewan and Alberta, will have their own capitals bye and bye." The community's position in the midst of a vast wheat-growing area was, however, to be its main justification. Moose Jaw Creek was on the edge of the best farm land but Wascana Creek was in the very middle of the area of heavy, stone-free soil which was to produce so much cereal wealth. It was fitting that the capital of an agricultural territory and, later on, an agricultural province, should be chosen for its potentialities as the market centre of a tributary farming area.

Many of Dewdney's contemporaries (especially those who were his political opponents) were not convinced that the rich soil of the neighbourhood compensated for the several defects of the site. Sceptical observers believed there was a different reason behind the Governor's choice. Dewdney and several friends had formed at least two syndicates early in 1882, and had bought approximately twenty-eight sections of Hudson's Bay Company lands adjacent to the future route of the C.P.R. in Assiniboia. Hudson's Bay Company lands were the only property along the railway route that could be purchased at this time, as the rest had been reserved for railway and governmental purposes. One parcel of land owned by one of these syndicates consisted of the south half and the north-west quarter of section 26, township 17, range 20, west of the second principal meridian. The members appear to have gone to a great deal of trouble to conceal their identity, but documents in the Land Titles Office reveal that there were eleven participants, including Dewdney, two members of parliament, a former Manitoba cabinet minister, the comptroller of the Mounted Police, a high official of the Hudson's Bay Company, a son of the Honourable A. T. Galt, and a future Manitoba judge. Their property later became part of Regina, bordered on the south by Dewdney Avenue and on the east by Pasqua Street. This was just north of where the railway crosses Wascana Creek—the very spot selected as the centre of the capital by Dewdney himself!

Had the capital developed near the creek crossing as Dewdney wished, then section 26 would almost surely have become an important portion of the town. If the 480 acres, which were later subdivided into approximately 6,500 lots, had been sold at $250 per lot (the average sale price of townsite lots in 1882-83) the Dewdney syndicate stood to make a tidy fortune. As the land was purchased for only $3,360, a handsome profit of $1,000,000 could have been made by the sale of only two thirds of the lots. Future developments were to prevent the syndicate from making any substantial profit, but in the meantime there was much caustic denunciation of the Lieutenant-Governor and his capital.

Dewdney denied that his property interests had influenced his choice. He explained to the Prime Minister that he had only "a small interest in the twenty-eight sections of Hudson's Bay Company lands" and that "my interest in the Hudson's Bay Company section on the Bell Farm [at Indian Head, a rival site] is more than double what it is at Pile of Bones and they both lie in the same position to the town sites." Existing evidence substantiates these statements. This was an era of widespread dabbling in real estate; Dewdney was an intelligent and diligent official; and so he apparently convinced the Prime Minister and others that his personal speculations had no bearing on the performance of his public duties. However, even one of his political allies, the Winnipeg *Times*, declared, "He may say that he is or was interested in section 26 at Regina and that he holds shares in the Bell Farm, not as Lieutenant-Governor but as plain Mr. Dewdney. It is impossible, however, to distinguish between the two entities more especially as Lieutenant-Governor Dewdney and Mr. Dewdney have a common pocket."

Some of those associated with the C.P.R. were convinced that Dewdney was seeking personal gain and said so, even though they had previously approved the site. It was difficult for them to be calm about the matter because the C.P.R. at this time was in deep financial distress and desperately anxious to make every possible profit. Townsite property, especially in a capital city, was a most valuable asset, and the Railway was in no mood to share real-estate profits with outsiders (other than with its partner, the Government). A real-estate struggle was imminent.

Riel

MAGGIE SIGGINS

Louis Riel was born at Red River in 1844. He was educated in St-Boniface, then Montreal, before returning west in 1868. He found his fellow Metis were fearful of losing their land and rights to the intrusions of white settlers. The Metis established a provisional government with Riel as its leader, but he was forced into exile in the United States when Canada sent in a military force. Many of the Metis moved farther west, and some of them settled along the banks of the South Saskatchewan River in and around Batoche. In 1884, with white settlement pushing into this territory as well, the Metis sent a delegation to Montana to convince Riel to return to help them protect their rights in the Saskatchewan Valley.

JANUARY 1, 1885, must have been one of the most enjoyable days in Louis Riel's life. Two hundred residents of the St. Laurent community, from St. Louis de Langevin in the north to Tourond's Coulee in the south, gathered at Baptiste Boyer's house for a huge New Year's Day banquet in Riel's honour. Everyone, grandmothers, infants in arms, young girls, elderly men smoking pipes, attended. The fiddlers played all night and the dancing never stopped. The tables groaned under the weight of the feast dishes. Madeleine Dumont had arranged that a new dress be made for Madame Riel. Marguerite had developed a bad cough and had not been feeling well over the winter. The two children, Jean and Angélique, were thriving, though, and they were rambunctious with all the other kids. For Louis, the most wonderful part of the evening was when the letter from "the Inhabitants of St. Louis de Langevin" was read. It made very clear how much the Métis loved and honoured him.

We do not want to let the opportunity of this New Year pass by without acknowledging the respect, gratitude, and affection we have for the one who we justly regard as the true father of the French

59

populations inhabiting the vast territories of the Northwest.

To us, you are, as in the Roman days, the valiant leader of this population that is strongly confident that, God willing, you will one day bring to victory our just claims.

This was followed by many toasts. It was the year, they all said, that great honour and wealth would finally come to Louis Riel. He responded by saluting all the Métis women in the room, and Queen Victoria.

Life was rather pleasant right then. There was still hope that the government might respond to the petition. The war with the Oblate fathers had eased a little. And the Riel family finances were not quite as tight; a cash subscription had been raised for their immediate use. In November, the Riels had left the Nolin home at St. Louis de Langevin and had moved into a cabin on Moïse Ouellette's farm. For Riel it was a weaning away from the Manitoba émigrés and their emphasis on caution, and a move, both physically and intellectually, towards the Saskatchewan Métis dominated by the activist Dumont clan . . .

On January 28, 1885, the federal government finally got around to doing something about Métis land claims. A three-man Halfbreed Land Claims Commission was set up, but its only mandate was to compile a list of all those living in the Northwest Territories who might be entitled to receive land grants. Those who had received scrip in Manitoba were to be excluded from any such largesse in the Northwest. A telegram announcing the commission was sent to the lieutenant-governor and he was shocked by it. It gave the Métis almost nothing they wanted. Of the 1,300 who believed they had a claim, only 200 fit into the purview of the commission. To make matters worse, there was not a word about the thorny question of river lots. Nor was there a mention of Riel's personal claim. Dewdney thought it might very well incite the Métis to violence, and so he reworded the official version to vaguely read: "Government has decided to investigate claims of Half Breeds and with that view has already taken preliminary steps." This was passed on to the territorial representative, David Macdowall, who in turn gave it to Charles Nolin. Riel finally saw the Dewdney telegram on February 8. It was not until almost a month later that Dewdney showed Father André the original version from Ottawa.

The Dewdney version of the government's proposal caused much excitement. Another "investigation" was not what the Métis wanted, but at least it was a response to the petition. Riel himself felt that his job was all but done. In the second week of February, he made arrangements with Louis Marion to drive him and his family to Winnipeg in mid-March. He planned a visit to his family before he returned to his teaching job in Montana.

On February 17, a forty-hour prayer marathon took place at St. Laurent de

Grandin Church, concluding with the unveiling of a special dedication, written by Riel, of the Métis nation to the Sacred Heart of Jesus. Some thought it was a little like a war cry. "Sacred Heart of Jesus! Give us the light! Instruct us! Protect us! Defend us! Strengthen us! Save us! with all those to whom we are united by blood."

On February 24, 1885, a community meeting was held at St. Antoine de Padoue Church at Batoche. The place, as usual, was packed. Ostensibly the subject was Dewdney's telegram but the talk quickly shifted to the real concern that night. Riel told the crowd that the work he had promised to do—draft the petition—was completed and they had an answer of sorts from the government. Now, given his notoriety, he would be nothing but a hindrance to their movement. He had received reports that the NWMP were secretly conspiring to arrest him. He had always said he would return to the United States; now he planned to do just that. The entire church erupted with shouts of "No! No!" People jumped to their feet. One old Métis yelled, "If you leave, nephew, we will go with you!" A white settler from Prince Albert boomed out that Riel must stay in the country. Charles Nolin, according to his friends, "would have continued to clamour NO! forever if someone hadn't interrupted him." Even the priest, Fourmond, got in the mood and blessed Riel for his patriotism. When the racket had subsided, Riel asked quietly, "And the consequences?" Almost to a man, they answered, "We will suffer the consequences!"

On March 1, Riel addressed the congregation on the steps of the little St. Laurent de Grandin Church. According to the memoirs of Louis Schmidt, written after he had turned against his old friend, Riel upped the ante considerably. Peace and compromise had achieved nothing, he suggested; maybe it was time for the Métis "to bare their teeth". Then, according to Schmidt, he spoke quite irrationally, "For I have only to lift my finger and you will see a vast multitude of nations rushing here who are only awaiting the signal on my part."

The next day Riel, Napoléon Nault and Damase Carrière set off for Prince Albert. Twelve years before, Father André had assisted them in setting up a government in the newly formed St. Laurent district. Perhaps he could give them some advice, even his blessing, for some kind of provisional government. They obviously had no idea how much André loathed Riel, or they wouldn't have bothered. He hadn't stopped writing Lieutenant-Governor Dewdney pleading for bribe money to get Riel out of the country. His letter of February 8, 1885, was typical: "I am aware that his [Riel's] name has already caused you considerable annoyance, and that you would be glad to hear no more about this notorious character. I share your feeling in this regard . . . " Naturally, André was not going to sanction any government that Riel would lead. At first

Louis was polite towards the priest. But once André, in his usual condescending and sarcastic manner, began belittling the idea, Louis became enraged. He abruptly turned on his heel and left. From that time on there would be open warfare between the two men.

On March 3, Riel, with Dumont and sixty other intimidating-looking Métis, attended a meeting at Halcro Village with white settlers and English-speaking Half-breeds. Riel said the reason his companions were armed was that he needed protection; the Mounties, he had heard, were about to arrest him. Although he did not talk of open rebellion, he railed against the government. That night many of the settlers decided to distance themselves from the Métis and their movement . . .

On March 5, a secret meeting was held at Gabriel's Landing. Attending were Louis Riel and ten other Métis, including Gabriel Dumont, who was still very much in command of these people. Four others were members of the Dumont clan. A revolutionary oath written by Riel was taken and it was vintage Riel, a strange mixture of politics and religion:

> We, the undersigned, pledge ourselves deliberately and voluntarily to do everything we can to
>
> 1. save our souls by trying day and night to live a holy life everywhere and in all respects.
>
> 2. save our country from a wicked government by taking up arms *if necessary* (italics added).
>
> We particularly pledge ourselves to raise our families in a holy way and to ceaselessly practise the greatest trust in God, in Jesus, Mary, Joseph and Saint John the Baptist and in all our patron saints. For our banner we take the commandments of God and the Church and the inspiring cross of Jesus Christ our Lord.

There followed the mark X of ten men. Louis Riel's signature was not on the document, probably because he considered himself only an adviser. As George Woodcock points out, the coming together of this secret society indicated "the old Saskatchewan clans of hunters who had dominated the earlier council at St. Laurent were once again moving into the leadership."

There was a reason for the rising militancy in the early days of March. Bad news had been filtering into the St. Laurent settlement for weeks.

On February 20, the prime minister had finally made a decision about Louis Riel's own demands—the large sum André and Macdowall had said they would get him. Sir John A. was blunt: "We have no money to give Riel. He has a right to remain in Canada and if he conspires we must punish him. That's all." There was indignation throughout the entire Métis community.

On March 4, the full details of the government's telegram to Dewdney announcing the Halfbreed Claims Commission were, at last, released. For most in the community the idea of getting a few more acres of land in the vast Northwest vanished. The day after this announcement was made, March 5, the secret oath of Métis militants was taken.

But there was something even more serious to worry about. The summer before, in 1884, two hundred heads of households had submitted applications for patents to their river lots. All but forty-five land owners in the St. Laurent settlement area had finally caved in and made the boundaries of their land conform to the government's survey. Since they had done what was expected of them, they had assumed that, after years of pleading, they would finally get title to their land. However nine months had passed without a word. Finally in February the Prince Albert land office received its instructions. All but six had been allowed only the right to "enter" for their property. This meant they would have to perform further homestead duties—cultivate more land, remain on their properties for months at a time—and pay fees. If their farms were over the 160-acre limit, the maximum allowable under a "free grant", they would be charged $1 or $2 an acre, money most of them didn't have. Worse, they were required to go through the whole application process again, including inspection by a Dominion Lands Office agent. These bureaucrats were notoriously patronizing and often bigoted in their attitude towards Half-breeds and Indians. If they felt for any reason that an applicant was not living up to the Homestead Act—perhaps the fields were not ploughed neatly enough—they would recommend denial of the patent. And the officials in the land office in Prince Albert and in Ottawa's Department of the Interior were even worse tyrants. No wonder many Métis felt the chance of ever owning their land was slim indeed. Not only that, but about thirty families were still living on land the government had sold to the Prince Albert Colonization Company; that problem was simply ignored. The government could claim that it was acting within the rules and regulations set down by the Dominion Lands Act, but that meant nothing to these people. They were desperate. With the buffalo gone for good, and freighting jobs shrinking every year, their only chance for survival was on their land. To lose it would be to face an unspeakable future.

Blood Red the Sun

WILLIAM BLEASDELL CAMERON

When hostilities erupted between the Metis and the Canadian government in the spring of 1885, Cameron was a twenty-two-year-old Hudson Bay Company clerk at Frog Lake, near Fort Pitt. The tense situation in the North-West, combined with years of depri-vation among Big Bear's band, led to violence. The old chief attempted to prevent bloodshed but lost control of his younger men, who killed nine people. Only Cameron and the two white women at Frog Lake post were spared. He became a writer and well-known as the "lone survivor of Frog Lake," a story that he told and retold.

THE DOOR OF THE CHURCH WAS OPEN. Several armed and painted Indians stood before it. Father Marchand stepped down to close it, but Father Fafard stopped him. Big Bear and Miserable Man stood inside at the back. The chief told me later that he was there to prevent bloodshed and I believed him; for though outwardly calm, well do I recall the suppressed feeling and determination on the old warrior's face. I am convinced Big Bear would have flung himself upon the first of his savage followers to point a gun and fought for our lives.

All the whites were assembled, as well as the half-breeds. The priests were celebrating mass, for it was a holy day of their church—the day before Good Friday.

I stepped across to the row of pews opposite the door and took a seat . . .

The congregation was kneeling, and I knelt with the others.

A moment later there came the rattle of musketry from the door and looking out from beneath my arm I saw Wandering Spirit enter. He moved cat-like on his moccasined feet to the centre of the church and dropped on his right knee there, his Winchester clutched in his right hand, the butt resting on the floor. His lynx-skin war-bonnet, from which depended five large eagle plumes, crowned his head; his eyes burned and his hideously-painted face was set in lines of deadly menace. Never shall I forget the feelings his whole appearance and action excited in me as I watched in stupified amazement while

64

he half-knelt, glaring up at the altar and the white-robed priests in sacrilegious mockery. He was a demon, a wild animal, savage, ruthless, thirsting for blood. I doubted then that we should any of us ever again see the outside of the chapel.

Prayers ended, the priests warned the Indians against committing any excesses and we were allowed to leave the church. Those of the Roman Catholic faith dipped their fingers in the font at the door and crossed themselves as they passed out. I returned to the shop and the other whites were soon after taken by the Indians back to the agency. King Bird, Big Bear's second son, accompanied me.

"*N' Chawamis,*" he asked, "with whom do you side, Riel or the Police?"

"Cousin," I replied, "the half-breed war is far from us. Let them fight it out between themselves. Here we are all friends." It did not answer to be too candid on this second of April morning. He asked for the loan of the Hudson's Bay Company's flag for the dance he said they intended holding later in the day and I allowed him to have it. Quinn, cool and self-possessed, his Scotch cap on the back of his head, came in and we spoke together for a few minutes. Leaving, he said to me: "Well, Cameron, if we live through this we'll have something to remember for the rest of our days."

Wandering Spirit appeared in the door. "Go to the instructor's where the other whites are," he rapped out.

I hastened to obey. The Indians were sacking the Mounted Police barracks and as I was passing it Yellow Bear came out and stopped me. Earlier in the day he had asked for a hat, but after thinking a moment had replaced it on the shelf, saying he would get it later. It was now ten o'clock. "I want to get that hat," he said.

King Bird danced up to me, the Hudson's Bay flag over his shoulders. We had always been good friends. "*N' gowichin!* (I'm cold!)" he said. He shook, but not from cold; the day was warm and pleasant. It was from suppressed excitement. He came closer and added meaningly, in a whisper: "Don't stop around here!"

I turned to Yellow Bear. "You can have the hat," I said. "Come with me."

He balked; he did not wish to miss his share of the police plunder. "Won't you bring it to me?" he asked.

"Wandering Spirit has just ordered me here," I answered. "If he saw me going back he might shoot me."

"Yes? I will go with you then," said the Indian.

The shop was not much more than a hundred paces distant. Half way we were stopped by Wandering Spirit. He was running, carrying his Winchester at the trail.

"I told you to stay with the other whites!" he exploded, his rifle poised suggestively in front of him as he stood for an instant regarding me darkly out of his evil eyes.

Yellow Bear interposed quickly. "He's going with me to get a hat. The sun's hot and I have none."

Whatever may have been the question engaging the mind of the fiery leader it had, for the moment at least, been resolved. Flinging at me a last significant admonition to "Hurry back," accompanied by another disconcerting stare, he ran on.

Thinking over the situation since, I have reached the conclusion that the only thing that saved me at this pregnant juncture was Yellow Bear's instant grasp of my peril. Wandering Spirit had all morning endeavored to keep me constantly with the other whites and he was now clearly exasperated by his failure to do so and as a result was ready at once to begin the massacre as he proved to be ten minutes later. I do not think he foresaw the climax coming quite so soon as it did and he therefore expected me to be back with the other victims in time to share their common fate, for there is no room whatever for doubt that he had then no thought that I should escape a bullet.

As I passed the Hudson's Bay house I saw Big Bear talking with Mrs. Simpson in the kitchen. Yellow Bear got his hat and I was locking the shop again, when Miserable Man appeared with an order from the Indian agent. I glanced across and saw Quinn standing on the hill I had just quitted, faced by Wandering Spirit.

I turn to an old scrap book and from a piece of foolscap pasted in the back copy the faded lines, the last writing of my brave friend. It is worn and soiled, for I carried it in my waistcoat pocket for many weeks. It is undated, but to me nothing done on that fateful 2nd of April needs a mark. It reads:

> Dear Cameron,
> Please give Miserable Man one blanket.
> T.T.Q.

Miserable Man was, I think, the most brutal-looking Indian I have ever seen. His face was deeply pitted by smallpox, and the yellow ochre with which it was coated made it appear even more repulsive than usual.

"I have no blankets," I said.

He did not reply but stood regarding me doubtfully, an ominous cast in his rat-like eyes.

"What are you looking at him for?" demanded Yellow Bear. "Don't you hear him say he has no blankets? They've even taken the blankets off his own bed."

Miserable Man was as great a coward as he was huge in bulk. His belligerent mask dropped from him at once. "Well, can't I have something instead?" he enquired humbly. I said he might.

He selected a small shawl, a "carrot" of tobacco and a balance in tea. I dumped the tea into the shawl (our customers did not expect to receive their purchases wrapped) and he was tying up the parcel when a shot, sounding as if just outside the building, brought my heart for an instant into my mouth. Two more followed in quick succession.

At the first report the eyes of Miserable Man opened wide. At the third he snatched his bundle from the counter and dashed out of the shop. I followed with Yellow Bear, locking the door behind me and putting the heavy brass key in my pocket. Two months later, on the day of my escape from the Indians, I left that key in a discarded pair of trousers hanging in a poplar bluff near Frenchman's Butte. It was the sole substantial relic to escape destruction of what had been the Hudson's Bay Company's trading post at Frog Lake.

On the hill before the police barracks which I had quitted only ten minutes before lay the form of a man. It was the lifeless body of poor Quinn.

Dust and smoke filled the air; whoops and shrieks and the clatter of galloping hoofs blended in a weird and ghastly symphony. High over all swelled the deadly war-chant of the Plains Crees, bursting from a hundred sinewy throats. I heard the peculiarly-ringing voice of Wandering Spirit calling on his followers to shoot the other whites and burst after burst sounded the death knell of other of my friends. Walking Horse, staring out of the Company's house, muttered savagely, but half-scared: "*Atim-eenawuk!* (Dog-men!)"

Big Bear rushed out of the kitchen doorway and toward his followers, shouting at the top of his tremendous voice:

"*Tesqua! Tesqua! (Stop! Stop!)*"

As well might he have shouted at the wind. The smouldering fire of inherent savagery had burst into flame and he was powerless to quench it; the spring of blood of the old chief's dream had broken forth and spurted through his futile fingers!

Skyscrapers Hide the Heavens

J. R. MILLER

N THE TREATIES OF THE 1870s many western Indians had been promised that they could have schools on their reserves when they wanted them, and in the years following the making of the numbered treaties some steps were taken to support the schools that missionaries had already established or wished to erect near or in Indian settlements. In the 1880s the educational policy for western Canada and British Columbia shifted from day schools to boarding institutions.

The theory behind residential schooling had not changed since Ryerson's day: it was still an experiment in social engineering. As the DIA 1889 Annual Report put it: "The boarding school disassociates the Indian child from the deleterious home influences to which he would otherwise be subjected. It reclaims him from the uncivilized state in which he has been brought up. It brings him into contact from day to day with all that tends to effect a change in his views and habits of life. By precept and example he is taught to endeavour to excel in what will be most useful to him." The underlying purpose of residential schooling was what the Americans called "aggressive civilization."

Initially, Indians welcomed offers of education for their young in western Canada as they had in the east. They understood the significance of the coincident arrival of whites and disappearance of bison: they would have to adjust to new ways and to new methods of earning a living. A young Assiniboine who "at the age of twelve years . . . was lassoed, roped and taken to the Government School" later recalled that he had been sent to school to acquire "the whiteman's magic art of writing, 'the talking paper.'" But Indians wanted enough schooling to enable them to cope with the new order, not what they got. From 1883 onward the federal government established "industrial schools" off the reserves at which Indian children would be educated and trained far from parental and band influence. As a federal cabinet minister explained in the Commons: "If these schools are to succeed, we must not have them too near the bands; in order to educate the children properly we must separate them from their families. Some people may say that this is hard, but if we want to civilize them we must do that." A parallel system of boarding schools, which were less ambitious and less well financed than the industrial schools, persisted after 1883. Industrial and boarding schools both aimed at the assimilation of the Indian children.

The residential schools were operated in uneasy tandem by government and the missionary societies of the Catholic, Anglican, Methodist, and Presbyterian churches. Part of the unease arose from denominational rivalries among churches in various locations. More stemmed from the tug of war over funds between Indian Affairs and the missionaries. Although it was originally the department's intention to concentrate its efforts among the western Indians in the industrial schools, finances made it impossible to do so. The industrial schools were very expensive, and parliament was forever complaining about the heavy costs of Indian Affairs. In 1892 an attempt was made to control expenses by shifting to a new financing system, but costs continued to spiral well beyond the results that school inspectors could turn up in their annual visits. Moreover, both teachers and officials encountered substantial Indian opposition to residential schooling. In some cases parents complained that their children worked too long in fields and shops, while learning too little in classes. In other cases they objected to the harsh discipline, including corporal punishment, and the poor food. By the early twentieth century the escalating death rates in the schools were becoming a public scandal as well as a reason for both parental and student refusal to cooperate with the residential schooling experiment. Not even the 1894 introduction of compulsory schooling regulations proved sufficient to keep some of the schools full.

The department's response was to contemplate exerting even more control over young Indians. As early as 1892 Indian Affairs considered the establishment of "colonies" where graduates of the industrial and boarding schools might be sent to keep them longer from the influence of home and reserve. One such farming community was set up in the File Hills area of southern Saskatchewan at the turn of the century, and others were contemplated. Although the File Hills experiment lasted almost to mid-century, it by no means realized the complete assimilation of the "colonists" that was intended.

Because the industrial schools, though much more expensive, proved little better in educating children than the boarding schools, Ottawa shifted away from the costly experiment. The Liberal government in power after 1896 was particularly unsympathetic to ambitious plans to train children in trades and agriculture in the industrial schools, the minister responsible for them saying flatly that "the attempt to give a highly civilized education to the Indian child . . . was practically a failure. I have no hesitation in saying—we may as well be frank—that the Indian cannot go from school, making his own way and compete with the white man." The federal government reduced funding to the schools, looked for ways to close some and move their students to "new, improved day schools," and, finally, gave up the distinction between industrial and boarding schools. In 1923 both industrial and boarding schools were amalgamated into a single category known as "residential schools." By then the system had grown quite large. Where in 1883 there had been three government-financed industrial schools and an unknown number of boarding establishments run by the churches, by 1907 there were twenty-two industrial and fifty-three boarding schools. The system still reached only a minority of school-age children, however. These schools would persist till the 1960s.

The failure of Indian education in general, and residential schooling in particular, was attributable to government parsimony and Indian resistance. As Ottawa's refusal to continue for even a decade the high level of funding required for industrial schools illustrated, the government was not prepared to pursue assimilation through education if the struggle was going to be lengthy and expensive. From 1892 onward it tried regularly to shift an ever larger share of the cost of running these schools onto the shoulders of the school children and missionary organizations that, for their part, were becoming increasingly disillusioned with Indians, schools, and their government partners. The government preferred, as in the compulsory attendance provisions, to move to coercion rather than to invest in the schools to such an extent that Indians would want to send their children there. But Indians did not want to, because the schools were ineffective, harsh, unsafe, and interfered with the development of the Indian child into a being with a sense of identity and a place in society. Most graduates found there was no work for them; many returned to the reserves and psychological limbo.

The Indians resisted coercive education in a variety of ways. Most simply they refused to surrender their children to the school and Indians Affairs authorities, no matter what policeman or agent said. Those who were still nomadic or semi-nomadic, as was often the case on the west coast, could simply remove themselves from the reach of those who enforced the compulsory attendance provisions. The parents could disrupt the school by making unauthorized visits or by failing to return their children after holiday visits home. On the Blackfoot reserve in 1895 an Indian Affairs employee was killed and the missionary-principal of the school forced to flee in fear for his life. At the Kamloops school the Shuswap chiefs came to the school and drove out an instructor who had abused a girl. When the offender returned the next year in clerical garb, the "chief came and really raised hell with him, told him 'I don't care if you come camouflaged in a priest suit . . . we told you to leave. We don't want you back. Get.'" The children were even more effective at resisting. They could—and did—misbehave, violate rules, refuse to learn, defiantly continue to speak their own languages in spite of official prohibitions, run away, and in the ultimate case, indulge in acts of arson against property and violence against the staffs of the schools. One particularly ambitious break-out involved "planning for weeks on end, packing stuff and hiding it outside." The girls involved in this escape managed to evade capture for some time.

While some students of these residential schools were thoroughly converted by the experience, many more absorbed only enough schooling to resist still more effectively. It would be from the ranks of former residential school pupils that most of the leaders of Indian political movements would come in the twentieth century. Unfortunately, yet another large group—probably more than one-quarter of the pre-1914 students—succumbed to disease during or shortly after their stay at the schools. By any reasonable standard of evaluation, the residential school program . . . failed miserably.

Beginnings in Canada

Maria Adamowska

By late in the century Indian people had been confined to reserves and the Metis pushed to the margins of the new society. Following the election of the Laurier government in 1896 aggressive attempts were made to lure settlers to the North-West. Among those recruited were Europeans from Britain, Germany, Hungary, Russia, Scandinavia, and Ukraine. Most came as individual settlers, but others, like the Doukhobors, Mennonites, and some Germans, settled in groups or colonies. Saskatchewan, already home to various aboriginal nations and the Metis, became an even more multi-ethnic society also comprising many European races.

MY PARENTS AND I left our native village of Mykhalkove, the familiar thatched cottage, the beautiful orchard, and all those lovely scenes of my early, carefree childhood. Inexpressible grief seized my young heart when all our relatives and everyone from the village met in our yard to wish us Godspeed into the faraway, unknown world. The parting and the mournful keening were heartbreaking. Old and young wept as they bade us farewell, perhaps forever. And little girls, my schoolmates and girlfriends, wept with me.

The mere mention of school broke my heart. It was as if my soul presaged the loss of the most valuable treasure in my life, one which I would never recover. I loved school and learning as I loved my dear mother. But cruel fate had decreed against me.

Amidst tears and despair, we seated ourselves in the wagon and set out for Cherniwtsi. When we reached the hill on the outskirts of the settlement, we paused for a last look at our dear native village, nestled proudly in the midst of its cherry orchards as if decked with garlands. Overcome by grief, none of us had the strength to utter a single word . . .

In Cherniwtsi, we boarded the train and proceeded on our way.

My father was a man of firm resolve. He was glad to tear himself away from the Polish yoke once and for all. Hence, having temporarily borne the pain of parting with his homeland, he began to take an interest in the beautiful scenery as it flashed past the windows of the train and began to weave golden visions of that fabulous land, Canada.

Mother, on the other hand, was tenderhearted. Of all the trials that had been her lot in life, this one was the most bitter. Whenever father had mentioned going to Canada, she had started to cry. And she cried all the way on the train and missed seeing the lovely sights in God's good world.

We arrived in Hamburg. Here we had to wait a few days for our ship. My childish fancy was captured by the sight of huge dogs hitched to carts full of large milk cans. The milk vendors shouted as they went about making their deliveries.

Finally, our ship arrived. It anchored some distance away from the shore, and we were transported to it in a small boat.

Aboard the ship, we met more of our countrymen from Galicia and Bukovina who were also on their way to Canada. We were assigned to cabins with bunks placed one above the other. The journey had its ill effects on a number of passengers. Many suffered from seasickness and had trouble holding food in their stomachs. Some ugly scenes took place, especially at night. If a person in the lower bunk forgot himself and stuck his head out, he ran the risk of being plastered with vomit from the bunk above him. When it happened, the sight was more deplorable than funny . . .

Finally, we sailed into port at Halifax. On the shore, a crowd of people stared at us, some out of curiosity, some out of contempt. Our men, particularly those from Galicia, were dressed like gentlemen for the voyage, but the women and children traveled in their everyday peasant costumes. The older men from Bukovina attracted attention to themselves by their waist-length hair—greased with reeking lard—and by their smelly sheepskin coats. Perhaps that was the reason why the English people stopped their noses and glued their eyes upon us—a strange spectacle, indeed.

In Halifax, we boarded a train and continued on our journey. As we sped across Ontario with its rocks, hills, and tunnels, we were afraid we were coming to the end of the world. The heart of many a man sank to his heels, and the women and children raised such lamentation as defies description.

At last we arrived in Winnipeg. At that time, Winnipeg was very much like any other small farmers' town. From the train we were taken to the immigration home. Here one great source of consolation was Kyrylo Genyk. He spoke with each one of us and offered his kind advice. And he inquired of those from his native village about his schoolmate Mykhailo Dorundiak . . .

From Winnipeg, we went to Yorkton, Saskatchewan. There we hired a rig which took us more than thirty miles farther north. At long last, after a miserable trip—we were nearly devoured alive by mosquitoes—we managed to reach our destination, the home of our acquaintances.

Our host, who had emigrated to Canada a year or two before, had written us to boast of the prosperity he had attained in such a short time. He said that he had a home like a mansion, a large cultivated field, and that his wife was dressed like a lady. In short, he depicted Canada as a country of incredible abundance whose borders were braided with sausage like some fantastic land in a fairy tale.

How great was our disenchantment when we approached that mansion of his and an entirely different scene met our eyes! It was actually just a small log cabin, only partly plastered and roofed with sod. Beside the cabin was a garden plot which had been dug with a spade. The man's face was smeared with dirt from ear to ear, and he looked weird, like some unearthly creature. He was grubbing up stumps near the house, and his wife was poking away in the garden. She reminded us of Robinson Crusoe on an uninhabited island. She was suntanned like a gypsy and was dressed in old, torn overalls. A wide-brimmed hat covered her head.

When mother saw this scarecrow, she started crying again. Later on, father reprimanded the man for writing us such nonsense. But his only answer was, "Let someone else have a taste of our good life here."

Quest for a New Homeland

ℱATHER ℬRUNO ᗅOERFLER

*In 1902, with open land becoming scarce in Minnesota, a group
of German Catholics were looking for a place where many of them
could settle in the same locale. Father Bruno Doerfler led a small
group on a trip through the Canadian North-West in search of
fertile land. In this excerpt from Father Doerfler's diary, the group
sets out in an easterly direction from Rosthern, guided by Gerard
Ens, a Mennonite from the Rosthern area.*

O N THE MORNING OF AUGUST 30, 1902, our party set out from
Rosthern to investigate the district that had been so highly recommended by Mr. Gelley, of the Immigration office at Winnipeg. The
preparations for the trip having required a longer time than we had anticipated,
we did not get started before 10 o'clock. The road led eastward for a few miles
and then turned in a southeasterly direction over a fine level prairie, well
cultivated and partly covered with a splendid crop of grain which was about
half cut. After we had travelled for six or eight miles, we found the soil getting
lighter continually, as we were nearing the South Saskatchewan River. Near
Rosthern, the settlers were all German Mennonites, but soon we came into a
region settled principally by Galicians, who had taken homesteads within the
last three or four years. When they arrived they had been poor as beggars, but
now many of them were already well to do.

In about an hour and a half after setting out from Rosthern, we reached
the banks of the river and were surprised to see what appeared a fine village on
the opposite bank, with a good-sized Catholic church and a commodious
residence for the pastor. Mr. Ens explained that this was the half-breed
settlement of St. Laurent at Fish Creek. The ferryman, a half-breed named
Fidler, took us across the magnificent river, which here has about the size of
the Mississippi at St. Paul, for the usual fee of 15 cents per team. A steep climb
on the opposite high bank brought us onto the plateau of the settlement. The
latter consists of a single street running parallel to the river for a distance of
several miles. The holdings of the half-breeds all extend to the river, having a

width of only a few hundred yards and running back for two miles. Their houses are built along the street. Thus they secure the advantages of village life without the drawbacks of having their farms away from their dwellings. All the inhabitants are Catholics, and two priests, the Revs. Krist and Forner, O.M.I., reside in their midst. The latter has charge of the numerous Galicians and Hungarians in the surrounding country.

As we drove by the church, the Angelus bell rang, but we continued our journey towards the stream from which this settlement received its ordinary appellation of Fish Creek. On the banks of this creek was fought the first battle between Gen. Middleton and the half-breeds in the second Riel Rebellion in 1885.

Before arriving at the creek, we turned eastward and drove through a magnificent country with rich black soil, nearly level and interspersed with beautiful groves of poplars. This would have been an ideal spot for founding a colony if all available government lands had not already been taken by Galicians.

About five or six miles from the river, the country became more rolling, though the soil in general was quite good. Mr. Ens explained that we were coming into the Menaginous Hills, a range which extends from northwest to southeast for many miles. For a considerable distance we followed the western edge of this range on an old Hudson Bay trail. In the northeastern part of Township 40, Range 28, west of the second meridian, we stopped at the house of a Galician friend of Mr. Ens to feed the horses and to take dinner. The woman prepared some tea for us and, with the victuals we had brought with us, we had a splendid dinner. The well contained excellent water, the garden had splendid vegetable, the house, though small and built of logs, was neat and clean. We were, therefore, not surprised to see that our hosts were happy in spite of their evident poverty.

After dinner we departed from the old trail and turned our faces directly towards the east. The country became more and more hilly and wooded, and the soil poorer. After driving for six or seven miles, our friend Moritz began to express a fear that the beautiful country promised us, existed only in Mr. Ens' imagination. That gentleman, however, advised him to hold his peace for a short time longer and then to judge for himself.

Suddenly we emerged from the hills and a beautiful panorama spread out before us. A plain, about six miles in diameter, lay before us, sloping uniformly towards its center which contained a circular lake over a mile in diameter, whilst the outer edge of the plain seemed to rise gradually to the very summit of the chain of hills by which it seemed bounded. Small groves of poplars were scattered about on the plain in profusion. Mr. Ens halted the horses, jumped up and throwing down his coat cried out enthusiastically that any man who did not think this a splendid country would have to fight him. Needless to say, nobody picked up the gauntlet, for this was indeed a most splendid location for a colony. We all agreed that nothing finer could be found, provided the soil was of the right quality and provided the district was large enough.

We now headed for the only building in sight, the unfinished house of a Galician who had squatted on section 28, Township 40, Range 26, about a mile northwest of the lake. As we advanced we became more and more enamored with the district, for the soil was indeed of splendid quality. As the Galician had dug a well about twelve feet deep, we sampled the water, which we found very good. We noticed that the rich black soil was about two feet deep and underlain by yellow clay, separated into layers by occasional thin sheets of sand to the very bottom of the well.

We had now driven about 40 miles and, as the afternoon was well advanced, Mr. Ens advised us to move on, since he wished to spend the night at Olivier's Ranch, near the old Hoodoo mail station, 12 miles further northeast.

We drove directly eastward for about two miles in what evidently was once a part of the lake bottom. Apparently the lake had formerly occupied this entire beautiful plain, but had in the course of time receded to its present bed which had no visible inlet or outlet and, as a result, undoubtedly contained salts in solution. On the north shore we noticed an elevation, several acres in extent, which was at one time an island and which was now covered by a fine growth of poplars. Closely adjoining were the decaying buildings of an abandoned ranch. The lake has since been christened St. Bonifatius Lake, and within less than a year after our visit the village of Leofeld has risen on the southeastern slope of the lake. The parish of Leofeld, under the efficient charge of Father Meinrad Seifermann, O.S.B., of St. John's, now has an imposing church, splendidly furnished and equipped, a fine parsonage with ten rooms, a large school with an attendance of some 60 children, two stores and hotels, a smithy etc. Altogether, the village forms an imposing appearance on account of its prominent location, being visible across the plain for a distance of from eight to ten miles.

Our way now led up the slope towards the northeast for several miles, and as we proceeded, our enthusiasm increased over the found treasure, for we found the soil to improve continually. When finally we arrived at the summit of the slope, we were greeted by a gently rolling plain, studded with beautiful groves and chrystal lakes. The soil on this plain was of the very choicest, for it was a deep black humus, covered with a heavy growth of pea-vine vegetation, an evident sign that it was entirely free from alkali. Several miles ahead we observed a prominent hill rising from the plain. For this hill we headed. At its foot we found a long, narrow lake containing good drinking water. An abandoned ranch stood on the wooded bank of the lake, and a fine spring burst forth in a wide deep ravine which ran in a northwesterly direction. The soil in this vicinity was still unsurpassed in quality.

Our course followed the west shore of the lake for some distance and then led across the plain in a northeasterly direction to Olivier's Ranch for four or five miles. We arrived at the ranch at sunset and were hospitably received by the owners. Our horses were stabled and good supper prepared for ourselves. Mrs. Olivier, a very kind elderly lady, was delighted to see her old friend, Mr. Roy, and Mr. Pitet once again had an opportunity to have a chat in his native language, which caused him infinite delight. The rest of the party, however, had to take second place, as the Oliviers were old country French and not conversant with English.

Homesteader

JAMES M. MINIFIE

THIS LAND! My father looked around. To the north the land fell away in a gentle slope to the grassy verges of the Big Slough. Beyond it, a slow rise took the khaki-coloured grasslands to the horizon, marked by a low range of hills over which he had driven yesterday. Westwards there was a flat, possibly wet, but showing no signs of the dangerous white alkali which destroyed fertility. As far as he could see, there was neither tree nor bush—nothing to clear away before you start to plough, my father reflected. He was already plotting out his farm. A little cluster of low hills suggested a site for house and barn, if only because it was good for nothing else.

First, however, it would be necessary to find water. Slough water could not do for household use, and wells were tricky. There was no spring, nor any obvious depression which might indicate an underground water-course. However, at the foot of one of the small hills there was a heavy growth of buffalo-willow and plenty of waterweed, a low plant of the genus glycerrhizia, or wild licorice, whose roots were supposed to go down to water within fifteen feet. There were in addition a couple of ant-hills, which was also a good sign. Like the badgers, ants were supposed to go down to water not too far below the surface. My father built another small cairn to mark his trial well-site, and then realized that he was very hungry, and that his wagon and the food were half a mile away. Even as he headed back north-east, however, he noted the little ponds scattered among the hills, and determined to make this his pasture—good forage and water, and with luck, a well.

He headed for the stone cairn he had built at the corner of his half-section and then struck east, figuring he would find his wagon easily enough. He hoped so, for the mosquitoes arose from the grass like smoke, and while he slapped at them the enormity of his task began to overwhelm him. He tried to marshal his work in order of importance: prairie to be broken, crop seeded, well dug, barn built, cellar dug, house built, pasture fenced.

As he walked he collected horse-dung for his cook-fire. Weathered "prairie coal" makes a quick, hot fire, soon ablaze, soon dead; on it he put a pot of water for the inevitable porridge, and grilled a couple of rashers of bacon on the tines of a pitchfork. Between layers of toast these tasted good, but the porridge was lifeless—he had forgotten to put salt in it. However, the water in the double-boiler was good for tea once the duck-feathers and mosquito larvae were strained out. Porridge and bread were dull and my father noted: Should have bought some jam—or corn syrup would perhaps be better; it would go on porridge as well as bread. He began to realize that porridge would be his staple diet for some time. He had no disposition to linger over the meal, even had the mosquitoes permitted.

As soon as the porridge was consumed, he hitched up and drove back to the well-site. Taking a handful of laths, he strode west from the boundary cairn, driving in a lath every fifty yards. These would be markers for his plough; without them he would have little chance of ploughing a straight furrow to the west end of his land; dog's leg furrows made a man a laughing-stock and the land unfriendly. Anxious to run a straight furrow at the start, my father chose the single-share sulky rather than the gang-plough, as easier to handle for the first trip. He hitched up four of the oxen, Buck and Bright, Blackie and Jerry. Oxen were preferable to horses for the heavy task of breaking the prairie. They were slow, but when they felt an obstacle they stopped, where horses would jump into the collar and strain until something gave, either the harness, the evener to which they were hitched, or the plough. This could be expensive to repair and put the rig out of action until it was done.

At the top of the little rise where he had placed the marker, my father let the blade down. It scraped the gravel for a few feet, then bit in, furrowing the three-inch sod bound together with the roots and remains of grasses, flowering plants—roses, yellow bean and prairie crocus. This sod had kept the surface intact for ten thousand years of wind and rain, frost and sun and snow, since the retreating ice-sheet abandoned its hundreds of feet of debris shorn from rocks of the northern shield to form the happy hunting ground of a succession of nomad wanderers until the farmers came, intent on destroying that millennial ground-cover to produce a year or two of intensive crops until the exhausted fabric began to unravel and fall into ruins before the incessant beating of the wind.

There was no hint of all this in the brisk north-west breeze which rippled the Big Slough and drove the mosquitoes away from the straining oxen. There was no ominous flight of birds, no thunder on the left to suggest caution in disturbing the stable life-pattern of the short-grass prairie. The plough bit into the turf and turned it over in a long dark ribbon. At the foot of the hill the share struck a boulder buried in the turf. The eveners creaked, the oxen stopped in their tracks and allowed their chains to go slack. My father struggled to keep his seat and tripped the share out of the ground. The obstacle was an ice-borne intruder of grey granite which had lain there from time immemorial, almost invisible, with only a rounded tip protruding among the grasses. Fortunately for him the oxen had halted when they felt the extra weight. It would not be wise to risk another encounter between plough and boulder. He took the crowbar from the wagon and walked along the line of laths, watching carefully for other half-hidden impediments. He was learning the first prairie lesson, picking stone. All along the line he had marked for ploughing he unearthed small boulders, less than a foot across, weighing ten to twenty pounds each and showing great variety: limestone, pink, grey, and blue granite, an occasional piece of slate, and even old basic brown trap rock. He left them in a line, to be moved away on a stone-boat—whenever he found time to build one. That was another priority beating remorselessly on him—a stone-boat: two runners under a two-by-six platform, and a two-horse hitch.

He began to be aware of the ruthless pressure of time that bears down on the shoulders of every farmer and particularly of every new farmer. There is never enough time on the prairie. Ploughing cannot start until the frost is out of the ground, for the prairies freeze a foot or more deep during the long winter. Once the land is ploughed, seed must be thrown in as fast as possible at what the farmer guesses or senses is the optimum soil condition. Planted too early the seedlings can be damaged by late frost, frequent in May. Planted too late they risk frost damage before the grain has matured in August. Then the crop must be cut and stooked, again in a wild rush to secure optimum conditions, and threshed as soon as possible to get a good price before the new crop deluges the market and sends the price sliding downwards. In between seeding and binding, hay must be cut, cured, and stored against winter; summer-fallow must be worked, granaries and bins built, harness and machinery repaired, seed cleaned for next year, fences built and repaired, and all the thousand and six daily chores performed—cows milked, stables cleaned out, eggs collected, chickens feathered, peas picked and shelled, gardens weeded, leaks in the roof mended, wells cleaned out, potatoes dug and stored, hogs butchered, sausage ground, bacon cured, horses shod, shares sharpened, cream skimmed and churned, outhouse moved to a new pit and last season's Eaton's mail-order catalogue hung on the wall . . .

In some ways the oxen looked after themselves better than their drivers did. Towards noon, after a hard morning's breaking, their patience began to wear thin. They were thirsty after hours in the hot sun, drooling long ropy saliva. There was a beautiful rippling slough just beyond the end of the furrow, but instead of slaking their thirst they were required to turn around for another trip. At noon the oxen revolted. With one accord they refused to turn at the end of the trip; they headed straight for that beautiful, shining water. My father set the plough deeper; the oxen put their weight into the collars and plunged on, cutting a six-inch furrow straight into the slough. There the team stopped, dipped their muzzles thankfully into the water, and drank their fill; then they moved quietly out, ready for another trip. The deep furrow persisted for years, a testimony to bovine determination to be their own master. My father cherished this memorial of his pioneer days, and refused to allow it to be obliterated. He had much in common with the oxen, he felt. At the time he was amused and thankful that the oxen had slaked their thirst and then moved on, instead of lying down, as horses were apt to do when they felt put upon.

My father was glad enough to make the oxen an excuse to quit. At the end of the next trip, he unhitched, gave them some hay and a bundle of straw, and left them to their ruminations until it was time to start the afternoon's breaking. He might have been wise to take a leaf from the oxen's book, but he submitted instead to the ruthless pressure of his calendar.

At the end of his day's ploughing, as the sun neared the horizon, he gouged holes with the crowbar into the tough prairie; then he hammered in the willow stakes he had brought from Sintaluta for fence posts. It was essential to be able to turn the oxen into pasture in the evening. After two hours of this, and little enough to show for it, he was too tired to do anything but spoon up the cold remains of the morning's porridge, and wash it down with slough-water, regardless of the wigglers and the feathers. He had no time or strength for refinements such as tea or a fire for himself—just something filling to eat; for the oxen hay and straw. Then he would roll up in his blankets under the wagon—a shelter against the dew. It is not hard to rise at sun-up from such a bed.

Fence posts in, barbed wire had to be strung. Barbed wire is diabolical. It cuts and tears, trips and slips, tangles in knots, and breaks with a savage backlash. My father unrolled a length of fifty yards, wound one end to a solid corner post, and tied the other end to the wagon. Then he drove ahead until the wire was taut, but not so strained as to break. Then, as quickly as if he were securing some wild beast, he stapled it to the posts, always careful to keep his head turned away, lest the wire snap and lacerate him. It is like trying to tie up a tiger with bare hands . . .

After putting it off for three days my father took the fateful decision to start on the well, there where the buffalo-willow, waterweed, badger holes, and ant-hill augured for success. Using the crowbar and spade alternately, he removed the turf from a circle six feet in diameter. This was a generous width, but he knew that, once he got down to his own level, he would need a wide hole in order to have room to throw the earth up over the lip. But it meant that for each foot he sank the hole, he would have to move 28.26 cubic feet of earth. He could not expect to strike water short of twelve feet down—lucky if he did then—which meant moving very nearly 340 cubic feet of soil. The tough glacial clay, studded with stones like plums in a pound cake, challenged his strength and endurance. It was too much after a day's ploughing, so he limited himself to one hour every evening, reserving his major effort for Saturday and Sunday. As a Lord's Day occupation it was not in the same class with St. Modwen's or reading W.G. Grace on cricket.

As he excavated deeper, the stones began to thin out, and the earth became more closely packed. At four feet it occurred to him like a thunderbolt that he was digging himself in with no way of getting out. But using his spade as a stepladder, and grasping desperately at the buffalo-willow growing near the lip, he pulled himself out and collapsed on the grass, sweating in panic at having so nearly buried himself.

To prevent any repetition, he built a ladder of two-by-fours with cross slats for rungs, and let this down into the pit. It was comforting, but it took up so much space that he found it difficult to toss the earth up over the lip. At length he was forced to the wearisome and time-consuming alternative of hauling up a bucketful of earth, then descending the ladder to fill it up again. It was back-breaking toil.

At ten feet he was encouraged by the appearance of sand, moist sand, which might indicate that he was reaching an aquifer. Another foot, and the crowbar sank easily into the sandy stratum. When he pulled it out, water welled up in the hole. That was it! He had found water! He hastily scooped a hole and watched, fascinated, as the trickle of sand and water oozed in from the south, very cold, as if it had just melted from eternal snows. "You and I, Water," he said, "came a long way to meet here. You look after me," he went on, addressing the water as if it were a living sentient thing, "and I'll look after you, give you a good roof over your head, and a strong cribbing so there will be no cave-in on top of you." You have to dig a well, he said to himself, and find your own water, to know why men used to worship at wells.

He filled a bucket with the muddy sand and dragged it to the top. In half an hour the sediment had settled, leaving half a bucket of clear water. He tried it. It was so cold it made his mouth ache; but it was sweet water, not saline, not alkaline, a little earthy still, but good for man and beast. He took a long draught of his water—his water! His mind went back to his youth, and a cold spring bubbling out at the foot of the Malvern Hills from which he had once drunk on a walking tour. He would call this Malvern Link, after that cold spring found on a sunny day so long ago. He consecrated it then and there, pouring a little onto the ground, like a tithe. He looked down into the pit and rejoiced at the gleam of water at the bottom.

Greenhorn

R.D. SYMONS

Symons was born into an educated family in England. After reading Colonel William Butler's The Great Lone Land, *which fired the young man's imagination, Symons decided to head for the Canadian North-West. At age sixteen he arrived by train in Maple Creek, alone and unannounced, determined to find work on a ranch.*

AT THE BOTTOM OF THE MAIN STREET was an enormous hip-roofed building painted red, with the name "A. Gow Livery and Sales Stable" painted in foot-high letters across the front.

I went into its cool shady interior with the rows of horses munching, and the sweet smell of hay and grain. A short, thickset man was watering a team at a big trough in the alleyway. He looked at me and grinned. I said, "Hello."

He said—"Hello, young fellow, you don't belong 'round here, do you?" I said no, I'd come here looking for a job—on a ranch. He looked me up and down—"You're light, and you're young—know anything about ranch work?"

"Not a thing," I said.

"Good," he said—why he said "good" I couldn't imagine. "There's Scotty," he went on, "as owns this barn—I'm looking after it for him, you'll understand—there's Scotty out on Box Elder Ranch"—he jerked a thumb to the southwest. "He told me to look out for a young fellow that'd learn. You might be that—but mind you, he won't pay much to start."

"Where is he?" I asked.

"I told you—out at the ranch—but he'll be in tomorrow. You be here before noon." I thanked him and helped him fork down some hay. I found his name was Geordie Griffin.

Just before noon the next day I went to the barn. Geordie said, "I didn't think you'd come—well, that's him—there in the office. Tell him I sent you."

In the office sat a heavy, aging man with blue eyes, the complexion of a boy, and a heavy down-curled moustache. He was looking over some papers at a cluttered desk; and a broad-brimmed hat was pushed to the back of his head.

"Are you Mr. Gow?" I asked.

"Oh, aye, that's me." He looked up and smiled. "Forbye they call me Scotty," he added, "and ye'll be the laddie as Geordie here was speaking aboot—the laddie that's for a job?"

I said, "Yes, I'm looking for a job."

"Weel," said Mr. Gow, "I'm not wishing to pry, ye'll understand, but you look but a wean and it's a rough way we have oot here . . . I doot ye'll suit the job or the job suit ye, for it looks to me that fair spoke as ye are you'd be better in a store like—a counter jumper. Could ye no find a better place to come to? And besides, laddie, ye wouldna be in trouble would ye? Did ye run away and leave a mither grieve for ye?"

"Oh, no," I stammered, "my mother and my brothers let me come. You see, I like horses and, well, everything about the country, and actually I've done a lot of gardening and I'm stronger than you may think; and I like horses and I've ridden a bit, and then I met a fellow in England who'd been here and he told me I wouldn't get much wages, but he said the ranch people were awfully nice, and . . . " I came to a lame halt and felt very confused beneath Mr. Gow's steady gaze.

"So ye like horses?" he said finally. "And ye're willing to take small wages and learn to work?" I nodded. "Weel, I'll take ye on. It'll be but twenty dollars a month and board, an' ye'll understand, if ye think better o' it, ye can give a month's notice, an' if ye'r nae good, I'll do the same. I'm that short o' gear I'll have to get ye a saddle and ye can pay me back oot o' your wages."

I said, "Oh, I've got enough money—I think—for a saddle, and perhaps if you'd be good enough to show me what to get . . . ?"
My employer asked my name. I told him. "But I'll just call ye Charlie . . . for we call young lads wi' schooling 'Charlies,' and ye look and talk like one," he said. And that was my introduction to a man who has long since passed on, but whose memory will always be green with me.

Scotty gave me five dollars to "seal the bargain"—as he said—and took me to the saddlers and then to Dixon's store for blue denim pants and one of the short jackets we called a smock. We were to be ready to leave by noon. It was thirty-five miles to the ranch.

The winding, rutted trail seemed endless, but some time after dark I stumbled sleepily to a table and stuffed myself with hot biscuits, syrup, and bacon. I was shown a bed and in seconds was asleep, dreaming of the sway and rattle of the buggy and the soft clip-clop of the ponies' hooves . . .

The summer of 1906 saw the Canadian short-grass ranges stocked to capacity. It was a wet summer and the grass made a green carpet from Moose Jaw Creek to the Milk River. Even the sheepmen were forgiven that year, for the grass sprang up behind the cropping bands as if the prairies were a watered lawn . . .

The cow country faced the future with high hopes that fall. Those range yearlings and two-year-olds, no less than those off-colored dogies only had to keep their cud-cheeks full for another year—mebbe two—and Pat Burns would pay "cash on the hoof" to keep his beef contracts with the railroad companies. Not that the ranchers wanted any iron roads in their domain. The C.P.R. main line, anything up to a hundred miles away, was plenty close enough—or they could ship on the Great Northern in Montana.

The puff from the northwest that sent the 76 [a Crane Lake ranch] cowboy loping into camp was nothing to what followed. On November 11, the wind shrieked again. This time the blizzard lasted three days and the thermometer hit the below-zero mark—and kept going. When it blew itself out the range was deep in snow. Cattle—the luckier ones—had drifted into the Cypress Hills; others had gone into the valley of Frenchman River—the Whitemud, as the ranchers called it. But the riders, weary from the saddle, shucking off their sheepskin coats and woolly chaps in the warmth of the bunkhouses, could still laugh and chaff. The chinook would come, they said, looking at the inscrutable skies.

But the chinook didn't come. It was held back west of the mountains, and now storm followed storm. The cattle were plunging knee-deep, their muzzles snow-wreathed to their eyelashes, their legs weary. Riding became limited to a few hard-won miles. Even fed saddle horses couldn't go on, plug-plug, all day.

Fetlocks began to bleed and the gaunted ponies began to leave red tracks.

"Uncle" Tony Day, who'd brought the Turkey Track outfit up from Dakota, was beginning to think that maybe the homesteaders he'd left behind weren't the only enemy he and his fifteen-thousand cattle would ever face. He was an old-timer—one of the cow-hospital haters, and he didn't wean his calves—"Range weanin'," he'd say—"nature's way is good enough."

North, across the South Saskatchewan, the boys of the Matador—the Flying U—told of what they'd seen in the sand hills. Antelope drifting into the breaks—perhaps across the river. Cattle dying. Too many wolf tracks. Perhaps those "loafers" smelled something in the frosty air—something the little pronghorns knew about, that they'd shared with the buffalo. But the hump-backed Indian cattle had already fallen prey to a worse enemy than Old Keewadin.

The T Down wolfer, Jack Brown, saw the wolf-sign, too; saw it as he squinted across the white glare of the high plains, his weathered and whiskered face crinkled into a thousand lines. No chance for his hounds here; they'd soon play out. No chance to make a circle with his poison bait either. In this weather, that would be sowing a harvest he couldn't reap. He spat and turned back to the bunkhouse. The boys dropped their dog-eared books, their out-of-date papers, and their "Hambly Saddle Catalogues," as above the lash of the wind those mournful wolf howls told them that another critter had given up the fight out there in the cold and dark.

The boys looked at each other. One ran his mouth organ softly across his lips, another stoked the stove noisily, still another reached for the thumbmarked pack of cards at his bunk-head. "Laugh Kills Lonesome" said the print tacked on the log wall—it was Charlie Russell who had said that, for sure—yes, and he'd painted the picture. *He* knew!

Well, Harry Otterson, the T Down foreman had said, "We'll make 'er till March. They's enough hay at Stone Pile for the bulls and calves." *He* knew, too. This outfit—the Bloom Cattle Company—were running ten-thousand head, but on a big range. But a lot of 76 cattle and stock from the smaller ranches had drifted onto their range, and these extras sorely taxed the resources of the brush coulees and other sheltered spots. And March was a long way off.

Christmas dinner on the far-flung ranches of Southwest Saskatchewan was the best the owners could provide. But many a cowboy as he sucked on a drumstick or heaped his tin plate with pudding could not keep his thoughts from the critters who wandered and plunged aimlessly in the white fury that was beating them down, blinding their eyes with ice, and stripping their ribs to washboards till they could only stand and dully watch their companions go down.

Tom Carr, at the Forks of the Red Deer, could not sleep nights for the click of cattle hooves which rang like castanets above their bawling as they tramped round and round his barnyard, keeping the snow packed, probably thinking they were going some place where they could eat. They did go some place, into the ground in time, starved to death. And Tom had to vacate his premises when the hot weather came at last, for that stench of death was more than any man could put up with.

New Year's Day of 1907 was cold, real cold, with the thermometer at sixty below zero. Harry Otterson remembered how, on January 10, it took him fifteen hours to ride thirty miles to Stone Pile. He wrote: "I noticed a few dead ones all the way. The boys at Stone Pile . . . were riding all the time, picking up the weakest cattle and trying to get them to the ranch, probing the coulees looking for bunches that were snowed in."

And so it went, riders coming and riders going, tramping the snow with their saddle horses to make a way out for drift-bound cattle which would mostly die by spring anyway. But cowboys aren't spawned by accident. They are born that way. Men who love freedom, who stand up to a challenge, who love nature and animals and wind-swept places. Not for them the ease of the armchair, the boredom of the office. They worked from an inner compulsion and even if, like the Matador boys, they did not personally know the owners of their spread, they were loyal to "the outfit," to the range boss, to each other, and to the sacred cows that had walked by the side of man since the dawn of history.

Theirs was not "unskilled labor"; theirs was a craft that Jacob knew, that the Scottish beef breeders understood, that had come to America with the Spanish language; theirs was a freemasonry of dedication that still operates from the Chihuahua Desert north to the Peace River. Not one of these men, despite the grumbling around the bunkhouse stove, would have chosen to be elsewhere during the bitter months of that epic winter.

Wheat and Woman

GEORGINA BINNIE-CLARK

Binnie-Clark, an educated Englishwoman, activist, and writer,
settled near Fort Qu'Appelle in 1905 and began life as a farmer.
Wheat and Woman is an account of her first three years in
Saskatchewan, and of the many obstacles she faced. Not the least
of these was a homestead law that excluded most women from its
terms and benefits.

HE FAITHFUL CHRONICLE of one's own difficulties may at first
thought appear but a poor foundation for one's hope and firm belief
that agriculture will prove to be the high-road and foundation of
wealth and independence for Woman, but the strength of a chain is in its
weakest link. To command complete and uninterrupted success for an
agricultural experiment on the Canadian prairie or anywhere else, a certain
amount of training in the theory and practice of agriculture is necessary, and
also some knowledge of stock-raising, capital in adequate relation to one's
proposition whether it is to be worked out on five or five hundred acres of land,
a commercial instinct and a true vocation for life on the land, an innate love
and understanding of animal and vegetable life. I had no training, inadequate
capital, and my commercial instinct, though strong in theory, is weak in
practice—I fail to hold my own in buying or selling, and should never discuss
price except on paper. But in spite of this, and the fact that I am still behind
my conviction that three hundred and twenty acres of good land in Canada can
be worked to produce a net profit of £500 per annum to its owner, my weak link
is very much stronger than at the time I set out for Ottawa to claim the right of
women to their share in the homestead land of Canada . . .

   . . . I learned that Canadian women had already taken up the matter of
Homesteads for Women with a deep sense of the injustice of a law which,
whilst seeking to secure the prosperity of the country in enriching the stranger,
ignores the claim of the sex which bore the brunt of the battle in those early
and difficult days when every inch of our great wheat-garden of the North-West
had to be won with courage and held with endurance. No pen can depict the

fine part that Woman played in the spade work of expansion in Canada, although history throws many a search-light over the past, which discovers her claim to an equal share in the land which over a hundred years ago she helped to win by travail and hold by toil.

It is still among the pleasing traits of Canada that "men in great place" are easy of access; throughout the Dominion there rules between man and man a common respect for Time. When I reached Ottawa, Mr. Scott, the Commissioner of Immigration, received me at once, told me his full mind on some facts and conditions of immigrants and immigration, and listened to all I had to say about women-farmers and homestead land. I learned with regret that the Hon. Frank Oliver had left Ottawa that day for the Christmas recess, but Mr. Scott advised me to see the Deputy-Minister—Mr. Cory, with whom he fixed an appointment for the following morning.

Mr. Cory was kind and wore the anxious-to-please air of the professional politician which is always soothing, but I think he knew rather less of the practical side of agriculture than I of Blue books, and, just as I had anticipated, firstly, lastly, and all the time came the argument, "She can't." However, there was also a promise to place the matter before the Minister of the Interior on his return. But I never discussed the matter personally with Mr. Oliver. Not long before the fall of the Liberal party I heard that Miss Cora Hind had seen him on the matter, and that he had arrived at a decision to refuse to recommend the expansion of the homestead law in order to permit women to homestead because he considered it would be against the main interest of the country. He argued that the object of granting the land-gift to men is to induce them to make home on the prairie—home in the centre of their agricultural pursuit. He held the first requirement of the genuine home-maker to be a wife: he marries, he has a family, etc., etc. Women, he assumes, are already averse to marriage, and he considered that to admit them to the opportunities of the land-grant would make them more independent of marriage than ever . . .

Exploring the North

FRANK CREAN

While plans for settlement focused mainly on Saskatchewan's parkland and prairie areas, there was also a great interest and

*enthusiasm for settling and exploiting northern regions. In 1908
and again in 1909, the federal government sent Frank Crean on
excursions to assess the agricultural, mineral, and logging potential of the land between the North Saskatchewan and Churchill
Rivers. Government officials promoting northern agricultural
settlement hurried to issue Crean's reports and printed glossy
pamphlets based on them.*

OTTAWA, APRIL 10TH, 1909

O THE HONOURABLE FRANK OLIVER,
Minister of the Interior, Ottawa.

Sir,—I have the honour to report on my exploration during the last
season. By the foregoing letter of instructions to me, dated August
6th, 1908, and signed by Mr. R. E. Young, D.L.S., Superintendent
of Railway Lands, I was to make an exploration of that part of
Saskatchewan north and west of Prince Albert as far north as the
Churchill River covering as much of this country as time would
permit . . .

Topographical Features

The topography of this tract varies very much as one travels north. In the more
southerly portion, on the west side, along the valley of the Big River, the country
is broken by deep coulees, and the prairie is rolling with round topped hills,
admirably suited for ranching; farther north it becomes flat and low. In the
northern part of the tract it is all flat, very few ridges occurring. In this latter
country the construction of roads would not be easy as swamps occur
frequently. Winter roads of course might be built in almost any direction by
simply clearing the way.

Climate

The climate conditions seemed to be most favourable. The expression "Frozen
North," sometimes used, is a misnomer. Of course the winter is cold but not
any colder nor longer than the winter in some of the settled portions of
Saskatchewan. In August, 1908, a frost occurred almost all over the settled parts
of Saskatchewan but did not apparently affect the northern portion which I
explored. Locally this frost may have been felt but it was certainly not felt all

over. I was not in the district at the time but the first frost registered by my thermometer was on October 2nd, when the thermometer fell to 24 degrees F. I was at Portage la Loche on September 17th, and the potato tops were not frozen in the least.

The garden was also quite untouched. Cabbages, carrots, parsnips, etc., all looked well. Nor had I seen any frozen vegetables on the way up. At La Plonge Mission the wheat was touched, but it was grown close to the river and caught any frost there could have been. The vegetables in the garden here were quite untouched and looked well on September 4th; the tomatoes had been removed from the garden in case frost might come.

The lakes began to freeze on October the 20th, but remained open for perhaps two weeks, the weather turning quite mild again. There was not sufficient snow for travel with dogs until November 20th, and even then there was very little. The snow was not deep until about December 15th.

The rainfall in this district is ample, though not excessive, and its uniformity from year to year is a valuable feature. As far as I could learn the heaviest rains occur in the early summer just when rain is most needed for agricultural operations. The snowfall is not generally heavy, seldom exceeding 18 inches and as with the rainfall, is uniform.

Ranching

Along the Big River in the southern portion of the tract, is a splendid ranching country. Hay abounds and water and shelter are easily obtained. The country is principally open, dotted with bluffs of poplar, and hay is to be had everywhere. The grass cures here and the rolling hills would be blown clear of snow which would afford a winter range for stock almost equal to the Porcupine Hills in Southern Alberta. Farther north, however, the country is too flat until Portage la Loche is reached. The valley of Clearwater River below Portage la Loche would furnish a cattle range that to my thinking would be hard to beat.

I am informed that there is even a better cattle range in the valley of the Pembina River, southwest of Portage la Loche, but I did not see it. Generally speaking in my opinion mixed farming would be the industry best adapted to the entire tract explored.

Hay

Everywhere I travelled there was an abundance of hay and along the main routes hay was stacked in quantities in many places but always with an eye to proximity to the trail. Sometimes the meadows would be small but always numerous. At Green Lake there were particularly fine meadows, and I am told to the west of it is even better . . .

The tract of country explored in the season of 1909 was particularly well supplied with hay. In the southeasterly portion, the Meadow Lake district, hay is extremely plentiful and the quality of it is the very best. Several of the natives living between Green Lake and Cold Lake have cattle and horses. Further north, around Whitefish Lake, there are very large hay meadows which are cut by the Indians with scythes and the hay put up in small stacks. Towards McMurray, although there is still ample hay, I did not see any stacks. South and north of Lac la Biche there is ample hay, in fact all that large strip of country between Lac la Biche and Clearwater River west of the 4th meridian is abundantly supplied with hay. At Cowpar Lake hay is easily obtainable and several head of cattle and horses are fed there . . .

I have, in my previous report, mentioned the fine ridge of country around the Big River. I passed through it again this year and had no reason to change my opinion of it as a cattle country.

At Meadow Lake there are two or three large herds of cattle which are thriving well. The grass at Meadow Lake grows perfectly, and is of the very finest quality for feed. The snow may be deep here, but hay is so easily procured that I am of the opinion that it would balance the scarcity of winter range.

Along the Pembina River there are fine hay meadows which should enable anybody who desires to keep cattle to procure ample feed for the winter.

To the west of Cowpar Lake there is a large prairie which would certainly afford magnificent summer range, though I am informed that in the winter the snow is too deep for cattle to range out. Northwest of Cowpar Lake I saw some horses grazing in December. Their owner had made no arrangement to winter them, and I am told that the horses thrived.

Close to Lac la Biche the country is more rolling and therefore, in my opinion, should afford an excellent winter range.

Mixed Farming

Mixed farming would appear to be an industry which most readily adapts itself to northern conditions.

Wheat can be grown in almost any part of the north which I have explored. It is undeniable that northern latitudes increase the likelihood of summer frosts. If, however, live stock is kept, the larger yield of grain to the acre, even if slightly frosted, will pay quite as well converted into beef or pork as a smaller yield of the better quality grain in more southern latitudes.

At Meadow Lake the few settlers agree that two loads of hay will winter one animal, that is, two loads for each head of stock, whether yearling or full grown. Hay grows in such profusion that two loads to the animal could easily be obtained for even a large herd of cattle. There is little doubt that cattle fed and finished make better beef than range cattle, and the opportunity of procuring finishing food (ensilage) is always present in the northern latitudes.

I do not know if any statistics are available which would show the number of cattle at present produced in Southern Alberta and the numbers which were produced when Alberta was a range country, but I feel sure the passing of the cowboy has not lessened either the quantity or the quality of beef.

Pigs will, I firmly believe, thrive well in the north, and sheep will at any rate suffer from the raids of the coyote.

Although the North may never seriously compete with the more southerly latitudes in the wheat market, still, by mixed farming, it will eventually be equally productive and support a dense, thriving population.

Boom and Bust

DON KERR & STAN HANSON

Saskatoon draws its name from the Cree word for the delicious Saskatoon berry, and the site was home to aboriginal hunting tribes at least six thousand years ago. White settlement began when the area was chosen as a Temperance colony by Rev. John Lake. The first white settlers appeared in 1883, and commercial life began in earnest when a railway arrived in 1890.

FROM THE SPRING OF 1910 until the fall of 1912, Saskatoon experienced its great boom and the spirit of speculation rather than the spirit of temperance ruled the town. Like other western Canadian communities Saskatoon became a gold rush town, only the gold was land, and for three years there was nothing more real in town than real estate. Everything went up and up and up—land values, buildings, hopes. All the graphs of growth shot off the top of the page: population—about 10,000 in 1909 and about 28,000 in 1912; building permits—$1,002,055 in 1909 and $7,640,530 in 1912; assessment—

$8,156,357 in 1909 and $36,897,498 in 1912; real estate firms—37 in 1909 and 267 in 1912. Approximately ten subdivisions had appeared on the Saskatoon market by the end of 1910. By 1912 real estate maps showed over a hundred subdivisions, although the number actually marketed was probably closer to sixty. The 1912 city had, as the board of trade proudly announced, 41 miles of cement sidewalks, 35 miles of sewers, 37 miles of water mains, 11 miles of street railway (scheduled to open January 1, 1913), 4 miles of paved roads, and over 400 acres devoted to parks. It also had 9 architectural firms and 8 photographers, 12 automobile dealers and 16 livery stables, 13 banks and 14 pool rooms, and 5 employment offices, 2 massage parlors and 9 theatres. Saskatoon looked just like a city.

In 1909 the one building of suitable stature for a metropolis was the International Harvester building. There were twenty such buildings erected or under construction by the end of 1912 and physically the city went as high as eight storeys with Allan Bowerman's Canada Building. The elaborate five-storey King George Hotel replaced the three-storey Flanagan as Saskatoon's premier hotel. J.F. Cairns exchanged his 10,000 square foot store for one of 90,000 square feet, one of the finest department stores in the country, designed by the university architects, Brown and Vallance. Even a Chicago architectural firm, Hill and Waltersdorf, made an appearance in Saskatoon designing the Rumely warehouse. The three public schools opened by the end of 1909 were joined by seven more either open or under construction by the end of 1912. Almost all featured a kind of medieval tower that bespoke the primacy of the mother country, of the English language and British tradition—Saskatoon as an outpost of the Empire. By the end of 1912 construction had begun on three of the great downtown churches, Third Avenue Methodist, Knox Presbyterian and St. John's Anglican. They made their predecessors appear very humble indeed. In the Idylwyld area, along Queen Street, University Drive, Saskatchewan Crescent and Spadina Crescent, mansions replaced bush or prairie or shacks as wealth made itself manifest. Most often the manifestation included pillars.

The boom went up and up, like the Canada Building, which began as a four-storey idea in early 1911, was expanded to six storeys by January 1, 1912 and finally to eight storeys when construction began later in the summer—a literal example of rising expectations. Where would the boom itself end? Because the reality was so fantastic in these years, fantasy was in good repute. And it was not easy to separate the one from the other. It was widely predicted that Saskatoon would reach a population of 50,000 by 1915 and perhaps 100,000 by 1920. Since realtors made most of the projections, their optimism is suspect. However, as sober a group as the Church Union Committee made building plans on the basis of a forecast of 65,000 by 1921 and President Murray predicted a population of two million for Saskatchewan by 1931, at which time the University of Saskatchewan would rival the University of Toronto. Sometimes Saskatoon, like other western cities, was compared with earlier miracles in the "World Movement of Population" westward. "Saskatoon belongs to the great family of Western cities. It is in the class with Cincinatti, St. Louis, Chicago, St. Paul, Minneapolis, Winnipeg." However, since it has "within the first decade . . . shown greater growth than any of its elder sisters" it could outdo them all and become the "largest farmers' city in America". It is difficult to tell if a sentence like that is folly or knavery. Saskatoon was finally certified as important, however, when Bassano advertised itself as the "Saskatoon of Alberta".

Like population and growth predictions, the rhetoric of booming also went up and up, reaching its zenith in a series of advertisements run by B.E. Dutcher in the summer of 1912. It was the proposed coming of the streetcar that inspired Dutcher. (In the West, iron rails were always the single greatest occasion for poetic rapture.) Rapid transit, Dutcher said, will "remove the Chinese bandages from our feet and supply us with the seven league boots by means of which we can keep pace with our wonderful growth". Thereafter the sky is the limit:

Like a bolt from the blue it has dawned upon the people of this City of Destiny and certain greatness that TODAY the greatest opportunity of all the ages to amass certain and easy wealth has been thrust down among the people of this fortunate place—Saskatoon . . .

Look about you and see what grasping the village and town opportunities of the past has done for others in Saskatoon, and think what today means to you in the greater and grander opportunities which this revolution in transit and the commencement of a far greater and grander city of Saskatoon means to you if you but use your eyes and intellect to see and understand, and your will power and ability to act and grasp the wealth that is NOW within the reach of every wage worker in this budding and blossoming garden of industry and commerce just NOW breaking the bonds of the city of today to become the great and glorious metropolis of tomorrow. Saskatoon's growth and progress can not be checked and in her onward and ever-forward course she will scatter wealth and plenty among a worthy and deserving populace.

Breathless prose and a religious vision. Dutcher was selling Dutcher's Addition for $150.00 to $225.00 a lot. It was a piece of bare prairie beyond Preston and Taylor and not developed for sixty years.

What went up between 1910 and 1912 came down between 1913 and 1915. The value of building permits issued by the city plummeted from a high of $7,640,530 in 1912 to an all-time low of $20,200 in 1915, by which time building had come to a virtual standstill. Tax arrears increased dramatically from $25,000 in 1912 to $288,000 by 1916 and well over one million dollars by 1921. Between 1913 and 1915 the city payroll was reduced by more than half. Real estate speculation collapsed in the spring of 1913—there was no money to speculate with, and although city centre land and lots on sewer lines remained of value, outside lots became in many cases a liability for their owners who could neither sell them nor pay taxes on them. By 1923 the city had taken title to 12,267 parcels of land within the city against arrears of taxes. The 25,000 subdivided lots outside the city were returned to acreage and lots purchased for from $200.00 to $300.00 in 1911 were worth $10.00 each in 1923. Years later Sid Johns said it was the capitalists of foreign countries

> who proved Saskatonians' salvation when the boom collapsed. The foreign investors continued to pay their taxes and retain possession of their property 'when local owners went to the wall', could no longer pay their taxes and turned the property back on the hands of the city. 'Had all the property here belonged to local people, the city would not have been able to carry on.'

The bust in Saskatoon was in every way worthy of the boom.

Yet in 1913 and early 1914 people did not know what the future would bring and to a degree remained optimistic. To some it looked like the brief depression of 1907-08 all over again, a useful tightening of the belt. As in 1907-08 when the new railroad bridges promised a better future, 1913 saw three important initiatives in Saskatoon. The city opened its street railway system on January 1, 1913, the provincial government began construction of a traffic bridge to the new university and the Dominion government chose Saskatoon as the site for an inland grain terminal. In terms of building and general retail trade, 1913 was a good year (building permits were over five million dollars). As well immigration remained in full flood. Board of Trade Commissioner Sclanders called the decline "a little lull" and looked to a bright future—"our thoughtful people have pulled the silver lining from behind that small cloud, and in the gleam of that lining there is no cloud". But money was tight, as everyone kept saying, and there was indeed a cloud in Sclanders' silver lining, the enormous storm clouds of World War I. In fact the city would not expand substantially again for another dozen years, until the mid-Twenties.

The causes for the financial stringency were much discussed in 1913 and early 1914. Externally the great cause was said to be the shortage of money in Canada's major money market, London, a shortage caused by the great demands placed on London by world development and by Canadian development in particular. The dominion, provincial and municipal governments of Canada, and especially the railroads, all placed their major financial demands on the London market. A more important drain on money, however, was said to be the demands of war, the Balkan War and later the re-arming of Europe . . .

Financial men agreed that credit had been too easily come by: "Last year the banks would give a large line of credit to anyone with a few thousand dollars." In 1913 they were calling in the loans and sounded positively pleased about one result of the financial stringency—the end of speculation and of the speculator, the "cheap curb brokers whose only asset was their ability to sell real estate on a commission basis". Speculators had helped attract capital to the West and been well repaid for their efforts but now they impeded further business and industrial development. So financial men saw the stringency as a blessing in disguise. Other causes for the stringency were suggested too: low wheat prices for the 1912 crop lost the West between thirty and forty million dollars; British capital that supported some of the loan companies had dried up; municipalities unable to market debentures at the end of 1912 had borrowed heavily from banks; western companies had expanded too rapidly and failed to build sufficient reserves for lean years and were asking for credit; and loans for building purposes had been previously made without sufficient caution and with very little cash invested by the builder—now he would need 50 per cent of the capital and have to prove the need for the building. For whatever set of reasons, money was tight and the boom over.

Coyotes and Grain Elevators

FREDELLE BRUSER MAYNARD

IRCH HILLS WAS TWO STREETS, a line of grain elevators, and a railway station. Not that I saw it so during the years I lived there. I was three when we arrived, nine when we moved away. We passed through many small towns afterwards, but Birch Hills has remained for me always The Town, the essential prairie experience. I can walk in my mind every foot of its wooden sidewalks, move through the rooms of our small brown house there as familiarly as if I had never left. Looking back, I am astonished to realize its cramping limitations. (My children would say, "What could you *do* in a place like that?") Yet though often lonely I was never, I think, bored. Bounded in a nutshell, I counted myself king of infinite space.

Strung out along Main Street (one could hardly call it "downtown") were four false-fronted general stores—rather a lot for a village whose population cannot have been more than five hundred. One Frenchman, one Scot, one Norwegian, and one Jew—my father. I remember them that way because that was their meaning in 1925. Only the Norwegian prospered. There was a fascinating butcher shop, sawdust-floored, where whole sides of beef and pork hung from great ceiling hooks. In the barbershop, Sammy Horton's father sheared creamy froth off rough cheeks with a straight razor. Children didn't much go to barbershops; a familiar billboard of the time, advertising cooking fat, showed a boy with an inverted lard pail on his head, his mother solemnly cutting round its edge. The legend: *Domestic Shortening.* We had a cafe (pronounced to rhyme with *safe*), a blockish-looking bank, the town's only brick building, and a bakery that smelled in all seasons of moist heat, yeast, and flour.

On the border line between Commerce and Sin stood the hotel, which I was forbidden to enter even when, briefly, I had a friend who lived with her proprietor parents in one of its dingy rooms. The hotel's chief *raison d'être* was its beer parlor. Certainly it entertained no "guests" in the usual sense of that word, though salesmen alighted there on their way to other, equally dreary spots . . .

It is strange to recollect that our town had no policeman. Such trouble as occurred—a drunk on the rampage, somebody's wife "gone crazy"—would be dealt with by the Mounties, the red-coated members of the Royal Canadian Mounted Police. A Mountie's riding into town was an event. So was the occasional appearance of a wandering contingent of Salvation Army members, the women plain and lofty countenanced in their hard blue bonnets, the men a trifle seedy, making up on a rolling drum what they lacked in presence. Once, when the Army came, I disgraced myself terribly. They had been putting on a good show, those soldiers of the Lord, shaking their tambourines mightily and singing the risen Christ. But the response, in a devout Lutheran community, was embarrassingly lukewarm. When, at the climax of the street-corner service, the sergeant-major boomed out, "Who will COME and be WASHED in the BLOOD of the LAMB?" no one stepped forward. There was a long, awkward silence. He tried again, this time supported by a wail of women. Again, nothing. A reckless sense of social obligation overcame my normal shyness. I stepped forth, the only Jewish child in town, and presented myself for baptism.

Though we had a doctor in Birch Hills, his function was pretty much confined to delivering babies and making the diagnoses which resulted in the dread QUARANTINE signs being nailed to one's door. I suppose, given our lonely situation and the primitive pharmacology of the twenties, there wasn't much a general practitioner could do except sit by bedsides looking grave or wise. Minor illnesses were treated by mothers in accordance with generally esteemed folk practice. Most cures began with enemas or castor oil. The standard treatment for earache, I remember, was pouring hot melted butter into the ear. Tooth troubles meant oil of clove. If that failed, you tied a string to the aching tooth, attached the other end of the string to a doorknob—and slammed the door. The common cold, and all related afflictions, evoked an extraordinary range of comforts. In our house, at the first cough, we were put to bed under quilts and fed hot milk and honey. If the cough "developed," our chests were swathed in mustard plasters made from outgrown woolen underwear, very cheering. An aggravated condition called for the building of a bed tent. Then heavy blankets, supported by the bedposts, enclosed the patient in warm fragrant dark while heated eucalyptus and friar's balsam gave off their curative steams. This experience was especially pleasant if you could hear the wind howling outside and be assured, by ambulatory members of the family, that the thermometer registered fifty below.

Birch Hills had already a theater in those days. For ten cents on Saturday night you could see Lon Chaney in *The Hunchback of Notre Dame* or Colleen Moore in an orange blossom romance. There was no sound track, of course, but the local pianist thumped away in the dark, suiting her chords to the crash of a plane (*Wings*) or that thrilling moment at the end of a cowboy picture when Hoot Gibson leaned towards his lady love and held his hat before their canted lips. Occasionally we had live entertainment, a vaudeville road show. My chief memory here is of talcum-powdered limbs in pale mauve light and blackface dancers with wide watermelon mouths. Striped trousers, twirling canes, much eye rolling and finger snapping . . .

Once every summer Chautauqua rolled into town, a great event that began with a community parade (I and my friends wearing curtains) and ended in an evening's drama under the big tent. Years later, I was surprised to discover Chautauqua's connection with the temperance movement. So *that* was the meaning of those long dull speeches! To my family the occasion signified uplift of another sort—Culture, the Arts. Middle-aged ladies with wonderful bosoms sang "The Last Rose of Summer" or struck tragic poses to declaim, "Curfew *shall not* ring tonight!" . . .

Life in Birch Hills had a curiously static quality. Few people owned cars. Travel was by horse and buggy in summer, by sleigh in winter. Small children were pulled about snowy streets on sleds with high sides. One of my earliest memories is of lying back in just such a sled, snug under a white bearskin robe, observing the comfortable bulk of my father's back and hearing him whistle an old Low German courting song whose faintly salacious words I learned years later. "*Een oude paar ossen gevlekte koe, Gaf my myn vader wanneer ik vryen doe . . .* " (An old pair of oxen and a speckled cow, My father will give me when I go courting . . .) When I was five—that would have been 1927, the year Lindy flew the Atlantic—we heard, what dazzlement, a plane overhead, and everyone tumbled out to see it slice the sky. But for the most part I had no experience of speed, and little sense of world beyond. Sometimes beggars came to our door (we called them hoboes), and often, often, as the freight trains shunted through town, I saw huddles of ragged dirty men riding on top or peering out half-open doors. I had heard of gypsies, too—and how you had to watch your clotheslines when their caravans passed by. So I knew there was something besides our town. But my sense of place was vague indeed. Had I been asked to produce a Child's Own Geography, it would have gone something like this. Birch Hills, center. A long car ride away, Round Lake, where we waded in bathing dresses, and—farther still—Watrous, a beach for sick people. To the north, Prince Albert, its special distinction being Woolworth's, really a fifteen cent store in those days. To the west, Battleford, where crazy people were locked up. And to the east Winnipeg, the great city, grandparents, *our people* . . .

Summer evenings, so far north, were late bright. You could race out after supper any night and find a gang ready to play. In the brief democracy of those waning hours, children of all ages joined; it was the best moment for team games. That is how I see Birch Hills now, in dusky lavender light. We have gathered in the field by the skating rink; the town lies behind us, the woods thicken round. I smell crushed grass and clover and—from a nearby garden, heavy, sickish-sweet—the white night-blooming tobacco plant. Fireflies wink and fade. Someone calls, "Run! Quick!" All the others have made it, across a dangerous no-man's-land, to the safety of goal, and in the sudden dark I hear the leader's cry:

"Red Rover, Red Rover,
I call Freidele over."

Booze

JAMES GRAY

The temperance movement in Saskatchewan was in evidence from the early days of farm settlement, and there were several vigorously contested provincial plebiscites held on the issue of prohibition. In 1916 and 1920 people voted that the province should be dry, but another vote in 1924 toppled that result. Between 1920 and 1933, however, the United States was officially dry, thereby providing a golden business opportunity for some entrepreneurial Canadians to export booze into the United States. Southern Saskatchewan was one of the main sources of supply.

IN 1922 HARRY BRONFMAN could look back on perhaps the most remarkable three years in his life. From operating a small-time wholesale drug warehouse and makeshift liquor-blending plant in Yorkton, he had grown to dominate completely the whisky trade on the prairies. Of the more than sixty competitors who had rushed to get into the mail-order booze business during the 1919-20 hiatus, only he and a half-dozen others remained. A several-times-over millionaire he was now established in the biggest house in Regina at 2326 Sixteenth (College) Avenue . . .

From Regina southward the stores supplied the rum-runners from the United States, and in the southeast became the base from which thirsty Winnipeggers drew most of their supplies . . .

Instead of transporting the stuff to them in his own or hired vehicles, he adopted a "here-it-is, come-and-get-it" system. He established a string of export stores in the towns most convenient to the border. His customers were invited to bring in their own vehicles and load them at his store, thus avoiding splitting their profits with truckers. It also reduced the risk of having a double-crossing driver steal either the bootleggers' money or the Bronfmans' booze.

The North Dakotans at first were reluctant to venture north of the border into the wilds of Canada where North West Mounted Policemen were reputed to be lurking behind every bush. In plain truth the Mounties were so thinly scattered across the prairies that few natives, let alone American rum-runners, ever caught sight of them. To allay their fear, Harry Bronfman set up an all-coverage insurance scheme. If the liquor were seized while the Americans were in Canada, he would replace it. If their cars were seized, he would put up the double-duty bond required by the customs department for the release of their vehicles. In later years, Bronfman disclaimed credit for devising this "free ingress and egress" insurance plan. The testimony of those who operated under it, however, leaves little doubt as to the scheme's inventor . . .

The actual running of the booze across the border, while not completely an American monopoly, was nearly so. Occasionally adventurous Canadians drove carloads of whisky as far south as Omaha and Denver. Despite the blood-and-thunder tales of hijacking and murder of the later years, such risks were not great. The main problem for Canadians was to find buyers for their smuggled booze, once they got to population centres, without running afoul of local law enforcers in a strange and unfriendly environment. After the business had shaken down into established avenues of trade, Canadians did begin to participate more, but much more often as hired drivers and guides rather than as principals in the traffic.

The Americans gradually overcame their fear of Canadian officialdom, but they were never really comfortable until they were back in their own country. They usually came into the country in the late afternoon and in summer hid out in their cars until it was time to load their cargoes. That was invariably done at night after the natives were long since in bed, and it was done in pitch dark both by choice and by necessity; few of the towns had street lights. The financial arrangements would be completed and the liquor collected in the boozoriums behind well-draped windows. Then it was lights out while the stuff was carried outside into the cars. On bright moonlit nights they often drove without lights and otherwise took great pains to attract as little attention as possible. They kept always to the back roads and trails and when they saw cars following them they had lengths of heavy chains bolted to the rear axles which they could drop down to drag along the dirt roads, creating such clouds of dust that pursuers were forced to slow almost to a halt . . .

It was not long before a number of extra-legal aspects of the North Dakota booze trade began to spill over into Canada. The American rum-runners were reluctant to carry around the large quantities of cash needed in their Canadian purchases. A fully stripped-down Studebaker whisky six could carry up to thirty or forty cases of whisky when fully loaded. Three or four such cars in a convoy would be carrying five thousand to six thousand dollars' worth of whisky at fifty dollars a case. In the first transactions cash was demanded and produced. Then the practice developed of paying with cashier's cheques drawn on United States banks. These were similar to Canadian marked cheques and the forerunners of traveller's cheques. It took the small-town banks, and the liquor stores, time to become accustomed to United States cashier's cheques. As they were doing so they were cheated out of tens of thousands of dollars. Several pads of blank cheques were stolen in a hold-up in the United States and then passed to the rum-runners, who used them to pay for Canadian whisky.

As time passed and the Americans lost some of their fear of Canada they moved farther north for their supplies. In the process they discovered the small-town banks. They noted that the banks carried substantial quantities of currency and seemed able to cash bank drafts for any amount. Yet they went completely unguarded, except for a revolver lying in a corner of the teller's cage, which was empty most of the time as tellers doubled as ledger-keepers, accountants, and janitors. Sooner, rather than later, the vulnerability of the Canadian small-town banks became bruited about the North Dakota and Minnesota underworld, with the inevitable result.

Until 1921, the small towns of the Canadian west had little need for local police protection. In the rare event of a crime being committed somebody telegraphed the nearest Mounted Police post and a Mountie caught the next train. Robbing banks was therefore the merest child's play for American bandits. They cut the telephone and telegraph wires, brandished their guns at the bank managers, scooped up the available cash, and left. By the time anybody in the town could make his way to the nearest working telephone or telegraph office, the bandits had a long head-start back home. Sporadic bank robberies in the small towns of both Manitoba and Saskatchewan had occurred in 1920 and 1921. In 1922, two Manitoba towns were raided in August, another, along with three Saskatchewan towns, was held up in September, and there were more robberies in Saskatchewan in October and November.

Sapiro and the Pool

GARRY FAIRBAIRN

From the earliest days of settlement Western farmers believed that they were being victimized by the private grain trade. Farmers had been attempting to establish a wheat pool for years, but the spark that ignited a successful organizing drive was a whirlwind speaking tour in the summer of 1932 by Aaron Sapiro, an American cooperative organizer.

"When will you learn that you are not dealing with wheat? What you are dealing with is human lives, what your children will eat, what your children will wear, how you will pay the doctor, how you will send them to school, whether you will have taxes to pay for roads, whether you will even have taxes enough to start and pay off the national debt. It is not wheat at all! It is all of your standard of life wrapped up in the doings of a little gang of men at Winnipeg, a larger gang of men at Chicago, and a cleverer gang of men at Liverpool."

Aaron Sapiro, 7 August 1923

N O ONE IN SASKATCHEWAN had ever seen his like before. Even many who later saw John Diefenbaker and Tommy Douglas in their full glory said they never again saw the equal of Aaron Sapiro on a public platform. Samuel W. Yates was then an SGGA official, later an historian of the pool movement. The opening words of Yates' book left no doubt as to his view of Sapiro's role:

In the month of August, in the year 1923, there came to the Province of Saskatchewan a missionary . . . he passed like a brilliant meteor from point to point, leaving behind him, as it were, a trail of light stretching like the tail of a comet across the heavens.

Neither in Canada nor the United States did the principles of producer-controlled commodity pools begin with Aaron Sapiro. But then, neither were the individual Ten Commandments unheard of before Moses. And Coca-Cola was just the hobby of one Atlanta druggist before someone with a flair for marketing discovered it. With Sapiro, the clashing imagery of Moses and Madison Avenue were rolled up into one dynamic force . . .

Decidedly mixed feelings awaited Sapiro. As late as 30 July, Premier Dunning told the Farmers' Union he could not say whether he would be at the meeting arranged for 7 August in Saskatoon. Earlier, Dunning had grumbled in a newspaper interview that Sapiro insisted on practical unanimity among farm groups before he came—a condition Dunning felt removed any need to bring in such a "high-priced marketing engineer." Meanwhile, there were squabbles within the Farmers' Union over whether and when Sapiro could speak in Regina and Swift Current. Sapiro himself had to rebuke his Union allies for their changeable schedules. And one Union organizer was charging that the SGGA was working with local business establishments to make Sapiro's meeting in Regina and Moose Jaw failures.

No matter how many times different groups promised different types of pools for 1923 or 1924, many farmers continued to feel that progress was being made with all the speed and vigor of sleepy old men pursuing petty, droning debates in the stuffy confines of their comfortable club.

On 2 August 1923, Aaron Sapiro kicked in the door of that sleepy club, a howling fresh wind at his back. To 3,500 assembled farmers and townspeople in Calgary, he bluntly declared that prairie farmers were only a few short steps away from an organization that would give them both decent prices and control of their own destiny. That, he added, would be only the start of a worldwide transformation: "I tell you that before two years are past there will be a pool of surplus wheat between the United States, Canada, Australia, and perhaps, even Russia." But by itself the Canadian pool would mean ten cents more per bushel to farmers. Who would put up the money to finance initial payments and storage costs until the proposed pool could sell the wheat? No problem, Sapiro said—Canadian banks would scramble to get shares of the financing for a soundly based pool. And if they did not, "I am authorized to say that there are American bankers who will lend you between $100,000,000 and $170,000,000." Applause from the hope-parched crowd overwhelmed his next words, erupting also as he gave a long, detailed account of how his co-operative strategy helped the tobacco growers of Kentucky break free of large tobacco corporations, become owners of their own warehouses, and raise their previously pathetic incomes by 800 percent.

It was the same story in three smaller Calgary speeches that same day, plus another three in Edmonton the next day. The magnificent orator seemed to answer every doubt, every fear in listeners' minds. Alberta government representatives were impressed at a private conference on 3 August, huge crowds heard him again on 4 August in Lacombe and Camrose. A bandwagon was rolling, speeded by newfangled radio broadcasts of his speeches and the through-the-night efforts of prairie newspapers to transcribe those speeches and print them in full . . .

It was time for Saskatchewan farmers to find out in person what a Sapiro speech was like. Veteran journalist Pat Waldron found no standing room within 100 feet of the large church when he arrived. He recalled that day well, even fifty years later:

> He was the most inspiring, invigorating speaker I've ever heard. He moved, he played on that audience like an artist. He controlled their emotions, they yelled and cheered. He could do anything with them. I never saw anything to equal what Sapiro could do on a public platform.

Premier Dunning gave a carefully-worded pledge as he introduced Sapiro: "the moral support of the Saskatchewan Government is assured for any sound pooling scheme having the support of the farmers of Saskatchewan."

Then it was Sapiro's turn, to repeat and embellish his themes from earlier speeches. In front of this crowd, which included many disgruntled members of the Co-op Elevator Company and the SGGA, he won heavy applause with such details as his advice on directors: "Elect them all annually, so that if they are unsatisfactory you can kick them out annually." But Sapiro also made it clear that the farmers themselves were the root of the problem—in the form of each fall's mad rush to dump all the grain in sight on the local elevators and thus on the Exchange: "The central problem of co-operative marketing, the central problem of the farm is to try to stop dumping by the farmers!" How could cash-short farmers, many of whom had minimal education, build the elevator empire needed to compete in the grain business? Not to mention create a sophisticated global sales network and hire expensive managers? No problem, said Sapiro—those same farmers were already paying for all that:

> Just remember this: Who is paying the salary of every man in the grain trade today—the grain trade of Canada? Who is paying his travellers, and his expenses, and his dividends? Who is paying the salary of his office boy, and of his clerks? Who is paying for his book-keeper? Who is paying for his stenographers? Who is paying for all his equipment? Who is paying for all his bonuses? He? No!

YOU ARE PAYING EVERY CENT OF THAT! But you have no right to choose them; you have no right to say what they will receive; you have no right to fire them when they do not make good. You are paying their expenses, and salaries, and profits, and bonuses, and commissions, and dividends—every penny out of your pocket!

Sapiro freely threw his advice into internal details of the embryonic pool organization, insisting at a breakfast with McPhail, George Edwards and George Robertson, that McPhail must be the man in control of the organizational drive, regardless of who might be the titular head. By coincidence or otherwise, the next day McPhail wrote Violet McNaughton about Sapiro: "The more I see of this man, the more intense becomes my admiration for him." That was one of McPhail's last admiring comments, however. His strong distaste for Sapiro that became virtual hatred in the late 1920s, was to begin forming that fall and winter.

More conferences and equally powerful speeches in Regina, Moose Jaw and Swift Current rounded out Sapiro's five-day Saskatchewan tour, a tour that helped change the nature of the province's society and economy . . .

The Dry Land

"I'll get you some water," he said,
and ran over to a homemade water wagon that stood near the barn.
"Our well's been dry for a long time. My dad gets the water from the lake.
We sure have to watch we don't run out of water
before my dad gets back."

JAMES GRAY
The Winter Years

Desolation

Edward McCourt

THE WORLD-WIDE ECONOMIC DEPRESSION that began in 1929 affected all of Canada; Saskatchewan bore an additional and dreadful burden—nine successive years of drought and crop failure. 'The people of Saskatchewan have suffered a reduction of income during the last decade which has probably been unparalleled in peacetime in any other civilized country,' the Royal Commission on Dominion-Provincial Relations reported in 1939. (Incredibly, the net agricultural incomes for 1931 and 1932 were reported in *minus* figures.) 'The land was a landscape of almost incredible desolation,' a Regina newspaper reporter wrote after driving through southern Saskatchewan in the midsummer of 1934, 'as lifeless as ashes, and for miles there was scarcely a thing growing to be seen . . . Gaunt cattle and horses with little save their skins to cover their bones stalked about the denuded acres, weakly seeking to crop the malign Frenchweed which seemed to be maintaining some sickly growth. When the miserable animals moved it seemed as if their frames rattled. The few people in evidence in the little towns appeared haggard and hopeless.'

At first Saskatchewan was an object of concern and charity to her sister provinces, most notably Ontario; but as the long years continued to weave the unvarying tragic design with no end in sight the charitable impulse weakened—as it always does over the long stretch—and government relief alone kept many Saskatchewan people alive. Captain John Palliser had been right, it seemed, when he reported in 1859 that the southern plains area of the North-west was unfit for cultivation, and there was talk in eastern Canada of moving the Saskatchewan farm population to the northern Ontario bush.

The year 1937 brought the worst disaster of all. No rain fell, the wind blew what little topsoil remained in the fields into road-side ditches; dust-clouds—black, sinister, shot through here and there with eerie shafts of light—wavered all day and every day between earth and sky, and the heat was appalling. In

Weyburn on a July day the temperature rose to 114 degrees above zero—a record which still stands. On the Moose Mountain Indian Reserve old Chief Sheepskin, nominally a Christian, summoned his braves to perform a rain dance. He died shortly afterwards, no doubt confirmed in the faith of his fathers, for the day before he died a heavy shower fell on Moose Mountain. In Regina, bathers in Wascana Lake found themselves unable to reach the bath-houses from the water without being coated with dust and in the end went home to scrape the mud off themselves in their own bath-tubs; and in a small town near by, a baseball player—now an archetypal dust-bowl figure—lost his way running round the bases and was later found three miles out on the prairie. The wheat crop that year averaged two and one half bushels to the acre.

But there was little thought of quitting—and none at all of moving to the Ontario bush. The bewilderment and despair of the earlier years had by 1937 given way to a sterner emotion, and the people now took a kind of defiant pride in showing the world their strength to endure, without flinching, the worst that nature could do to them. 'The country is dismal, scorched, smashed,' the mayor of Assiniboia said, 'but the people are magnificent.' He was right. No one could survive nine years of hell without courage. Nor without faith—not in a benevolent god but in one's own capacity to endure.

Nor without scars. The rains fell at last and the erstwhile desert rejoiced and blossomed like the rose; but no amount of rainfall could ever wash away dreadful memories of the agonizing struggle to survive. For the people of Saskatchewan that nine years' sojourn in a dust-darkened wilderness was a genuinely traumatic experience which has left its mark not only on those who actually lived through the Dirty Thirties but to some degree on their descendants.

The Saskatchewan man has thus been shaped by a sterner physical environment than that of most Canadians. Having been compelled to adapt himself to that environment, he has made his own rules for survival and looks with suspicion on traditional values cherished in softer lands. He tends to take a less optimistic view of life than do his neighbours, particularly those who live in Alberta. He is less ebullient and more independent. To the stranger, Saskatchewan cities may appear dull and colourless, and in many respects they are, but at least what character they do possess is honestly their own. (In this they are to be distinguished from Calgary, now an outpost of Texas, and from Edmonton, striving frenetically to become a suburb of Dawson City.) The Saskatchewan man is politically-minded but distrustful of all political parties, remembering that no government did more than keep him barely alive during his time of greatest need—hence his willingness to indulge in far-out political and social experiments and his refusal to conform to any voting pattern that makes sense to the orthodox outsider . . .

The Winter Years

♪AMES ♪RAY

Gray was a newspaper reporter in Winnipeg when the Depression struck. He reported on it and later wrote books about it. Here, he and fellow reporter Bob Scott are making a trip by car from Winnipeg into the Saskatchewan dust bowl. It is hot and sticky, their car has been overheating, and they are thirsty. They pull into a forlorn farmyard near Carlyle. Ellen Simpson, the young woman there, says her husband has gone north looking for hay for winter feed. Though obviously very poor, she invites the two men in for a meal.

ESPITE SCOTT'S FOREBODINGS, our dinner that day was both nicely cooked and served. It was then well into the afternoon, and we began to suspect that she had eaten her own noon meal, whether 'lunch' or 'dinner,' and that she had cooked especially for us. Or perhaps she cooked an early supper. Anyway, while we were preparing to wash up at the bench at the back door, the boys took the kitchen table around to the verandah and Mrs. Simpson got out her best tablecloth. There were two tin wash-basins hanging on hooks on the outside wall, and I took a pail from under the bench and went looking for water. The three rain-barrels were all dry. Then I spotted the pump and was heading for it when Billy ran up and took the pail.

'I'll get you some water,' he said, and ran over to a homemade water-wagon that stood near the barn. 'Our well's been dry for a long time. My Dad gets the water from the lake. We sure have to watch we don't run out of water before my Dad gets back. That's why we don't give much to the horses. We gotta give part of theirs to the cow, because if you don't water the cow she can't give milk very good.'

He drew a quarter of a pail and carried it back to the bench. Bob Scott and I stripped off our shirts and went at it. When we were finished, Bob carried the water that was left in his basin over to the garden and threw it on the carrots. I simply emptied my basin on the ground. Bobby, who had been watching, rushed into the kitchen.

'Mommie,' he shouted in a hoarse whisper, 'Mommie, the man threw the water away! He just threw it away!'

His mother shushed him. 'It's all right, Bobby, don't worry about it. Mr. Gray just didn't know about saving water.'

Water disposal came back into the conversation at dinner. Since their well had gone dry, Joe had hauled water from the lake eight or ten miles away. Like other thousands of water-poor people in Saskatchewan and Alberta, they had reduced water conservation to a fine art.

'It's a real gyp,' said Billy, 'because Bobby always gets to get the first bath 'cause he is the smallest. Then I get to bath and then Mom and then Dad. But Bobby always gets the clean water and I never get the first bath.'

'What you should have done,' our hostess explained with a laugh, 'was to empty your basins into that barrel by the back door. That's my clothes water. Perhaps you won't believe it, but the dirt quickly settles to the bottom of the barrel and the water on top is quite clean although some of the soap still stays in the water. A funny thing I've noticed—I get my clothes a lot cleaner with less work and less water since we had to start saving wash-up water. After I'm through with my wash, the water goes on the garden. If it had not been for the wash water, there'd have been no garden this year. It's hard to believe such a little bit of water could make such a big difference.

'Oh, and another thing,' she went on. 'There was an article in your paper about cooking-water. I used to empty all the dishwater and cooking-water into the slop pail, and we'd feed it to the pigs. The pigs loved it. Then I read where there is great food value in the cooking-water, that we'd be better off to drink the water and throw away the potatoes. Well, we tried drinking the vegetable water, but none of us really developed a liking for it. Anyway, Joe said if there was a lot of food value in the water, we'd get it eventually from the pork and the chickens.'

'The most fun,' said Billy, 'was last year when it rained, remember, and the water barrels all got full. My Dad pushed the wagon over near the big barrel and Bobby and I jumped into the barrel. Boy, it was keen! We'd jump in and get wet and come out and put soap on and jump in! Boy! My Dad said if it rains again this summer, we can do it again. We sure hope it rains, don't we, Bobby?'

Dustbowl Baseball

ℒES CROSSMAN

HE NEXT SUMMER—my statistics now being fifteen years, six feet, 126 pounds—I was once more driving a six-horse outfit during the day and spending as many evenings as possible on the baseball diamond near the country schoolhouse. One evening late in July a burly giant of a man named Tod Crocker, who normally spent the day driving six horses on a farm a mile or two north of me, called me aside and said, "How'd you like to go to Zealandia Fair with a few of us on Friday?" "Sure, great!" I said, too flattered to ask who else was going, or why I was being invited. Tod went on to say that he and his buddy, Danny Ryan, had entered a team in the baseball tournament—"not the regular tournament where there'll be teams like Ruthilda and Delisle," he explained, "but a special tournament called Farmers and Farmers' Sons." Then came the shocker. "We want ya to pitch fer us. . . "

When the umpire shouted "Play ball!" I had a painful-pleasant sensation in the pit of my stomach. This was (I hoped) the worst diamond I would ever play on, and nobody but the other seventeen players and the umpire would be on hand to admire my curve, but this was senior baseball—none of your highschool stuff. I was dead lucky to get this chance, and I mustn't muff it. Next year or the year after I'd probably be trying out with the Rosetown seniors, and maybe even get a chance to pitch an inning or two against Milden or Outlook in a one-sided game. The big danger today was that I'd get too keyed up and not be able to get the ball over the plate.

While these thoughts were going through my mind I noticed that our lead-off man was behaving like no batter I had ever seen in my brief baseball experience. When the umpire called a strike on him he backed out of the batter's box and stood for several seconds holding the bat horizontally with both hands, high above his head. Before bringing the bat down he did a kind of jig that I thought made him look foolish—downright silly. The pitch might have been a bit high, but I saw no reason for this unusual form of protest. When a second strike was called, a pitch or two later, he seemed about to go through the same routine, but the umpire walked over to him and said—a little more politely than necessary, I thought—"Get back into the batter's box or I'll have to call you out." The batter took a vicious swing at the next pitch and missed it by half the length of his bat. I couldn't believe it when he went back to the bench laughing. What was worse, everyone on the bench was doubled up with laughter. "What's so funny about striking out?" I asked myself.

The antics of our next batter were as ridiculous as the lead-off man's, though in no way similar. He hit what should have been a sharp single to right field, but the force of his swing carried him through a full 360 degrees, and he ended up sprawled in front of the catcher. It was a close play, but the right fielder got the ball to first base just ahead of him. Danny Ryan, our best hitter, swung very hard and very late at three consecutive pitches, all of them out of the strike zone. I began walking toward the spot where the mound should have been.

In those days the umpire of this kind of tournament usually stood behind the pitcher—for obvious reasons. As I walked toward him he tossed me the shiny new ball that had made contact with a baseball bat exactly once. I was looking at its stitches, wondering whether I'd have my 24th of May curve going for me, when the umpire said quietly, "Are you sober, Slim?"

"Am I what?"

"Are you sober?"

"I don't know what you mean."

"Well," he said, "everyone else on your team is drunk. I just thought you might be too."

The painful-pleasant sensation left my stomach. There was a moment of disbelief, followed by embarrassment—embarrassment for myself, at first, and then the whole team. But the embarrassment soon gave way to anger. I think I was as much annoyed with myself as with Tod, Danny and the others. How could I have been so stupid? What would I say to my brother Ralph when he asked, as he certainly would ask, "Didn't you know they were drunk until the umpire told you?" Maybe I'd try to think of something sarcastic, like: "I don't get a chance to see all that many drunks, you know." But that combination of ignorance and injured innocence was no defence, really. In fact, there was no defence. I decided that if Ralph called me stupid I'd just do my best to remain silent. I had left myself open to ridicule, and I would simply have to endure it when it came.

The game was soon over. We never did get the side out. The farmers from Feudal hit me pretty hard, but they'd have scored plenty of runs even if I had struck out every batter I faced. Every second pitch got away from Danny, and runners were advancing unmolested. Once when I threw a soft round-house Danny dived far to his right and the ball hit him on the wrist. As he writhed there on the now trampled grass the umpire called time. I walked down to him to see if he wanted someone else to go in and catch, but in a minute or two he had the mask and mitt back on and was saying, "Don't throw no more of them Stan Douglas curves, kid. Just let 'em hit. We're all behind ya."

I've forgotten at precisely what stage the umpire called the game. I remember that two lazy fly balls that should have been caught landed near the centre fielder and were never retrieved from the long grass. In the absence of ground rules covering balls lost in the abundant hay crop, both batters were credited with home runs. I suppose I was the only person on the field who failed to see the funny side of that centre fielder's plight as he hunted around for the second of those lost balls. The nine members of the other team were holding their sides, and most of the Bevis Creek team joined the centre fielder in the futile search, all of them guffawing and falling over one another like so many tumbling clowns. Even the umpire had a wide grin on his face as he said to me, "Don't take it too hard, Slim." But all I could say was, "The stupid clodhoppers. And they don't even care." "Where'd you learn to throw that curve?" he asked, but he obviously wasn't looking for an answer. "You want to work on that pitch, but don't overdo it. And you need to get more zip on that fast ball." Then looking out toward the revelry in centre field he said to me, "I'm gonna call this game on account o' bootleggers." I think he liked the sound of that phrase, because he turned toward the other team and said in a loud voice, "Game called on account o' bootleggers and lost balls." I walked, head down, toward the page-wire fence.

....

Nature Conquers All

ℱARLEY ℳOWAT

In 1933, young Farley Mowat moved to Saskatoon where his father, Angus, became the city librarian. Mowat was a naturalist even then, as this selection from his book Born Naked *indicates.*

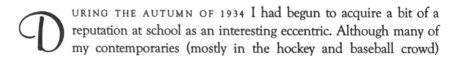URING THE AUTUMN OF 1934 I had begun to acquire a bit of a reputation at school as an interesting eccentric. Although many of my contemporaries (mostly in the hockey and baseball crowd)

continued to deride me as a "sissy nature kid," others were impressed by the remarkable relationship which existed between me and Mutt, one which seemed to verge on the paranormal. It was claimed by some (and who was I to deny it?) that I could communicate with beasts by means of mental telepathy, something which was all the rage in those times. My possession of a witch doctor's bundle composed of dried tarantulas and poisonous centipedes (a present from my uncle Jack who had picked it up in Africa during the war) did my reputation no harm, and the fact that I was known to share my bedroom with bats was thought fascinating by some, if in a repulsive sort of way. These things produced a sufficient measure of regard from a small group of other youngsters to enable me to create the Beaver Club of Amateur Naturalists.

Initially the club consisted of four boys and three girls, one of the latter being Tom McPherson's daughter, Kathleen. All candidates for membership (excepting Kathleen, with whom I was enamoured and who therefore had dispensation) were required to submit to a rigorous initiation. Each had to be able to list from memory one hundred birds, twenty-five mammals, and fifty fish, reptiles, or insects. Each had to undertake at least one ten-mile nature hike a month. Each had to write, then read aloud at one of our regular weekly meetings, a four-page essay about nature. Finally, each had to donate a natural object of some considerable value to the Saskatchewan National Animal Museum.

I had actually begun the museum some time before founding the club and shortly after my first exploration of the professor's house. In the basement I had found a large, wood-panelled room whose walls were lined, floor to ceiling, with glass-fronted book shelves. Recognizing their potential as display cases for my ever-growing collection of bits and pieces of animate creation, I staked my claim on the room (which had been the professor's study) as a place in which to do my homework. Since neither Angus nor Helen had any other use in mind for it, they let me have it.

One of the first things the Beaver Club did was to devote a Saturday afternoon, when my parents were absent from home, to pulling the professor's hundreds of academic tomes off their shelves and hauling them out to the garage. We stacked them between the lawn mower and the lawn roller where nobody but mice was likely to discover them until spring. Then we began filling the bookcases with our exhibits.

Kids love collecting stuff, and enthusiasm amongst the club members reached fever pitch. During two successive weekends we laboriously hauled home scores of clay-coated bones from a landslip a mile away on the river bank. I identified these as dinosaur bones. They may actually have belonged to buffalo, but more probably cows. We also scoured barns, back sheds, and attics in the neighbourhood, from which we abstracted some rare and wonderful objects.

Until a few years ago I still had the "acquisition catalogue" in which was carefully inscribed a list of our exhibits. It has now gone from me but I remember some of the more interesting entries. There was, for instance, the joined skulls of a two-headed calf. There was an enormous umbrella stand made from the lower leg and foot of an elephant. And there was a gruesomely discoloured human kidney in a jar of alcohol, "borrowed" from his doctor father by one of our members.

We also had a stand of mounted tropical birds which had originally been protected by a glass bell jar. The jar had since been broken and the birds had become home to legions of moths and a myriad of skin-bone-feather-eating little beetles called dermestids. The display had, in fact, become a sort of mini-menagerie whose enterprising members quickly colonized the professor's house.

Another prize possession was a decrepit stuffed black bear cub which had languished for too long in a damp basement. It stank with a peculiarly penetrating pungency.

It was our intention to hold a grand opening of the museum during the Christmas holidays. We planned to invite the mayor and other dignitaries. I had even written an announcement to be sent to the *Star Phoenix*, in which I extolled the uniqueness of our endeavour: "It is the most stupendous collection of natural and unnatural curiosities of all sexes ever gathered in Saskatoon."

Disaster struck before we could go public. The moths and beetles precipitated things by invading the cupboard where Helen kept her raccoon coat and establishing a lively colony there. And a week of wet weather brought the bear to such a peak of pungency that my parents finally got wind of what was happening below decks. Angus made an investigation which was immediately followed by an ultimatum. We were given twenty-four hours to disperse the Saskatchewan National Animal Museum or it would end up in the rubbish bin behind our house.

I was not entirely devastated by the loss of my museum. The collecting phase had come to an end in any case, and my tribe was losing interest. Moreover, I was already preparing to engage my little band in another enterprise.

In December of 1934 a new magazine joined the ranks of Canadian periodicals. As is the Canadian way, it did so without fanfare. *Nature Lore–The Official Organ of the Beaver Club of Amateur Naturalists* came quietly upon the scene. The cover portrayed a bloated sea-gull about to bomb a very shaggy beaver. The club's motto was inscribed below the beaver. *Natura Omnia Vincit* which, if my Latin is to be trusted, means Nature Conquers All.

The first issue contained: *"Stories and Articles and Poems About Animals, Birds and Reptiles, Together with Various Illustrations and Anecdotes by Members of the Club. Price 5 or 10 cents the Copy."*

The variable asking price was, I submit, an act of genius. Those were Depression times so we dared not charge more than a nickel but, by giving the purchasers the *option* of paying ten cents in a good cause, we shamed most of them into doing just that.

It will come as no surprise to learn that Billy Mowat was the editor-in-chief. He wrote an impassioned editorial for the first issue, from which I quote:

"Birds and animals do not get heard enough in this country and are not treated well. The Beaver Club intends to do something about this. Every 5 cent bit contributed to this magazine will be spent on the betterment of the birds and animals of Saskatchewan . . . "

I also wrote most of the text, although I attributed many of the pieces to my loyal tribesfolk. It was the least I could do. They fanned out all over Saskatoon in fine weather and foul, hawking copies of the magazine to all and sundry.

The public's reception astounded us. Within a week the entire first issue, amounting to fifty copies, had sold out. The three subsequent issues, with press runs of a hundred copies each, did almost as well, earning a grand total of $25.45, which was more than many people were then being paid for a week's labour. This sum was almost pure profit because I had persuaded Angus to print *Nature Lore* on the library's mimeograph machine (using library ink and paper) as a charitable contribution to a worthy cause.

I believe it *was* worthy. The articles may have been a little didactic: "Planestrius migratorius [the robin] is a prominent local insectivor"; or somewhat overblown: "The crow can talk extremely well and is as intelligent as most people." Nevertheless, the effect was to at least engender some interest in and sympathy for wild creatures amongst people who had never previously given a thought to the possibility that they might have something in common with other animals.

As promised, we spent our money on good works. Each winter the discharge of hot water from the city's coal-fired electric generating plant maintained an open pond in the otherwise frozen river. This provided a haven for ducks and geese which were unable to join in the great south-bound migration because of sickness or, more usually, because they had been wounded by hunters. In previous years, most of these unfortunates starved to death long before spring came, but during the winter of 1934-35 the Beaver Club saw to it that they were well-supplied with grain and corn. In so doing we set a precedent which, I understand, is still being followed by some of the worthy citizens of Saskatoon.

The Trek

RONALD LIVERSEDGE

During the depths of the Depression, in 1935, young men in federal relief camps in British Columbia hopped freight trains and headed for Ottawa, where they intended to lay their claims before Parliament and Prime Minister R.B. Bennett. Bennett decided to have the police stop them in Regina. Ronald Liversedge was one of the on-to-Ottawa trekkers.

DOMINION DAY, 1935, our country's birthday, and what a birthday celebration it turned out to be. The meeting that evening on Market Square, while not being as big as most meetings we had held, still had a substantial audience. There were probably fifteen hundred men and women, townspeople, some with their children, on that nice summer evening. It hadn't been thought necessary for a full turnout of the trekkers, as the meeting was to inform people of Regina what we, the trekkers, already knew.

There were probably four or five hundred of us on the Market Square, and there would be two or three hundred still having supper, or walking around town. The vast bulk of our men were watching two ball games out at the Exhibition Grounds.

The meeting wasn't long under way. Evans was speaking, when four large furniture vans backed up, one to each corner of the Market Square. A shrill whistle blasted out a signal, the backs of the vans were lowered, and out poured the Mounties, each armed with a baseball bat.

They must have been packed very tightly in those vans for there were lots of them. In their first mad, shouting, club-swinging charge they killed Regina City Detective Miller, who had evidently come onto the Square to help them. In less than minutes the Market Square was a mass of writhing, groaning forms, like a battlefield.

As we retreated I saw one woman standing over an upturned baby carriage, which had been trampled by these young Mounties, and I saw four Mounties pulling at the arms and legs of one of our men, whom they had on the ground, while a fifth Mountie continued to beat viciously at the man's head. This man they had down spent the next year in the mental institution at Prince Albert.

The surprise was complete, and it was a victory for the Mounties, the only one they had that night. Even at that, they were unable to follow up, as there were also not a few Mounties writhing on the ground, and it took about half of their number to arrest Evans and the few boys on the platform.

The word went around quickly, for the trekkers to assemble on one of the main streets to march back to the stadium. I think it was either Eleventh or Sixth Avenue. Here is where our long stress on organization and discipline paid off.

A couple of men were dispatched to thumb a ride out to the stadium, to warn all trekkers there to stay in the Exhibition Grounds, not to come down town, but to post strong guards at all entrances. On that street in Regina, we assembled under group leaders. Hilton and Paddy O'Neil took the head of the column and we had just started our march when somebody in a car coming towards us told us that there were two hundred horsemen lined across the street ahead of us, and then unmistakeably from away behind came the clop-clop of a large body of horsemen.

It was to be a squeeze play. We were not going to be allowed to get out of town. We were to be smashed up. How incredibly stupid. Immediately orders were given us to build barricades, and there was plenty of material to work with.

The street was lined with parked cars and we simply pushed them into the streets, turned them on their sides, and piled them two high. The barricades were built quickly, solidly, across the street, from wall to wall, with one narrow opening wide enough for one man at a time to pass through and we built quite a few, a couple of hundred feet apart.

It was then, before the first futile charge was made by the Mounties, that the miracle happened. The young boys, and even some girls, of Regina, organized our ammunition column. Without being asked, they came riding bicycles in from the side streets, their carrier baskets loaded with rocks, which they dumped behind the barricades, and then rode off for another load.

The Mounties never reached the first barricades, that is, the ones at each end of the street, and the attempts which they made to get behind and in between the barricades from the side streets were all beaten back. Our defense was simple: in front of the barricade, two lines of us formed, one behind the other, right across the street, each with a good armful of big rocks. As the line of horsemen charged, we waited until they were quite close, and then the front rank let go a barrage of rocks, and as soon as their rocks were finished, down on their knees they would go, and the row of men behind had a clear field to let go their barrage.

There were casualties in every charge, and the horses couldn't face the heavy rock barrages, and always turned down the side street in front of us, often with the rider lying on the horse's neck.

Besides this main battle, there were skirmishes going on all over down town. Some groups had left the Exhibition Grounds for town before the general order to stay there had been given, and these men were trying to join us on the main street. Some of the men from the Market Square, who had fought the rear guard action from the square, were trying to join us from another direction, and meeting roving squads of Mounties on foot.

The police must have had orders to beat and rout us thoroughly that night, for there can be no other explanation for the senseless continuation of those stupid horse charges.

We were not a rabble. We refused to be beaten up. We had tried desperately to avoid combat, even after the first unprovoked police attack. Whatever order was brought out of the chaos that night, then it was us, and not the police, who brought the order . . .

Our group arrived at the Exhibition Grounds at two o'clock in the morning, and lay down in the straw to sleep, for we were so exhausted, so drained out, so stiff and sore, that it was a day or two before we could relax sufficiently to sleep.

It had been some day, and some night, and I was bewildered trying to weigh up the score. About a hundred of our members in jail, including Evans and some of our valuable comrades, forty of our comrades suffering from gunshot wounds, one man killed, scores of other casualties, of whom I think the Mounties could claim the majority, and material damage in the heart of Regina amounting to hundreds of thousands of dollars.

What a price to pay for the defeat of a government and extinction of a political party, for although Richard Bedford Bennett was too great an egotist to admit the fact, he had, on that Dominion Day in 1935, signed the death warrant of his government and party for the next two and a quarter decades.

North to Cree Lake

A.L. KARRAS

When southern Saskatchewan dried out in the 1930s, many
farmers abandoned their land, loading their buggies or trucks and
heading for areas farther north where they hoped to reestablish
themselves. A.L. Karras had a different idea. He was a teenager
when he and brother Ab left Yellow Grass, near Weyburn, in
1932. For the next seven years they lived as trappers, first near Big
River, then near Cree Lake.

WHERE THE RIVER FLOWED INTO THE LITTLE LAKE was the site
chosen on which to build our home cabin. The area was heavily
wooded with black spruce standing tall and thick at the river's edge
while jack pines of suitable size for cabin walls grew all along the slopes of the
river valley. The ground was covered with caribou moss so thick that when we
walked among the trees there was the feeling that we travelled on a vast
grey-green, deep-piled carpet. The absence of underbrush, the fine green forest
unmarked by humans, the fresh, clean appearance of the countryside gave us
a sensation of enchantment so that we decided at once that this was where we
wished to build our cabin . . .

It was time to set our traps. Working our own traplines, we went our
separate ways stringing out the steel traps, blackened by a minute coating of
paraffin wax that helped to prevent rust and covered man-scent. Likely-looking
places were set along the river, on the shores of Cree Lake, Long Bay, and the
lake to the north where my outcamp stood. This lake, we discovered from the
ice, was the northwesterly extremity of Cree Lake, joined to the main water body
by a very narrow channel.

Our bait was lake trout. Hacked into convenient chunks these were buried in
the sand, a V-shaped pen fashioned from weathered dead tree limbs, and the trap
set at the entrance or on top of the bait, all camouflaged with caribou moss. We
hoped that foxes would be lured to the putrefying fish which, even when buried
in frozen sand, soon deteriorated into a green gangrenous mass that stank as an
abomination to the highest heaven. Light snows covered all traces of the sets.

The foxes migrated to our country. For a time fox tracks could be seen almost any place foxes frequent or on the ice. These tracks crisscrossed the countryside in a great pattern that eventually led past the river and far to the south. They were not planning to stay, for, coming to open channels in the river, they plunged into the water, shook their fur dry on the other side and continued on their way. Soon the tracks diminished so that their fresh tracks were only occasionally seen. The big move had lasted for about two weeks.

Our trapping success was beyond our fondest hopes. We "lifted" foxes until Christmas by which time we had collected thirty-seven foxes, five mink, and two coyotes. The awful-smelling bait attracted foxes from afar—for their tracks could be seen diverted from their normal course of travel—mesmerized so that they stupidly stepped into the traps. The sly fox of the children's story book had been discredited.

We were financially stable for the next year.

Adding to our good fortune, the barren ground caribou arrived in their thousands, in November, assuring us a glut of meat, along with warm and thick-pelaged hides for sleeping comfort.

The time for our prearranged rendezvous with Frank Fisher was upon us, the place, Cree Lake Outpost. We hiked the twelve miles across the lake ice which we judged had not frozen solidly until mid-November. Following Frank's directions of last summer, we skirted all the islands we encountered until we made for a larger island near the east shore.

We had no trouble finding the outpost. This Hudson's Bay Company establishment was under the charge of Jim Buchan, an Orkneyman, capable, congenial, and well chosen for his lonely charge. He made us welcome in true northern style, plying us with good store food, hot coffee, and boiled caribou. Alex, his big assistant, was half Cree, half white from Île-à-la-Crosse way, a great talker and entertainer, with a fine sense of humour. We all spent a leisurely and most enjoyable two hours over the meal. We had not had the company of our fellowman in nearly five months!

Just before dusk Frank arrived from his cabin on the American River. He was fully bearded now, but with his ever-present grin, and we greeted each other warmly for we were all genuinely glad to see each other. The evening and most of the night was spent in lively conversation and good fellowship. Towards morning we rolled into our bedrolls and were so late in rising next day that we were persuaded to stay another day . . .

Frank had a snug little cabin, with everything neat and clean. However, he had not done so well at trapping for he had gathered only a dozen foxes, even though he worked hard and travelled far. Somehow there had been no big movement of foxes through his area. It turned out that Ab and I had made the best catch at Cree Lake that winter, according to Jim Buchan.

In two days the time for visiting ended. With two dogs to pull everything the whole distance to our cabin was made in one day's travel after a brief stop at the outpost.

Well into the season of long nights and low temperatures, we took a good deal of interest in reading our thermometer. A good-quality Fahrenheit thermometer hung on a spruce near the cabin. This instrument was graduated down to -60˚ with a blank space above the ball. One morning I stepped outside, pursed my lips and blew a breath into the tremendously cold air. The sound was similar to that of a sheet of paper being slowly torn in two. Curious, I went over to read the thermometer. The red mercury column ended well below the graduation marks. I estimated that the reading was -72˚ or over 100 degrees of frost! Prince Albert, far to the south, has recorded a low of -70˚.

We knew that it was dangerous to travel in such weather. Fur-bearing animals knew it, too, and their tracks vanished altogether for a time; holed up to keep from freezing. We likewise remained in our cabin. We rested and ate well from our store supplies and the flesh of caribou. Books and magazines had been swapped with Frank and Jim Buchan and were now read and reread. The radio receiving set continued to function flawlessly on cold, clear nights. We tuned in weekly to the "Northern Messenger," a program beamed to the North and by which we received many personal messages from our relatives in the south. Dr. Brinkley still exhorted us very loud and clear on the virtues of his medical clinic from his powerful transmitter just across the southern United States border in Mexico. In this weather our dogs were allowed at large, but they did not stray from the cabin.

The cold lessened after several days. Now the snow fell steadily until it lay four feet deep in the bush. Affected by an almost complete absence of wind, the snow clung in great blobs to the pines all winter long for rarely did we experience a winter thaw. Average temperatures were well below that of Rat Creek area.

We were greeted by the croaking of ravens as we travelled our traplines. The big black birds were ever present on the cold desolate scene of midwinter. They eyed us while flying just above the trees and sometimes lit on nearby trees for a closer look. One day as I worked on a fox set, a raven glided silently over and perched on a dry snag almost at arm's length, looking me over with black beady eyes. I was reminded of Barnaby's raven, but the resemblance was in appearance only, for this one was probably viewing its first human, possibly having mistaken me for a sick caribou and hoping that I would lie down and die so that it could pick out my eyes. As I travelled on I saw the bird rise and disappear over the hills. We had to cover our meat well, for one caribou carcass, hastily covered and left for two weeks, was stripped to the bones by ravens although the meat was frozen rock hard. I have watched their flying antics which include the "loop-the-loop." I will always associate ravens with this land in the dead of winter—a country of wild and desolate beauty.

Tales of an Empty Cabin

WA-SHA-QUON-ASIN (GREY OWL)

By the early 1930s the conservationist Grey Owl had earned an international reputation as an author and speaker. He lived in Beaver Lodge, a tiny cabin on Ajawaan Lake in Prince Albert National Park. He saw his task as one of saving the beaver from extinction and generally raising consciousness about the wilderness and its creatures.

MAN, THAT IS CIVILIZED MAN, has commonly considered himself the lord of creation, and has been prone to assume that everything existing on this planet was put there for his special convenience, and that all animals (to say nothing of the "subject" races of his own kind) were placed on earth to be his servants. And this in spite of the fact that members of many of the "backward" races are often just as intelligent as he is, and are generally far superior to him physically, and that there are myriads of creatures extant, any one of which could, on even terms, as man to man so to speak, trim him very effectively on less ground than he was born on.

But a wider dissemination of knowledge of the worthwhile attributes, and a growing recognition of the rights of these lesser creatures, has worked, in later days, a somewhat sweeping change in public opinion among the more tolerant and sportsmanlike races of men. So that, whereas kindness and understanding as applied to those supposed to be so far below ourselves in the scale of life, would twenty years ago have excited ridicule, cruelty towards innocent, helpless animals, and the oppression and subjection of free and happy, if somewhat undeveloped peoples, are to-day regarded with stern disapproval.

The Wilderness should now no longer be considered as a playground for vandals, or a rich treasure trove to be ruthlessly exploited for the personal gain of the few—to be grabbed off by whoever happens to get there first.

Man should enter the woods, not with any conquistador obsession or mighty hunter complex, neither in a spirit of braggadocio, but rather with the awe, and not a little of the veneration, of one who steps within the portals of some vast and ancient edifice of wondrous architecture. For many a man who considers himself the master of all he surveys would do well, when setting foot in the forest, to take off not only his hat but his shoes too and, in not a few cases, be glad he is allowed to retain an erect position.

End of a Legend

ᗡONALD ᗺ. ᏚMITH

Historian Donald Smith wrote this article to mark the fiftieth anniversary of Grey Owl's death in 1938. It was only after Grey Owl died that the true story of his origins emerged.

THE NORTH BAY NUGGET KNEW HIS TRUE IDENTITY, so Grey Owl, the most famous Canadian Indian of his day, was living in constant fear of exposure.

He had an international reputation. His four books on the Canadian North and its animal and human inhabitants had won a devoted readership throughout the English-speaking world. On a four-month lecture tour of Britain, he had spoken to a quarter of a million people on Canada's northern forests and wildlife. Audiences throughout the British Empire, the United States and Europe had seen his films on the beaver.

In his second and perhaps best book, *Pilgrims of the Wild*, he had movingly told the story of his conversion from trapper to conservationist, his beginnings as a writer, his debut as a lecturer and his appointment as the protector of animals at Prince Albert National Park in Saskatchewan. He wrote his celebrated children's book, *Sajo and the Beaver People*, at the park in 1935, and completed *Tales of an Empty Cabin* in the summer of 1936.

For almost a decade Grey Owl had campaigned to save the beaver from over-trapping. He had devoted his life, he wrote, to saving "this useful and valuable animal, representative not only of all North American Wild Life but of the Wilderness itself."

A line in his preface of *Tales of an Empty Cabin* contained his whole outlook: "Man should enter the woods, not with a conquistador obsession or mighty hunter complex, neither in a spirit of braggadocio, but rather with the awe and not a little of the veneration of one who steps within the portals of some vast and ancient edifice of wondrous architecture."

But a threat to his reputation had arisen. Grey Owl had visited North Bay, 360 kilometres north of Toronto, on his way to Abitibi in northern Quebec, where he would shoot a film about the wilderness in winter.

Always anxious to spread his conservationist message, he had agreed to meet reporter Mort Fellman at the Empire Hotel on that afternoon in early March, 1937. The reporter, a veteran of four years in the *North Bay Nugget's* newsroom, was greeted in the hotel room by the tall, hawk-faced Indian writer and lecturer, mocassined and dressed in buckskins. "I was impressed by him," Fellman said later. "He was one of those men with a mission in life." The meeting with Fellman was to haunt Grey Owl until his death the following year.

Bert Bach, Grey Owl's cameraman, recalled what happened at the interview. "A young reporter from the local paper in North Bay was talking to Grey Owl and mentioned the name Archie Belaney, associated with the Temagami district. This changed Grey Owl's attitude and brought the interview to a definite close."

When Fellman reported back to the paper, *Nugget* city editor Ed Bunyan faced a tough decision. He knew Grey Owl's story of his background from the preface to his first book, *Men of the Last Frontier* (1931): "His father was a Scot, his mother an Apache Indian of New Mexico, and he was born somewhere near the Rio Grande 40 odd years ago." Other accounts elaborated: After a lengthy visit to Britain as a knife-thrower with Buffalo Bill's Wild West Show, he had come to Northern Ontario where the Ojibwa Indians had adopted him and transformed the plainsman into a woodlands Indian.

But Bunyan now knew that not a word of Grey Owl's account of his origins was true. His sharp reaction to the two words Belaney and Temagami proved it.

Two years earlier, the *Nugget's* city desk had received a tip from Temagami, about 100 kilometres to the north, that a local Ojibwa woman named Angele Belaney claimed to be Grey Owl's wife. Bunyan had sent a reporter to interview her at her home. While a big vat of rabbit stew simmered on the stove, the woman told him the true identity of Canada's most famous Indian. He was her legal husband, Archie Belaney, an Englishman who 25 years earlier had left her and their year-old daughter.

In his hands Ed Bunyan held one of the memorable scoops in Canadian journalism. And he knew first-hand how exciting a report of worldwide interest could be. Three years earlier, he had been the first journalist to send out the news of the birth of the famous Dionne quintuplets, an astounding story in those days. Yet this solid, dedicated newsman hesitated with the Grey Owl story. He had filed away the Angele Belaney item, unpublished, and now he decided again not to expose Grey Owl.

The events of the period must be remembered—the Great Depression still held the world in its grip. In Europe, Germany had occupied the Rhineland. Civil war raged in Spain. In Africa, Italy had attacked and conquered Ethiopia. Japan had seized Manchuria and was preparing to conquer all of China. Bunyan dealt with these stories every day. To a world plunged in depression and headed for another world war, Grey Owl presented a positive, refreshing message, calling for toleration and kindness, for the protection of the wilderness and its inhabitants.

At the invitation of Lovat Dickson, his publisher in Britain, Grey Owl returned to England late in 1937. Despite his private fears of exposure, he superbly delivered about 140 lectures, including a royal command performance at Buckingham Palace before the King and Queen and the two little princesses, Elizabeth and Margaret.

Ken Conibear, an Alberta Rhodes scholar who had grown up in the Northwest Territories and who knew Indians well, acted as Lovat Dickson's tour manager. Recently he recalled those extraordinary lectures, "each one so different from its predecessor that night after night I abandoned what I had planned to do while he talked and simply sat in the wings and listened, rapt. Yet each version had the same elements, the dry humor, the self-deprecation, the exaggerations necessary to give present impact to distant reality, the glorification of Indians and the Canadian North, and the final plea for understanding and compassion."

Fearing more than ever his exposure as an Englishman (his own mother had secretly approached him after his address at Oxford in late November), Grey Owl began a North American tour in January, 1938.

For three more months he maintained his gruelling pace. On the evening of his March 26 address in Toronto, for example, he arrived at Union Station from Buffalo minutes before 6 p.m., and two hours later appeared at a packed Massey Hall. Seconds after the enthusiastic final applause died down, the organizers of the lecture rushed him back to Union Station, where he boarded the Canadian Pacific transcontinental at 10:50

p.m., to arrive in Regina the evening before his lecture there on March 29.

Two weeks earlier, in Peterborough, Ont., he had told a reporter that "another month of this lecturing will kill me."

And so it did. A mild case of pneumonia carried him off in a Prince Albert hospital at 8:25 on the morning of April 13, 1938. His exhausted body had no resistance left.

Ed Bunyan ran the Nugget's three-year-old article on Grey Owl's true origins that same afternoon. It began with a quote from Angele Belaney: "No matter what they say, Grey Owl was my husband and the father of my daughter, Agnes."

The article continued "Grey Owl, Mrs. Belaney claims, is not a Indian but a full-blooded white man, probably of English descent, who settled in Temagami in the early days of the district."

Newspapers across the English-speaking world published the disclosure of the masquerade, and eventually the emergence of the Misses Belaney, two maiden aunts who had raised him in Hastings, England, led to the disclosure of the full story.

Archie Belaney's romantic tales of his Indian origins lay rooted in an unhappy childhood. Although he saw his mother occasionally in Hastings, he never saw his father, who was believed to have left for North America. Archie built a fantasy world centred on the North American Indians and he dreamed of going to Canada and living with them.

At 17, in 1907, he left for the Canadian wilderness where, apart from three years in the Canadian army, he spent the remainder of his life. Through his wife Angele Egwuna, he had learned about the Ontario wilderness he came to idealize. Knowing nothing of normal family life, he behaved as his father had and left his wife and their child in 1912, two years after their wedding in Temagami.

Archie Belaney was an actor playing in Indian costume. He took the part to achieve a noble end—the promotion of conservation.

Ed Bunyan, the humanitarian and fair-minded city editor, had carefully weighed his options and had chosen silence over disclosure in Grey Owl's lifetime. Only with the famous conservationist's death did he publish what remains, a half-century later, one of Canada's more extraordinary stories.

....

Sudeten in Saskatchewan

ℛITA SCHILLING

Hitler invaded an ethnically German region of Czechoslovakia (called Sudetenland) in 1939. About three hundred thousand Sudeten Germans, for reasons of democratic principle or religion, were potential victims of Nazi terror. The Canadian government agreed to accept a number of them. Approximately 150 families were assigned to the St. Walburg, Bright Sand, and Loon Lake areas of Saskatchewan.

ℬY THE TIME the Sudetens were about to arrive in Canada, in the early summer of 1939, the whole world was facing the probable outbreak of a world war. In Britain conscription had been introduced and the first recruits were already off to training camps. Air raid drills were being conducted, complete with blackouts, in large cities, such as Manchester and Hull. The British government's plan was to have its air force, fleet and army at peak power by August and September to ward off a crisis. At the same time there was still hope that international tension would ease.

Visible signs of war in the West were not restricted to Britain. In the heart of Paris, Britain and France displayed joint military might when planes, tanks, guns, motorized equipment and troops of both nations were paraded. In July an opportunity to show the national preparedness of the two allies had presented itself on Bastille Day in the observance of the 150th anniversary of the French Revolution. Along the Champs Elysées uniformed military attachés of all nations were present (including representatives of the Rome-Berlin Axis). A crowd of more than 1,000,000 milled around the parade areas.

Though the neutrality act was being examined in the U.S. Senate, a common sight was the motto added to American automobile license plates which read, "Keep U.S. Out of War." Meanwhile frantic talks were being held in London and Paris, where European leaders grappled with the question of how to oppose Germany.

In the meantime, Hitler had rearmed the Rhineland, absorbed Austria, and ravaged Czechoslovakia. Mussolini had conquered Ethiopia, Japan had invaded China, and the democracies appeared to have been rendered impotent. In Canada these turbulent events seemed alien and remote. This was something happening far away from the solitude and simplicity of life in Saskatchewan. That the world struggled with problems of nationalism and fascism was difficult to realize when, in their own private lives, western Canadians had so recently experienced the stress of seeing farms blown away by hot, dry winds, and livestock dying of starvation on their fields. For the people of Saskatchewan the effects of the Great Depression still hung like a grey cloud over the land . . .

Such then was the background against which the Sudetens made their first appearance in Saskatchewan. From the vantage point of the rumbling train, the bewildered refugees had had a preview of the prairie landscape. They had seen the horizon stretch across the sky—a thin pencil line which never ended. And they had seen the sun hang there like a great red ball. They had also travelled through endless rows of trees and gigantic rocks; it had seemed an eternity before they saw the thin line of the prairies. What were they to expect in this vast land with its awesome, frightening space? They had left behind the turmoil of an agonized continent and the terrible fear of violence. They had brought with them a small supply of personal possessions, a dream perhaps, at the very least a hope for freedom from political oppression. What now? . . .

At 3:45 that afternoon the refugees left Saskatoon for St. Walburg. It was a bright cool day in Saskatoon. The Dominion Drama Festival was on. Newspapers were filled with Il Duce's ten-year peace proposal plans. Preparations for the Royal Visit on June 3 were in full swing, while back in England, for the following day—April 21—Princess Elizabeth was preparing for a tea party to celebrate her first teen year.

The train pulled out of the CNR Station in downtown Saskatoon to begin the 200-mile northern trip to the refugees' new home. It was full speed ahead as patches of snow along fields and bushes whizzed by. The children were restless; they ran and jumped along the coaches keeping parents busy while they tried to get a good look at the Saskatchewan landscape.

At North Battleford the coaches were uncoupled from the train. They were shunted to and fro before they were finally joined to the local train to go further north. There was an overnight stop at North Battleford. As the citizens of the town slept, the colony coaches stood silently on the rail tracks. The new immigrants bedded down for the last time in their small bunk beds. The last hundred miles of the long journey would begin the next morning.

The following day the train stopped at the little hamlets of Meota, Turtleford and Spruce Lake before reaching St. Walburg. This slow journey must have seemed endless for both adults and children . . .

The train very gently came to a crawl. It had arrived at the "edge of the world," as one of the refugees described it. The conductor wearily called out "Last Stop. St. Walburg," and the children moved excitedly from their seats towards the entrances of the long coaches.

They saw the little wooden dwellings of St. Walburg huddled along the muddy streets. The wooden sidewalks were invisible beneath the great patches of mud and snow. They saw the primitive Post Office, the strange buildings called elevators, and huge barns, far bigger than the houses, on the outskirts of the community.

"Where is the town?" they asked, afraid to speak too loud for fear of appearing unappreciative in the eyes of the Canadians.

"A Haven in Canada" the newspapers had read. There had been a promise of beauty and freedom in those seductive words. They had imagined the splendour of the new world where they would settle near "a nice little town in northern Saskatchewan," as the immigration official had called it. Faraway St. Walburg had seemed charming, even glamorous. The image had travelled with them through the long tiresome journey.

"I never thought it would be this small," said a young woman to her companion in a Bohemian dialect. An elderly St. Walburg lady standing by smiled at the two young women. "Vait," she said in English, "After you'll be on the big farm for a few years, then Valburg will look pre-tty big."

But where was the promise? Where were the trees, and the lakes? They saw none of the things they had dreamed of as they scanned the pink map of the Dominion of Canada . . .

Understanding the Sudetens were Roman Catholics and possibly a fine expansion to his flock, the Reverend Anton Riffel, OMI, pastor of the church, called for the celebration of high mass. This idea was praiseworthy in the eyes of his parishioners and a great number appeared at the church. The villagers politely stepped aside to allow the refugees into the church where they were ushered to the front. A sermon by Father Riffel made reference to the newcomers and he appealed to parishioners to help the refugees in their adjustment to a new life far from the comforts of their former home.

A St. Walburg lady, at that time in her early teens, was present at the mass. She recalls that morning with a twinge of shame as she remembers that she and a friend had blatantly stared at the Sudetens during mass and that they had followed them back to the boxcars staring all the way. She feels uncomfortable simply thinking about the embarrassment of the new settlers in a strange church, in a strange new country.

The second transport arrived at North Battleford on May 6 and received a hearty welcome by the twin communities of Battleford and North Battleford.

When the 55 refugees arrived, a calvacade of motor cars sponsored by the Rotary Club took them for a cruise through the historic area of the Battlefords. Led by Mayors Holiday and Bowers, a reception took place first at the railway station and later at the town hall where many citizens turned up. Reverend Father Feist, Reverend Currant and Otis Jones, President of the Board of Trade, were a few of the speakers. They wished the Sudetens happiness and prosperity in their new homes, with an assurance of the cooperation of the community.

In a translated speech the newcomers expressed enthusiasm and gratitude. Professor George Simpson of the Saskatchewan Refugee Committee and Board of Trade members were also present and contributed to the welcoming speeches.

For the last night of the long journey the tired refugees bedded down in their bunks at the North Battleford Railway Station.

To some Canadians the newcomers brought forebodings and premonitions of war. The great majority knew little or nothing about the background and culture of the Sudeten Germans who were also referred to as the German Czechs. Nevertheless, Saskatchewan citizens displayed a remarkable interest in the first political refugees to arrive in the province in such great numbers for many years. Each group or "transport" was met by scores of people along the route at the railway platforms at Saskatoon, North Battleford and St. Walburg.

Many questions were asked. Were they really farmers? Were they Nazis? One Canadian was heard to ask his companion, "What the hell is a Sudeten anyway?" The answer was a question, "Aren't they from the Sudan?"

Described by journalists as "well-dressed, polite and attractive," they nevertheless bore the haunted look usually associated with refugees. The children were reputedly well behaved and engagingly shy. There was, of course, the language barrier, eased by a smattering of English picked up during their temporary stopovers in Britain where a few had attended English classes.

An article in the St. Walburg Enterprise on April 27 helped shed some light on the general attitude of the community of St. Walburg.

"Not one—not even those political acrobats who denounce immigration in all its shapes and forms—could quarrel with the decision of Ottawa to allow several hundred Sudeten German families to come to Canada this spring to settle on Canadian farms . . . these people are refugees in one sense, but there is nothing shabby about this label for them. They fled the Sudeten area when the shadow of the Swastika fell over it, when the democracy which had adopted them became merely another province of the Nazi Reich."

....

Last Days

ℛOBERT ℂOLLINS

SHAMROCK—The Victory Boosters Tobacco League held a variety concert at Rouen School May 29. The president of the local chapter of the league, McGowan Smart, was master of ceremonies and chief director of the program.

Features of the evening were vocal numbers by Jean Lightbody, Mildred Miller, Larry Collins and Mrs. Radcliffe. Instrumental music was supplied by Kenneth and Bill Lightbody. George Marriott submitted two humorous selections. Pupils of Rouen School presented a very cleverly conducted puppet show and a quiz contest completed the evening's entertainment. The purpose of the concert was to provide cigarettes for Canadian troops overseas and was a definite success. A sum of $15.50 was collected.

Regina Leader Post, June 6, 1942.

I TREASURE THAT FADED NEWS CLIPPING, not merely because I wrote it, as a *Leader* rural correspondent for ten cents an inch, but because it demonstrates how one small corner of Canada did its part in World War II. All over the land unimportant people like us were rallying to the war effort with knitting needles, bake sales, bingo games, variety shows and unflagging patriotism.

In every tangible sense the war was far away from our farm. A sprinkling of local boys enlisted, but few became casualties. Rationing, when it came in 1942, was almost meaningless: our coffee, tea, sugar and gasoline had been rationed by circumstances for a dozen years.

Emotionally, though, the war was present every waking moment in our red-white-and-blue household. In spite of all that the first obscene world war had done to him, my father was still a patriot to the depths of his soul. He was actively hating Hitler long before most of the Western world. As the Nazis gained strength in 1938 we visited Mister Adams and his radio to hear the news and bemoan the Empire's imminent peril. Once the Hitler voice ranted through the hiss and crackle of shortwave. As the news worsened in 1939 my father stomped angrily about the farm, wearing what we called his "fighting

133
....

face": tight lips, pugnacious jaw, icy blue eyes glinting under the red haystacks of his frown.

A radio became essential. He bought a thirty-four-dollar mantel Philco and paid for it in two-dollar installments. On September 3 he hunched grimly over it while the broken voice of Neville Chamberlain announced that Britain was at war. For the next seven days my father was unfit to live with—scowling, glowering, calling Mackenzie King unprintable things until the latter committed Canada's support. Then he wanted to volunteer for active service. Mother soothed him out of the idea. He was far too old and frail, of course, and I was too young to manage the farm even if the army had deemed him fit for Home Guard duty, guarding prison camps.

Well, at least we had the news and its fringe benefits. Thanks to Hitler we were now in step with the golden age of radio. Now we understood all the hoary gags about Jack Benny's Maxwell car and miserly ways, Edgar Bergen's smart-ass dummy Charlie McCarthy, the weekly opening and spilling of Fibber McGee's horrendously cluttered closet, and the acerbic wit of Fred Allen and the denizens of Allen's Alley.

For us, with our hyperactive imaginations honed over years of make-believe, radio drama was sheer wonder. We never missed "Lux Radio Theatre." We wallowed in the soaps: "Pepper Young's Family," "The Guiding Light" and Oxydol's cloying old Ma Perkins. On Saturday afternoons my mother fitted her mending and sewing around the Metropolitan Opera from New York. On Saturday night my father, Larry and I set new milking records beneath the astonished Old Reddy, so we could get to the radio in time to hear Foster Hewitt's clarion call: "Hello Canada, and hockey fans in the United States and Newfoundland . . . "

But the news had priority. Normally we monitored news at breakfast, lunch, supper and bedtime. During crises, such as the Battle of Britain, Dad came in early from the fields for extra bulletins and lived beside the radio on Sunday. We were steeped in the Hammond-organ tones of Lorne Greene, the cool urbane despatches of Edward R. Murrow and, of course, the plummy ponderous cadence of the BBC: "THIS . . . is LONDON calling . . . Now HEAH . . . is the NEWS . . . " Once after a heavy helping of BBC, Mother complained, "The English can say less in the most time than anyone I know." My father gave her a death-ray glance and strode from the house.

We hung on Franklin Roosevelt's every ringing word, on every tingling Churchillian phrase. We huddled, shocked, around the radio in the gray Sunday twilight of December 7, 1941, as reports tumbled in from Pearl Harbor. We were elated too, for now the United States would *have* to fight and surely our side would win. It made life infinitely more bearable for my American mother who, through two years of heckling from my father, had borne single-handed the heavy burden of the U.S.A.'s nonintervention.

When the war moved to North Africa we clipped newspaper maps and marked with pins each victory and defeat. When Shamrock High School offered a weekly twenty-five-cent War Savings Stamp for students most knowledgeable in current events, the village kids discovered that the scrawny country boy who always struck out at softball had *one* skill: I steamrollered over them all to win sixteen stamps, enough for a War Savings Certificate.

We hoarded all our savings for those certificates: every one-dollar Christmas gift from Uncle Dorlan in California, every penny from gopher tails, every ten-cents-per-inch fee from the *Leader Post.* It seemed a good investment: in seven and a half years a four-dollar expenditure matured into a five-dollar certificate. Besides, as the National War Finance Committee kept reminding us, we were "doing our part."

Some impeccable authority was *always* nagging us to do our part. The Department of Munitions and Supply urged women war workers to support their warriors ("Brave Men Shall Not Die Because I Faltered," cried plucky females in *Maclean's* magazine advertisements). National Revenue assured us that "income tax is fair to all" and that the enormous wartime bite was helping preserve our "very existence." The Wartime Prices and Trade Board scared hell out of us over sugar: "You need not hoard—you must not hoard—YOU MUST OBEY THE LAW."

Bell said its telephones were working for victory; RCA said its radios were. Parker's pens were writing letters for servicemen; Kodak was taking their pictures; Coke was keeping war workers refreshed. We accepted it all, enthusiastically and without question. But how could we, out in the boondocks, measure up? How could we, O Canada, stand on guard for thee?

We saved magazines to send to servicemen. We peeled tinfoil from cigarette packages and chewing gum wrappers, salvaged old aluminum saucepans and toothpaste tubes, and gave all to the war effort. My friend Mac Smart, as head of the local chapter of the Victory Boosters Tobacco League, maintained a constant flow of nicotine to Our Boys Over There. He was a wizard at ferreting out cash for this worthy cause.

He reached a pinnacle with the great scrap iron caper of 1942. The government offered $15 for every ton of scrap turned in. Mac cycled miles through the neighborhood soliciting old ploughshares, broken harrows, discarded cook stoves and sundry other junk. Even for $7.50 cash per ton, free pickup and a chance to help beat Hitler, some neighbors declined. One said he *needed* his junk. Another snarled that servicemen could bloody well afford their own cigarettes. A third, whose religion equated smoking with original sin, would never have yielded his rusty cultivator had not Mac astutely soft-pedalled the cigarette angle and murmured vague patriotic hints of "comforts for the troops."

Then in a series of back-breaking Saturday trips, Mac and I toured the district, gut-wrenched four tons of the stuff into kindly Wally James's truck, and netted about thirty dollars for the Tobacco League. For this and other missions Mac won the honorary title of Victory Crusader. I sold the story to the *Leader Post*. The junk presumably went into tanks and battleships to defeat the Hun. And Our Boys Over There got ten thousand cigarettes, many of which—as I eventually discovered overseas myself—were briskly bartered for souvenirs and sex.

By now I was near enlistment age. We had never discussed it but I always knew I would join up and that my father would be proud. War had ended the Depression. Wheat prices soared. Coincidentally, the rains came, grasshoppers dwindled and crops grew bountiful again. I could have stayed home—essential farm workers were exempt from military service—but the thirties had left a bitter taste. In 1942 my father began managing the Shamrock lumberyard, in search of a steadier income and an easier life. For a few months after, I managed the farm while we formulated our futures.

The thought of going away was frightening. I loved my home. I was agonizingly shy. I didn't want to get shot—at least nothing more than a glamorous flesh wound. But any offspring of Jack Collins had to have patriotism oozing from his pores. And every boy in those years was seduced by the high drama of war.

Airmen were my idols. Air force recruiting posters beckoned: I could be a "WORLD TRAVELLER AT 21." Every newspaper and magazine extolled the clean-cut lads in airforce blue. We all knew about Canadian ace Buzz Beurling and his twenty-nine kills. Roy Bien joined up, and came home with the aircrew white flash in his wedge cap and the wireless air gunner's single wing on his blue chest. Girls circled him like flies around honey. I was hooked.

The prairies were dotted with airfields under the Commonwealth Air Training plan. Sometimes training craft droned through our empty sky, such a novelty that we always ran to stare. Sometimes they hedgehopped. One autumn day as I stooked in a remote coulee, a yellow Tiger Moth with the RCAF rondel skimmed over a hill, maybe two hundred feet off the ground. I had never been close to a plane before. I stood transfixed, sweaty and earthbound in my overalls and heavy boots, and my heart went out to the helmeted figure in the cockpit.

The crop of 1942 was our best ever. I slaved over the stooks. They were caught in unseasonable snow and stood out all winter, but I had built them well. In the spring the threshing machine belatedly poured a torrent of wheat and oats into our granaries. My father paid off the mortgage and other debts that had lingered for twenty-three years. Then I sent away for the RCAF brochure. When it came in the mail everyone knew what was happening. We found a renter for the farm. I hitched a ride to Moose Jaw with the ever-dependable Hugh Adams and offered my body to the recruiters.

They betrayed not one tremor of excitement over the human prize that stood before them. They looked me over indulgently and passed out sheaves of paper. When I reached the bewildering dotted pages of the color vision test, I flunked. I was blue-green color-blind, enough to rule out aircrew or any ground job involving colored lights or wiring. I asked for another color test and failed again.

"We have openings for AFMs—airframe mechanics—and cooks," said the bored recruiting officer. AFMs, he explained, handled every part of the frame-and-fabric airplanes except the engine. It seemed a logical choice for a farm boy who knew a little about woodworking, nothing about engines and thought cooking was women's work. I took mechanical aptitude tests. A corporal stared at my score and said, "You sure you don't wanta be a cook, kid?"

But at last the indifferent air force accepted me.

"Go home for the harvest, you'll be needed there," said an officer. "Right after that, report to Brandon manning pool."

At home the family joined me in condemning RCAF color vision tests. I stooked and threshed more grain and began my private goodbyes to the places I had roamed for eighteen years. With delicious melancholy I reckoned I might never come back. I scratched my name for posterity on some favorite rocks, with soft yellow writing stone. Someday, beautiful girls with heroic breasts would come upon these inscriptions, pause and exclaim . . .

"R. J. Collins . . . Why, that must have been Wing Commander Collins, V.C., D.F.C., D.S.O. and Bar . . . !
"You don't mean . . . the one who was in all the newspapers??"
"Yes! The war hero! He lived here once, you know. They say he would have been a greater writer than Hemingway. But he was reported missing on his twenty-first birthday . . . "

Just how I would progress from airframe mechanic to air ace was a detail to be solved in later fantasies.

I rose on the final morning—after eighteen years, my last sleep ever in the farmhouse—and packed my father's worn club bag. We were all subdued. It was not just that I was going to war. The family was breaking up. Everything was breaking up. Soon the farm would be rented—this land we had loved so much, so long—and my parents and brother would move into Shamrock. Nothing would ever be the same again.

My parents' dream had come true. They were getting off the farm, seeking that easier life. Their great achievement was nearly over: they had raised a family well, in the worst of times. But now, at this last moment, we all sensed that those hard years had been the *best* years we would ever know together.

My father was wearing his fighting face. My mother performed her last loving act, the only really useful thing she could do now. She packed a huge lunch for the train trip: roast chicken, bread-and-butter sandwiches, cake, fruit. I put on my Botany Serge suit and the salt-and-pepper cloth cap that would instantly mark me as a rube upon arrival in Brandon. My dad revved the 1929 Chev and we pulled away.

When I looked back, my mother was standing on the flat stone beside the back door. It was only the second time in my life I had seen her cry.

A Hockey Legend

ℛOY ℳACℒKIMMING

Gordie Howe was born into a poor family at Floral, on the outskirts of Saskatoon. He went on to become perhaps the greatest hockey player ever during a thirty-two-year career in the National Hockey League and the World Hockey Association.

HOWE WAS JUST FIVE AND A HALF when one of the most storied incidents in Canadian popular myth took place: he got his first pair of skates. It's the earliest stage in the Howe legend, and the Canadian equivalent (to stretch a point only slightly) of little George Washington cutting down the cherry tree. It's a tale that was already being told in elementary school readers a generation ago; and it illustrates not only the economic desperation of the times and the necessity for mutual help among neighbours, but the crucial role Katherine Howe played in launching her son's hockey career—not out of any particular ambition for him but through her instinctive thoughtfulness.

At the very bottom of the Depression, a poor woman came knocking at the Howes' door . . . But better to let Mrs. Howe tell the story herself, as related to former *Globe and Mail* sports editor Jim Vipond a few years before her death in 1971:

"There were a lot of people on social aid . . . A neighbour lady, whose husband was sick, came to the door with a grain sack filled with things and asked me if I would buy it to help her feed her baby. I didn't have much to offer but I reached into my milk money and gave her a dollar and a half. We dumped the contents of the sack on the floor. Out fell a pair of skates. Of course Gord pounced on them.

"'They're mine!' he yelled. They were too big. Edna, his younger sister, and Gord each tried on a skate. They put on several pairs of stockings and out they went. The old Hudson Bay slough ran behind our house and the kids could skate for miles right out to what is now the airport. They kept coming in cold, bruised and crying but they'd go out again. Gord kept pestering Edna for the other skate until after a week he offered to buy it from her for ten cents. I gave him the dime to make the deal."

The skates were men's size six. In another interview at about the same time, Mrs. Howe added: "When Gordie first tried to skate with both of them on, he was happy but exhausted. A couple of years later I traded a package of his father's cigarettes for the next pair of skates . . . A man had brought them to the door." (We don't know what Ab thought about the trade.)

As the story of the neighbour lady and the grain sack was retold over the years, the amount Mrs. Howe paid increased with inflation. However little she spent in terms of today's dollars, she wasn't only offering charity; her family was large and poor enough that they could use some of the belongings in the sack, such as used clothing—as well, of course, as those famous skates.

Some hockey observers have reported hearing a variant of the story. In that version, it's the lady appearing at the door who is offering charity, saying, "I'm sure someone here could use these skates." But Howe himself corroborates his mother's version, in all but the detail of how he acquired the second skate. In a 1992 interview for the program *June Callwood's National Treasures*, aired on Vision-TV, he recalled, "They always say if you give, you'll get twice as much back. It was through the kindness of my mother—she took a couple of hard-earned dollars, either one or two or whatever it was. There was a lady who was trying to feed her family during the Depression and she needed some milk money, so my mother gave it to her. She in return gave her a gunny sack, and when that was dropped out onto the linoleum, there was a pair of skates fell out. My sister grabbed one, I grabbed one, and we went outside. We skated around on the pond at the back of the house. She got cold and went in and took the skate off, and that was the last she ever saw of it. I fell in love with hockey that day. I couldn't get enough of it. On the weekends, I never took the skates off."

On those weekends, Gordie and thirty or forty other kids would play on the frozen slough as long as they could. Using weighted-down jam tins for goalposts, they'd chase a puck up and down the immense natural ice surface and endure ravening cold that routinely descended to 25° F or 30° F below zero. The chill would be heightened by fierce prairie winds whipping into their faces and clothing, and whenever Gordie and his brothers or sisters caught a touch of frostbite, Mrs. Howe treated it with cold water on cheeks, fingers and toes. But weather was just weather. It didn't deter Gordie from playing the game he'd fallen in love with.

"I think I was immune to the cold," he says now. His mother would put newspapers down on the kitchen linoleum so that he and his brothers and friends wouldn't have to remove their skates while eating lunch. Then they'd go back outside onto the ice for hours.

But Gordie didn't have an easy time of it during those early years; he'd developed into a painfully shy child. Sometimes his sensitivity and self-consciousness were so extreme that he was nearly crippled socially. For a CBC radio documentary in 1966, Katherine Howe described her young son's difficulties in dealing with the other boys. "He was a little clumsy and awkward, you know, because he was growing so fast. The other boys used to tell him, 'Get out of the road!' or something, and he'd come home crying. And I'd say, 'Well, don't cry, you're strong enough, just get out there and look after yourself, because I can't be around all the time.'"

Somehow during those years, with all she had to do at home, Mrs. Howe did find time to encourage her son and even to be his playmate occasionally. She once told a Saskatoon television interviewer that Gordie would say, "C'mon, Mom, let's play hockey," and they'd find a couple of sticks and knock a stone around for a puck. Today Howe says he doesn't remember such times—perhaps the only point in recent memory on which he's contradicted his mother.

Ab Howe was less patient with his son. On the radio documentary just mentioned, Ab spoke in his gravelly voice, in the home-spun style of a born raconteur, about his own memory of Gordie's "backwardness":

"He was awful backward, you know, awful backward. Even after he played hockey, he wouldn't go into a store and buy an ice cream cone. We was going to stop for a drink one night, and we give him a quarter: 'Go on in and get yourself a pop or an ice cream.' And he come out, and we said, 'Did you get your ice cream, Gordon?' And he said, 'No. You go get it.' And I said, 'You'll wait a long time, boy—you got to get in there and hustle for yourself.'"

This was Ab's ruling principle, the primary lesson he felt he had to teach his bashful son. Just as young Gordie strengthened his physical backbone with exercise and, later, hard labour on construction sites, Ab tried to ensure, in the only way he knew, that Gordie strengthened his emotional backbone. With characteristic forthrightness, Ab stated his approach in another interview in the early 1960s. "The first time [Gordie] tried to join one of the small teams here they sent him home because he wasn't dressed properly or something and I was hopping mad. Ever since then I've always told him to never take any dirt from nobody, because if you do, they'll keep throwing it in on you. That's the way life is."

The old man's dictum eventually took—on the ice, at least. Howe was to make it his very own. No player ever took less dirt in the NHL, or so excelled at repaying dirty hits with interest.

But in a different sense, Ab's brusque approach could very well have had a negative, discouraging influence, to judge from another published remark: "[Gordie] was clumsy and backward and bashful. That's why I never thought he'd amount to anything."

If this assumption filtered down to young Gordie, as it inevitably must have, the fact that he later "amounted" to so much suggests a tremendous inner strength, a proud, stubborn determination to overcome the limits his father had placed on him . . .

Throughout Howe's youth, his most influential benefactors were female. His mother's support was crucial. At least two other caring women, Frances Hodges and Doris Crawford, also made a vital difference by understanding and appreciating the big, clumsy kid, whose "backwardness" seemed to irritate men while attracting maternal protectiveness.

Mrs. Crawford died in 1972, but Mrs. Hodges, now in her eighties, still resides in Saskatoon. Howe's sister, Joan Clark, recalls that, of all the adults who played a part in his early hockey career, it was Mrs. Hodges "who helped Gord the most."

There was a relative absence of male coaches and role models at the time because of the war. After 1939, many Saskatoon men, including Gordie's two older brothers, Vern and Norm, were away serving in the armed forces; others were like Ab Howe, working long hours to make ends meet in an era of scarcity. Hence the women were more likely to be available to help a boy growing up. This was the case with Frances Hodges, whose husband, Bert, was one of the organizers and coaches of the King George Athletic Club; since Bert's job with Canadian National Railways often took him away from home, Frances assumed his hockey duties more often than not.

With two hockey-playing sons of their own, the Hodges maintained a regulation-size rink in their backyard, near the small, two-storey frame house where the Howes now lived at 633 Avenue L South, kitty-corner from King George school. The Howes' house was cramped, and the children still living at home had to double up in the bedrooms. Mrs. Clark remembers her brother spending all his spare time on the Hodges' ice, playing shinny or just practising his moves. And as she also recalls, "Us girls wanted to play too, but we were never welcome—the guys wouldn't let us."

Mrs. Hodges, now a widow, retains crystal-clear images of "Gordon" from the age of about ten—images of his single-minded devotion to hockey and of his appealing personality. Indeed, if single-mindedness is one of the attributes of genius, Howe displayed it from an early age.

"We'd wake up in the morning to see Gordon out there skating on the rink," she recalled recently, "all by himself. He was a beautiful skater. Sometimes he had to clear the snow off first, but he didn't mind."

Circling the Hodges' ice, picking up speed as he perfected that rather peculiar kinesthetic process known as stick-handling—skating while moving a puck back and forth between opposite sides of a stick blade and simultaneously propelling it forward—the young Howe could leave his school difficulties and classroom humiliations so far behind that for a blissful while they ceased to exist. On the sanctuary of the ice, he was fulfilled, so totally absorbed by the pleasures of hockey that he often stayed on the Hodges' rink long after dark.

Tommy Douglas and the New Jerusalem

JAN & TOMMY McLEOD

Tommy Douglas was a Baptist preacher in Weyburn when the Depression hit Saskatchewan. The poverty and misery that he observed convinced him to forsake the pulpit for politics. He participated in the founding convention of the Cooperative Commonwealth Federation in 1933 and was elected to Parliament in 1935. He returned to lead the CCF in Saskatchewan, and with Douglas in charge the party won five consecutive mandates.

Tommy McLeod was a young student in Weyburn when he began to support Douglas politically, and later worked for the premier in Regina.

F OR THOSE CLOSE TO DOUGLAS, 1944 was a year of achievement. The days were filled with personal sacrifice but also with satisfaction. The work of building a new government with limited resources brought ministers and staff together in the kind of fellowship usually associated with a theatre of war. The government had made an amazing start. By year-end, it had issued cards to 30,000 people, widows, single mothers, and old people, giving them access to free medical care. It had introduced free cancer and psychiatric treatment, and raised mothers' allowances by 20 per cent. It had stabilized the farm debt situation, launched an insurance corporation, proclaimed a new day for labour, and started a massive program of administrative reform.

Douglas was sustained by a manic energy and a diet of raisin pie and coffee. In time his stomach rebelled, and he had to switch to milk and poached eggs. The strain told on other ministers as well. On cabinet days, regardless of what was on the agenda, the door opened at 10:30 sharp and the angel of the outer office appeared with a tray holding three half-pints of milk. Discussion stopped until straws had been inserted and first sips taken. This ceremony soothed three ulcers, but it threatened to create others, particularly in those who were interrupted while making a presentation. An exasperated Woodrow Lloyd commented, "If one more of you fellows would develop an ulcer we could buy a cow, and each of you could have a tit."

There was no half speed with Douglas. Every moment counted. One day, when McLeod chauffeured him to an appointment outside Regina, they got stuck behind a slow-moving truck on a country road, and Douglas fumed. Etiquette called for the truck to pull off and let the car go past; finally, McLeod made a lunge for it and crowded past on the outside. He turned to see the premier of Saskatchewan hanging from the open door on the passenger side, his head clearing the gravel by eighteen inches, trying to read the licence number on the truck.

Wherever he travelled in Saskatchewan during 1944, Douglas's followers lionized him as the man who had brought the CCF into its own. The party and the government enjoyed a honeymoon that year, highlighted by the remarkable fall session of the legislature when the government wrote much of the CCF's historic program into law. These were the party's greatest days. After this, the government would build up its own staff of in-house advisers and form new links with the world outside the party, and the CCF organization would lose its status as the main centre of influence . . .

Now facing the realities of office, the new premier found himself saying, in his first radio broadcast, that the CCF government had to serve all the people, not just members of the CCF. This marked the start of a discreet tug-of-war, with the party on one side and the cabinet and caucus on the other. The party's activists pushed for rapid and widespread reform. Over the years, however, Douglas and Fines would prove that they understood the limits to the public's appetite for change, and it would help them win five general elections in a row.

Douglas and Fines had to deal with a spectrum of pressure groups outside the party, including big business. Plans for a Farm Security Act and the new mineral taxes brought the government into sharp disagreement with several interests—mining, oil, mortgage, and insurance companies. Some major companies, such as Imperial Oil, would refuse to invest in the province for several years. The premier and the treasurer had to persuade those who would listen that the new government would act moderately and within the law.

Fines described Douglas in these meetings as "the smoothest customer I ever saw." The premier would rush from his desk, usher in his visitor, and spend several minutes on the weather and family matters. When it got down to business, he had a photographic memory for speeches, letters, and contracts, and often spouted a visitor's own words at him verbatim. Fines had a similar gift for numbers. He could pick figures out of the air, add, multiply, and compound interest, all in his head. The two leaders decided to fly to New York, Toronto, and Montreal in late summer 1944 to offset the scare stories about the socialist takeover. They reassured the financial houses that the new government intended to keep paying its debts. Most of the investment brokers received them cordially, but at Prudential Insurance in New Jersey the investment manager informed the pair that he had dumped $3 million in Saskatchewan bonds. Fines, as a Prudential policy holder, dressed the man down for his recklessness . . .

In mid-1945 Douglas found the planning expert he was looking for, and began negotiations to bring him to Saskatchewan. George Cadbury would play a leading role in sorting out the government's problems and in establishing the planning system that would let the CCF set long-term goals. Cadbury had been born into the world of business, and had worked for the family firm in England as well as for several other companies. He graduated in economics from Cambridge University at a time when giants such as Maynard Keynes and Joan and Austin Robinson were generating great intellectual excitement. Cadbury and his wife Barbara were committed socialists. Both were active in the Labour Party and in the co-operative movement, and were steeped in the ideas of international socialism. David Lewis had heard about Cadbury while he was at

Oxford, and advised Douglas to invite him to Saskatchewan. Fortunately, Cadbury consented.

On January 1, 1946, Cadbury assumed a double-barrelled title, chairman of the Economic Advisory and Planning Board and chief industrial executive. One part of his persona would be dedicated to planning, the other to bringing order to the crown corporations. Here was a public servant who could help to make the government into a rational institution "of the highest possible order," one that was both efficient and politically responsible. Until he left Saskatchewan in late 1951, Cadbury occupied a position just a step below that of a cabinet minister. Indeed, some cabinet ministers felt that he enjoyed a higher status than they did. He met freely with any of the ministers, particularly those who headed the crown corporations. For the most part, though, he dealt with Douglas, whom he regarded as "his minister," and with Fines, who had general responsibility for economic matters. Cadbury's two agencies, the Planning Board and the Government Finance Office—responsible for organizing the management of the government businesses—answered directly to the cabinet. Their governing bodies were twin cabinet committees, one headed by the premier, the other by the treasurer.

As premier, Douglas was the unquestioned leader in cabinet, in caucus, and party on matters of policy. He was the government's practical dreamer. The essence of his leadership, the source of his power over others, was his ability to dream and to cast his dreams in practical forms, to reduce his ideas to precise language, and to articulate them in such a way as to inspire those around him. He also had the ability to explore the ideas of others with an open mind, to analyse and to learn—and, at times, to act as a prodigious critic. The planning function, embodied in the Economic Advisory and Planning Board—the government's think tank—was built around his office and answered to him.

Fines, as treasurer, was the practical man who had the administrative skills and the manager's toughness that Douglas lacked. Luckily for the CCF, he had no desire to dump Douglas from the premier's chair. He understood his role, and was satisfied to complement Douglas's strengths with his own. If Douglas was the designer, Fines was the mechanic. During the almost twenty years that they worked closely together, from the time Douglas took the CCF provincial presidency in 1941, they probably never had a serious discussion of their unwritten contract, but both men adhered to it faithfully . . .

The work of the planners reached out to the field of economic development, but it also reached into the heart of the government, into the cabinet, the decision-making centre. The steps they took to streamline the flow of information—to insure that the cabinet remained up to date on what was going on, and could respond quickly to any hitches—were among the Planning Board's most important contributions to the province. Douglas and Fines not only accepted but promoted the recommendations for change. In doing so, each one sacrificed some of the traditional powers of his office for the good of the cabinet. The premier and the treasurer could no longer control events by keeping their colleagues in the dark, even if they had wanted to. Reports on the government's work and proposals for change now came to the cabinet as a whole.

The cabinet was surrounded by an array of specialized, professionally staffed agencies, each of them answerable from day to day to a cabinet committee. The Planning Board, as noted earlier, provided the overview of the provincial economy. The Government Finance Office watched over the crown corporations, while the Treasury Board advised cabinet on the annual budget. The Cabinet Secretariat pulled together the various streams of information and packaged them for the ministers. This high level of co-ordination and specialization marked a breakthrough in the art of government in Canada. Before this, most governments had been content to operate in a loosely structured, amateurish fashion, reacting to crises or to demands from pressure groups as they came up. The Patterson cabinet, like its counterparts across Canada, had kept no formal agenda and no record of proceedings beyond what might be contained in the premier's notes or in his colleagues' memories. With experience, the Douglas cabinet system became highly sophisticated, and, with a few minor changes, is still in operation in Saskatchewan today.

The CCF method of organization served as a model for other provinces, and veterans of the Douglas years took senior positions in Ottawa when the Thatcher Liberals smashed the Saskatchewan civil service in 1964. Tommy Shoyama, a British Columbia-born economist who served as chairman of the Planning Board after Cadbury, rose to become deputy minister of finance in the Ottawa of the 1970s. Al Johnson, a Saskatchewan native who succeeded McLeod as deputy provincial treasurer, also became a deputy minister in Ottawa, and then head of the CBC. Other members of the "Saskatchewan Mafia" moved into senior jobs in the federal Privy Council Office and in federal departments. Don Tansley and Jim MacNeill became deputies, and Al Davidson, Del Lyngseth, and Art Wakabayashi, among others, became assistant deputy ministers. The Mafia left its footprint on the public service of Canada.

Fundamental changes in the machinery of government brought changes in the role of the premier, changes that, for the most part, were highly compatible with Douglas's style of leadership. He sought to lead rather than to direct, and he preferred holding joint deliberations to giving orders. His method was essentially Socratic. He deferred to the specialized knowledge of the experts, and did not pretend to have all the answers. He did, however, have a gift for asking the right questions. He also had a remarkable ability to relate expert advice to the facts of real life, and to the real needs of his constituents. Shoyama, a brilliant economist who sat at the centre of many conferences, spoke almost in awe of the premier's ability to direct the flow of a technical discussion, and, by questioning, keep the experts' feet on the ground.

In working with his professional staff, Douglas tried to instill a sense of the music of the English language. Johnson and Shoyama once laboured to put together a speech for the premier, only to have him throw it aside with some irritation. Pacing up and down, Douglas dictated a new version with only minutes to go before he had to deliver it. He said later of the first version, "There was no rhythm in it."

Few things roused Douglas's ire faster than an attempt to cover uncertainty with a blanket of words. Sooner or later, most of those who worked for him got the lecture on verbal obfuscation. The premier wanted direct reports delivered in sparse, understandable language.

Douglas once highlighted his dislike of bureaucratese by pulling an item from his morning mail. He had his secretary bring in a letter from a voter who was angry about the Saskatchewan Power Corporation's method of putting up its power lines. Between the signature and the salutation there was one sentence: "Some bugger bust my fence." "There it is," said Douglas. "Subject, 'bugger,' verb, 'bust,' object, 'fence.' Why can't you fellows write like that?"

Mother of the CCF

J.F.C. WRIGHT

A farmer from near Assiniboia, Louise Lucas was an activist in the United Farmers of Canada and one of the founders of the CCF. She later ran for office several times, but was forced to withdraw from the 1945 federal election because of serious illness.

LIGHTS DIMMED IN THE REGINA-ASSINIBOIA BUS–couldn't read had you wanted to—must be nearing the crossroad because eight minutes back the bus driver had said, "We'll be stopping there in about ten minutes."

Her husband, Henry Lucas, would meet the bus at the crossroad.

It was six months since I had seen her. At that time she was preparing for the most formidable contest of what might have become a political career—the contest with the Hon. James Garfield Gardiner, former premier of Saskatchewan, then Agriculture Minister in Prime Minister William Lyon Mackenzie King's Liberal Government at Ottawa.

I had worked with her during the 1930s, and now in this late harvest-time of 1945 she was dying in the Lucas farm home close by Mazenod, a six-grain-elevator-village on Saskatchewan's open plain . . .

The car turned off the road into the Lucas farmyard. Light generated by the wind-electric (windmill) shone through this house of many windows, sunporch glowing in the night like a glassed-in deck of a ferry boat.

In the homey dining-room where ferns and flowers were growing, Henry introduced members of the family I hadn't met before; several had married during the war years I had been away. The hands of the cuckoo-clock showed after half-past ten.

We were sitting having coffee and a bite of near-midnight lunch, that prairie-farm-home institution of meetings and special occasions, when Dorothy Lucas, the youngest, a nurse-in-training, returned to the table, announced, "Mother wants to see you now, Mr. Wright."

I hadn't expected she would until daylight next morning, but none of the family looked surprised. Henry nodded, so I got up from the table and followed Dorothy along a short hallway to a bedroom on the same floor.

In a large double bed she lay propped with pillows, her greying dark brown hair parted in schoolgirl plaits with neat blue ribbons against the white pillow. Smaller now, she seemed like a little girl; her face had lost the lines of time. Only her dark, intuitive eyes were the same.

She lifted her good hand from the fresh white bedspread and, as I took it in mine, she nodded, then indicated a chair by the foot of her bed. A bright, orderly, inviting room, like the rest of the house.

"Jim," she said, "I'm not going to enquire about your wife and family, or ask about your work lately. You understand?", her eyebrows tilting in the expressive old way, mouth curved down at the skeptical I-see-through-you-and-all-your-worldly-tricks corner; up at the opposite and optimistic-faith-in-God-and-Humanity corner.

"You understand?", she repeated. Her vibrant voice had lost nothing of the determinative I-know-I-am-right quality, although the carrying power had diminished.

"You know I am interested, but I am going soon. Through you I must leave a message, a message in writing, to our women—especially our farm women—

and to the young folk. Do you see?" Eyebrows tilting again. "I must conserve my strength and voice for this. Have you your notebook and pencil?"

Hesitant, at first, to try her ebbing strength at this late hour of night, I was fascinated by her courage; inspired by the familiar crusading spirit in that now frail and shrunken, cancer-eaten body. As Dorothy left the room, I stood up. Louise Lucas nodded, "Go and bring your notebook and we will begin."

It was a command . . .

At the top of the page in my typewriter I had written: Page 1, dictated by Mrs. Louise Lucas, October 11, 1945.

In a clear voice and with precise—at times incisive mind, in startling contrast to her dying body, she began:

"Early that summer, after my first convention—the UFC [United Farmers of Canada] convention of March , 1927, I received a letter from Parchman, of La Fleche, inviting me to speak at the Wood Mountain UFC open-air rally. I replied, thanking him, but that I was no speaker, only an ordinary farm wife and mother—that I had never made a scheduled speech at a public meeting in my life, and didn't intend making a fool of myself now . . . "

She went on to relate how Parchman had not taken her answer as final. Like his fellow committee members, Parchman had been persistent, a necessary quality in an organizer, and after consultation with the committee, he got in his car and drove to Mazenod and the Lucas home.

He knocked at the door, introduced himself, was invited in.

" . . . now Mrs. Lucas," he said, "is that true? We heard you at the convention . . . not many could have got the attention of the crowd at that moment . . . you swung that tabling motion . . . just can't take 'no' for an answer . . . George Williams will be the main speaker, but we want you . . . "

"But Mr. Parchman, I wouldn't know what to say."

"Tell 'em what we want is two-dollar wheat," he said.

Her eyes flashed. "That would do no good," she shot back at him. "Prosperity does not depend on two-dollar wheat, or five-dollar wheat, or one-dollar wheat. Prosperity depends on what we farmers have left over for the welfare of our families, after we are through paying for the cost of producing the wheat. I am going to tell it again and again, because I know it is true—our welfare depends on parity prices for farm products . . . "

Parchman listening, nodded agreement as she developed this theme in that clear voice with its positive rhythm. Yes, he had her going now.

As if suddenly aware of his thought, and conscious she might be making a speech, she stopped abruptly, and seeing his fleeting look of "My God, does she read minds too?" she smiled and added "You see?"

"Sure, of course I do. That's the policy of our organization—parity prices.

Now there you have it. That's the speech for the rally. Couldn't beat it anywhere. Why, with that you'll . . . "

As Parchman got up from his chair to give a preview of the arrangements for the rally, " . . . we'll likely have a sound truck for the speakers to speak from," he was saying, she caught herself wondering if she really could make a scheduled address to a large audience without having stage-fright.

"All right, Mr. Parchman, I'll try. But remember, if I make a failure of it you have only yourself to blame. And next time you will burn up your gas on something more useful than driving over the roads to persuade *me!*"

And so, during her last ten days she continued to relate to me her story of struggle, attainment, distress—of how she first got into the "farmers' movement," humour spicing her crusade for a "better-price-for-wheat" and a better world.

Sometimes indignant at man's high-handedness, tolerant of stupidity but never of dishonesty; intuitive—always the mother—this was the woman who early in her married life had told her husband: "Politics are nothing but a dirty game for men crooks to play," yet, in the 1930s became known in Saskatchewan as "Mother of the CCF."

Wolf Willow

ᗺALLACE STEGNER

Stegner's family were homesteaders near the American border south of Eastend from 1914 to 1920. In winters they lived in town. When the farm failed, the Stegners returned to the U.S., where Wallace became an important writer. In the early 1950s he returned briefly to Eastend (which he describes as "Whitemud") and wrote a series of magazine articles later collected in his classic Wolf Willow.

ᑌNLESS EVERYTHING in a man's memory of childhood is misleading, there is a time somewhere between the ages of five and twelve which corresponds to the phase ethologists have isolated in the development of birds, when an impression lasting only a few seconds may be imprinted on the young bird for life. This is the way a bird emerging from the darkness of the egg knows itself, the mechanism of its relating to the world. Expose a just-hatched duckling to an alarm clock, or a wooden decoy on rollers, or a man, or any other object that moves and makes a noise, and it will react for life as if that object were its mother. Expose a child to a particular environment at his susceptible time and he will perceive in the shapes of that environment until he dies. The perceptive habits that are like imprintings or like conditioned responses carry their habitual and remembered emotions. Wolf willow is a sample, but things other than smells will do it. I can sing an old Presbyterian Sunday School hymn, "The Fight Is On, Oh Christian Soldiers," and instantly I am seven or eight years old, it is a June day on the homestead, the coulee is full of buttercups, and a flickertail's close-eared head is emerging in jerks from a burrow, the unblinking almond eye watching to see if I move. Only because I must have sung it to myself in that spot, a few bars of that tune can immerse me in the old sun and space, return me to the big geometry of the prairie and the tension of the prairie wind.

I still sometimes dream, occasionally in the most intense and brilliant shades of green, of a jungly dead bend of the Whitemud below Martin's dam. Every time I have that dream I am haunted, on awakening, by a sense of meanings just withheld, and by a profound nostalgic melancholy. Freudian implications suggest themselves, and the brilliant metallic greens of the dream could be an alarming symptom from my suprarenals. But the Freudian and endocrine aspects interest me less than the mere fact that this dead loop of river, known only for a few years, should be so charged with potency in my unconscious—why around it there should be other images, almost all from the river valley rather than from the prairie, that constantly recur in dreams or in the images I bring up off the typewriter onto the page. They lie in me like underground water; every well I put down taps them. If I must have Freudian dreams, and I suppose I must, why does that early imprinting, rather than all later experience, so often dictate their form? And if my suprarenals must cut up, why do the mescalin-vivid colors of my visions have to come, not merely from childhood but from a fraction of childhood?

I suppose I know, actually. As the prairie taught identity by exposing me, the river valley taught me about safety. In a jumpy and insecure childhood where all masculine elements are painful or dangerous, sanctuary matters. That sunken bottom sheltered from the total sky and the untrammeled wind was my hibernating ground, my place of snugness, and in a country often blistered and crisped, green became the color of safety. When I feel the need to return to the womb, this is still the place toward which my well-conditioned unconscious turns like an old horse heading for the barn.

Psychological narcissism is interesting enough to the individual who is indulging in it, but hardly to anyone else. There is something else here, and of a more general bearing. The accident of being brought up on a belated, almost symbolic frontier has put me through processes of deculturation, isolation, and intellectual schizophrenia that until recently have been a most common American experience. The lateness of my frontier and the fact that it lay in Canada intensified the discrepancy between that part of me which reflects the folk culture and that part which reflects an education imported and often irrelevant. The dichotomy between American and European that exists to some extent in all of us exists most drastically in people reared on frontiers, for frontiers provide not only the rawest forms of deculturation but the most slavish respect for borrowed elegances.

Man, being infinitely adaptable, does not perish of a mere discrepancy. The titanotheres whose fossil bones lie embedded in the Cypress Hills sandstones died off when a climatic change killed the mushy forage for which their chopper teeth were designed, but I shall not lose even sleep or efficiency because of the division in me. I shall only feel half an anachronism in an America that has been industrialized, regimented, bulldozed, and urbanized out of direct contact with the earth.

I may not know who I am, but I know where I am from. I can say to myself that a good part of my private and social character, the kinds of scenery and weather and people and humor I respond to, the prejudices I wear like dishonorable scars, the affections that sometimes waken me from middle-aged sleep with a rush of undiminished love, the virtues I respect and the weaknesses I condemn, the code I try to live by, the special ways I fail at it and the kinds of shame I feel when I do, the models and heroes I follow, the colors and shapes that evoke my deepest pleasure, the way I adjudicate between personal desire and personal responsibility, have been in good part scored into me by that little womb-village and the lovely, lonely, exposed prairie of the homestead. However anachronistic I may be, I am a product of the American earth, and in nothing quite so much as in the contrast between what I knew through the pores and what I was officially taught.

People in a frontier revert quickly, except when they are self-consciously preserving some imported nicety, to folk skills, and some of these are so primitive that they seem to have scarcely any national character at all. In their performance you cannot tell a Norwegian from a Dukhobor, or either one from an Ontario man. It is as if they came down to us from Neanderthal or Cro-Magnon ancestors—our way with simple hand tools, our way with animals, the simpler forms of social organization. On that level, every frontier child knows exactly who he is, and who his mother is, and he loves his alarm clock quite as much as if it had feathers. But then comes something else, a waddling thing with webbed feet, insisting that it is its mother, that he is not who he thought he was, but infinitely more, heir to swans and phoenixes. In such a town as Whitemud, school superimposes five thousand years of Mediterranean culture and two thousand years of Europe upon the adapted or rediscovered simplicities of a new continent.

We had our own grain, and our knots as well, but prairie and town did the shaping, and sometimes I have wondered if they did not cut us to a pattern no longer viable. Far more than Henry Adams, I have felt myself entitled to ask whether my needs and my education were not ludicrously out of phase. Not because I was educated for the past instead of the future—most education trains us for the past, as most preparation for war readies us for the war just over—but because I was educated for the wrong place. Education tried, inadequately and hopelessly, to make a European out of me.

Once, in a self-pitying frame of mind, I was comparing my background with that of an English novelist friend. Where he had been brought up in London, taken from the age of four onward to the Tate and the National Gallery, sent traveling on the Continent in every school holiday, taught French and German and Italian, given access to bookstores, libraries, and British Museums, made familiar from infancy on with the conversation of the eloquent and the great, I had grown up in this dung-heeled sagebrush town on the disappearing edge of nowhere, utterly without painting, without sculpture, without architecture, almost without music or theatre, without conversation or languages or travel or stimulating instruction, without libraries or museums or bookstores, almost without books. I was charged with getting in a single lifetime, from scratch, what some people inherit as naturally as they breathe air. And not merely cultural matters. I was nearly twelve before I saw either a bathtub or a watercloset, and when I walked past my first lawn, in Great Falls, Montana, I stooped down and touched its cool nap in awe and unbelief. I think I held my breath—I had not known that people anywhere lived with such grace. Also I had not known until then how much ugliness I myself had lived with. Our homestead yard was as bare as an alkali flat, because my father, observing some folklore fire precaution, insisted on throwing out the soapy wash water until he had killed off every blade of grass or cluster of false mallow inside the fireguard. Our yard in town, though not so littered with feathers and cans and chicken heads as some, was a weed-patch, because our habit of spending the summers on the homestead prevented my mother from growing any flowers except the Wandering Jew and Star of Bethlehem that she carried back and forth in pots.

How, I asked this Englishman, could anyone from so deprived a background ever catch up? How was one expected to compete, as a cultivated man, with people like himself? He looked at me and said dryly, "Perhaps you got something else in place of all that."

He meant, I suppose, that there are certain advantages to growing up a sensuous little savage, and to tell the truth I am not sure I would trade my childhood of freedom and the outdoors and the senses for a childhood of being led by the hand past all the Turners in the National Gallery. And also, he may have meant that anyone starting from deprivation is spared getting bored. You may not get a good start, but you may get up a considerable head of steam. I am reminded of Willa Cather, that bright girl from Nebraska, memorizing long passages from the *Aeneid* and spurning the dust of Red Cloud and Lincoln with her culture-bound feet. She tried, and her education encouraged her, to be a good European. Nevertheless she was a first-rate novelist only when she dealt with what she knew from Red Cloud and the things she had "in place of all that." Nebraska was what she was born to write; the rest of it was got up. Eventually, when education had won and nurture had conquered nature and she had recognized Red Cloud as a vulgar little hole, she embraced the foreign tradition totally and ended by being neither quite a good American nor quite a true European nor quite a whole artist.

Her career is a parable. If there is truth in Lawrence's assertion that America's unconscious wish has always been to destroy Europe, it is also true that from Irving to William Styron, American writers have been tempted toward apostasy and expatriation, toward return and fusion with the parent. It is a painful and sometimes fatal division, and the farther you are from Europe—that is, the farther you are out in the hinterlands of America—the more difficult it is. Contradictory voices tell you who you are. You grow up speaking one dialect and reading and writing another. During twenty-odd years of education and another thirty of literary practice you may learn to be nimble in the King's English; yet in moments of relaxation, crisis, or surprise you fall back into the corrupted lingo that is your native tongue. Nevertheless all the forces of culture and snobbery are against your *writing* by ear and making contact with your own natural audience. Your natural audience, for one thing, doesn't read—it *isn't* an audience. You grow out of touch with your dialect because learning and literature lead you another way unless you consciously resist. It is only the occasional Mark Twain or Robert Frost who manages to get the authentic American tone of voice into his work. For most of us, the language of literature is to some extent unreal, because school has always been separate from life.

In practice, the deculturation of a frontier means a falling-back on mainly oral traditions, on the things that can be communicated without books: on folklore, on the music and poetry and story easily memorized, on the cookery that comes not from cookbooks but from habit and laziness, on the medicine that is old wives' tales. Before it was more than half assembled from its random parts, the folklore of Whitemud was mine. I knew the going ballads, mainly of cowboy origin and mainly dirty, and because my father had a sticky memory and a knack of improvisation, I knew some that he probably made up on the spur of the moment. I took part and pleasure in the school cantatas and the town jamborees that were our concert stage and our vaudeville. I absorbed by osmosis the local lore, whether it involved the treatment of frostbite or the virtues of sulphur and molasses for "thinning the blood" in the spring. I ate my beef well done because that was the way everyone ate it, and only shame keeps me from eating it that way yet. But I also read whatever books I could lay hands on, and almost everything I got from books was either at odds with what I knew from experience or irrelevant to it or remote from it. Books didn't enlarge me; they dispersed me.

Naturally the books were not exactly what a wise tutor would have prescribed. We were not lucky enough to have in Whitemud one of those eccentric men of learning who brought good libraries to so many earlier frontier towns and who lighted fires under susceptible village boys. The books we saw were the survivors of many moves, accidentally preserved pieces of family impedimenta, or they were a gradual accretion, mainly Christmas presents, ordered sight unseen by the literary sightless from the catalog of the T. Eaton mail-order house.

Our house contained some novels of George Barr McCutcheon and Gene Stratton-Porter, a set of Shakespeare in marbled bindings with red leather spines and corners, and a massive set of Ridpath's *History of the World*. I handled them all, and I suppose read in them some, uncomprehendingly, from the time I was five. Their exteriors are still vivid to me; their contents have not always stuck. The gray binding and the cover picture of a romance called *The Rock in the Baltic* I recall very well, without recalling anything about the novel or even who wrote it. Until I began to get a few books of my own—Tarzan books, or the Bar-Twenty novels of B.M. Bower, principally—my favorite volumes were the Ridpath histories, because I liked the spidery steel engravings with which they were illustrated. It was my mother's inaccurate boast that I had read clear through Ridpath's volumes by the time I was eight.

Let us say that I had looked at the pictures, and learned a few names, and could parrot a few captions and chapter headings. Much of that random rubbish is still in my head like an impression in wax, and comes out of me now as if memory were a phonograph record. What strikes me about this in recollection is not my precocious or fictitious reading capacity, and not the durability of memory, but the fact that the information I was gaining from literature and from books on geography and history had not the slightest relevance to the geography, history, or life of the place where I lived. Living in the Cypress Hills, I did not even know I lived there, and hadn't the faintest notion of who had lived there before me. But I could have drawn you a crudely approximate map of the Baltic, recited you Tom Moore songs or Joaquin Miller's poem on Columbus, or given you a rudimentary notion of the virtues of Gracchi or the misfortunes of the Sabine women.

Though my friends and I sometimes planned gaudy canoe expeditions down the Whitemud, we had no notion where such a trip might bring us out, and no notion that there were maps which would tell us. The willow-fringed stream, after it left the Hills, might as well have been on its way to join the Alph. The Hills of which I was an unknowing resident were only a few fixed points: North Bench, South Bench, the sandhills, Chimney Coulee. The world I knew was immediate, not comparative; seen flat, without perspective. Knowledge of place, knowledge of the past, meant to me knowledge of the far and foreign.

I know now that there were some books from which we could have learned a good deal about our own world. Nobody in town, I am sure, knew they existed unless it was Corky Jones, and Corky's interest in history and other matters was never fully comprehended by his fellow townsmen. Certainly school taught us nothing in this line. The closest it came was Frontenac, Montcalm and Wolfe, and the Plains of Abraham. The one relic of the local past that we were all aware of, the line of half-tumbled chimneys where the métis village had once stood on the edge of Chimney Coulee, had in our mouths a half-dozen interpretations, all of them wrong. I remember my father's telling us that they were Indian signaling chimneys. He was, in his way, consistently creative. If he lost the verses of a song, he made new ones; if he was in doubt about the meaning or source of a word, he was fast with a folk etymology; if he was ignorant of the facts, as in the case of the chimneys, he did not let ignorance hamper his imagination.

In general the assumption of all us, child or adult, was that this was a new country and that a new country had no history. History was something that applied to other places. It would not have seemed reasonable to any of the town's founders to consider any of their activities history, or to look back very far in search of what had proceded them. Time reached back only a few years, to the pre-homestead period of the big cattle ranches. Some ranches had weathered the terrible winter of 1906, and to a child these survivors seemed to have existed forever, floating in an enduring present like the town. For that matter, I never heard of the terrible winter of 1906 until many years later, though it had affected my life for me before I was born.

So the world when I began to know it had neither location nor time, geography nor history. But it had a wild freedom, a closeness to earth and weather, a familiarity with both tame and wild animals. It had the physical sweetness of a golden age. It was blessedly free of most conventional restrictions, and its very liberation from the perspectives of time and place released our minds for imaginative flights into wonder. Our sensuous and imaginative education was exaggerated, but nobody told us much about what is now sometimes called "vital adjustment."

Under the circumstances it might sound fanciful to suggest that either the geography or the history of the Cypress Hills could have had any substantial part in making the minds and characters of children reared there. Certainly they could have no strong and immediate effect, as they might have upon a child who passes every day the rude bridge where the embattled farmers of Concord precipitated a new age with a volley of musketry; or upon a child who flies his kite in the Saratoga meadow where the bronze boot commemorates the nameless heroism of a traitor. In the world's old places, even the New World's old places, not only books reinforce and illuminate a child's perceptions. The past becomes a thing made palpable in monuments, buildings, historical sites, museums, attics, old trunks, relics of a hundred kinds; and in the legends of grandfathers and great-grandfathers; and in the incised marble and granite and weathered wood of graveyards; and in the murmurings of ghosts. We knew no such history, no such past, no such tradition, no such ghosts. And yet it would be a double error to assume that my childhood had no history, and that I was not influenced by it.

For history is a pontoon bridge. Every man walks and works at its building end, and has come as far as he has over the pontoons laid by others he may never have heard of. Events have a way of making other events inevitable; the actions of men are consecutive and indivisible. The history of the Cypress Hills had almost as definite effects on me as did their geography and weather, though I never knew a scrap of that history until a quarter-century after I left the place. However it may have seemed to the people who founded it, Whitemud was not a beginning, not a new thing, but a stage in a long historical process.

History? Seldom, anywhere, have historical changes occurred so fast. From grizzlies, buffalo, and Indians still only half possessed of the horse and gun, the historical parabola to Dust Bowl and near-depopulation covered only about sixty years. Here was the Plains frontier in a capsule, condensed into the life of a reasonably long-lived man.

Halfbreed

MARIA CAMPBELL

Maria Campbell is a Metis writer who grew up Saskatchewan. Her ancestors lived near Batoche during the war between the Metis and the Canadian government.

M Y PEOPLE FLED TO SPRING RIVER which is fifty miles north-west of Prince Albert. Halfbreed families with names like Chartrand, Isbister, Campbell, Arcand, and Vandal came here after the Riel Rebellion where the men had been actively involved. Riel was gone now and so were their hopes. This new land was covered with small lakes, rocky hills and dense bush. The Halfbreeds who came were self-sufficient trappers and hunters. Unlike their Indian brothers, they were not prepared to settle down to an existence of continual hardship, scratching out a scanty living from the land. They were drawn to this part of Saskatchewan because the region was good for hunting and trapping, and there were no settlers.

In the late 1920s the land was thrown open for homesteading and again came the threat of immigrants. By this time the lakes were drying up and the fur and game had almost disappeared. Having nowhere else to go, nearly all the families decided to take homesteads so that the land would belong to them. It was difficult to accept the fact that times were changing, but if there was to be a future for their children, the roaming, free life must be forgotten.

The land was ten dollars for a quarter section. Ten acres had to be broken in three years, along with improvements, before title would be granted. Otherwise the land was confiscated by Land Improvement District authorities. Due to the depression and shortage of fur there was no money to buy the implements to break the land. A few families could have scraped up the money to hire outside help but no one would risk expensive equipment on a land so covered with rocks and muskeg. Some tried with horse and plough but were defeated in the end. Fearless men who could brave sub-zero weather and all the dangers associated with living in the bush gave up, frustrated and discouraged. They just did not have the kind of thing inside them that makes farmers.

Gradually the homesteads were reclaimed by the authorities and offered to the immigrants. The Halfbreeds then became squatters on their land and were eventually run off by the new owners. One by one they drifted back to the road lines and crown lands where they built cabins and barns and from then on were known as "Road Allowance people."

So began a miserable life of poverty which held no hope for the future. That generation of my people was completely beaten. Their fathers had failed during the Rebellion to make a dream come true; they failed as farmers; now there was nothing left. Their way of life was a part of Canada's past and they saw no place in the world around them, for they believed they had nothing to offer. They felt shame, and with shame the loss of pride and the strength to live each day. I hurt inside when I think of those people. You sometimes see that generation today: the crippled, bent old grandfathers and grandmothers on town and city skid rows; you find them in the bush waiting to die; or baby-sitting grandchildren while the parents are drunk. And there are some who even after a hundred years continue to struggle for equality and justice for their people. The road for them is never-ending and full of frustrations and heart-break.

I hurt because in my childhood I saw glimpses of a proud and happy people. I heard their laughter, saw them dance, and felt their love.

A close friend of mine said, "Maria, make it a happy book. It couldn't have been so bad. We know we are guilty so don't be too harsh." I am not bitter. I have passed that stage. I only want to say: this is what it was like; this is what it is still like. I know that poverty is not ours alone. Your people have it too, but in those earlier days you at least had dreams, you had a tomorrow. My parents and I never shared any aspirations for a future. I never saw my father talk back to a white man unless he was drunk. I never saw him or any of our men walk with their heads held high before white people. However, when they were drunk they became aggressive and belligerent, and for a little while the whites would be afraid of them. Even these times were rare because often they drank too much and became pathetic, sick men, crying about the past and fighting each other or going home to beat frightened wives. But I am ahead of myself so I will begin again and tell of Dad's family.

Great Grandpa Campbell came from Edinburgh, Scotland, with his brother. They were both tough, hard men, and on the boat to Canada they got into a fight and disowned each other. They settled in the same area, both married native women and raised families. Great Grandpa married a Halfbreed woman, a niece of Gabriel Dumont. Prior to the marriage both brothers had wanted the same woman, and although Great Grandpa won, he was convinced that his only child was his brother's son and so he never recognized Grandpa Campbell as his own, nor did he ever speak to his brother again during his lifetime.

THE MIDDLE OF NOWHERE

He ran a Hudson's Bay store just a few miles west of Prince Albert and traded with the Halfbreeds and Indians around that area. When the Northwest Rebellion broke out in 1885, he was involved with the North West Mounted Police and the white settlers. He was not well-liked by his neighbours or the people who traded with him. Our old people called him "Chee-pie-hoos," meaning "Evil-spirit-jumping-up-and-down." They say he was very cruel and would beat his son, his wife, and his livestock with the same whip and with equal vengeance.

Grandpa Campbell ran away from home once when he was about ten. His father found him and tied him beside his horse. The old man then climbed in the buggie and whipped both the horse and Grandpa all the way home.

He was also a very jealous man and was sure his wife was having affairs with all the Halfbreeds in the area. So when the Rebellion broke out and he had to attend meetings away from home he would take his wife with him. She in turn passed on all the information she heard at these meetings to the rebels and also stole ammunition and supplies for them from his store. When he found out he became very angry and decided the best way to deal with her was by public flogging. So he stripped the clothes from her back and beat her so cruelly she was scarred for life.

He died not long after. Some people say her family killed him, but no one knows for sure. His wife went to her mother's people who lived in what is now known as Prince Albert National Park. Even though they were Indians they were never part of a reserve, as they weren't present when the treaty-makers came. She built a cabin beside Maria Lake and raised her son. Years later when the area was designated for the Park, the government asked her to leave. She refused, and when all peaceful methods failed the RCMP were sent. She locked her door, loaded her rifle, and when they arrived she fired shots over their heads, threatening to hit them if they came any closer. They left her alone and she was never disturbed again.

I remember her as a small woman, with white hair always neatly braided and tied with black thread. She wore black, ankle-length full skirts and black blouses with full sleeves and high collars. Around her neck were four or five strings of bright beads and a chain made of copper wire. On her wrists were copper bracelets which she wore to ward off arthritis. She wore moccasins and tight leggings to emphasize her tiny ankles. These were covered with bright porcupine quill designs.

Great Grandma Campbell, whom I always called "Cheechum," was a niece of Gabriel Dumont and her whole family fought beside Riel and Dumont during the Rebellion. She often told me stories of the Rebellion and of the Halfbreed people. She said our people never wanted to fight because that was not our way. We never wanted anything except to be left alone to live as we pleased. Cheechum never accepted defeat at Batoche, and she would always say, "Because they killed Riel they think they have killed us too, but some day, my girl, it will be different."

Cheechum hated to see the settlers come, and as they settled on what she believed was our land, she ignored them and refused to acknowledge them even when passing on the road. She would not become a Christian, saying firmly that she had married a Christian and if there was such a thing as hell then she had lived there; nothing after death could be worse! Offers of relief from welfare were scorned and so was the old age pension. While she lived alone she hunted and trapped, planted a garden, and was completely self-sufficient.

Grandpa Campbell, Cheechum's son, was a quiet man. No one remembers him too well, as the old people who are alive now seldom saw him or his wife. Grannie Campbell was a small woman with black curly hair and blue eyes. She was a Vandal, and her family had also been involved in the Rebellion. I cannot remember her ever saying very much and I never heard her laugh out loud. After their marriage, they lived miles out in the bush and never bothered much with anyone. Grandpa Campbell was a good friend of Grey Owl, an Englishman who came to our land and lived as an Indian. Grandpa loved the land and took from it only what he needed for food. Daddy says he was a kind, gentle man who spent a great deal of time with his children. He died when he was still young, leaving nine children, the oldest of whom was Daddy, aged eleven.

After Grandpa died, Grandma Campbell went to a white community and hired herself and Dad out to cut brush for seventy-five cents an acre. She wrapped their feet with rabbit skins and old paper, and over this they wore moccasins. They would put on old coats, then drive by horse and sleigh to work. Dad says that some days it would be so cold he would cry, and she would take the skins from her feet and wrap them around him and continue working.

In the spring after the farmers had broken the brushed land, they would return and pick the stones and roots and burn the brush, as the farmers wouldn't pay the seventy-five cents an acre until all this was completed.

In the fall they went to work harvesting. They did this until they had enough money to buy a homestead. She and Dad built a cabin and for three years tried to break the land. Because they only had one team of horses and Dad used these to work for other people, Grannie on many occasions pulled the plough herself. After three years of back-breaking work they still weren't able to meet the improvements required, so they lost title to the land. They moved then to the Crown lands along the road lines, and joined other "Road Allowance people."

As Daddy and his brothers grew older, they trapped, hunted, and sold game and homemade whiskey to the white farmers in the nearby settlements. When they each were married, they built their cabins beside Grandma's.

Grannie Campbell had a special place in our hearts. Daddy loved her a great deal and treated her with special tenderness. She was a very hard worker and it seemed as though she worked all the time. When Daddy tried to make her stop, as he could have looked after her, she became quite angry and said he had a family to worry about and what she did was none of his business. She brushed and cleared the settlers' land, picked their stones, delivered their babies, and looked after them when they were sick. Her home was always open to anyone in the community who cared to drop in, but in the forty years she lived there no white people ever visited her home, and only three old Swedes came when we buried her.

Daddy married when he was eighteen. He went to a sports day at the Sandy Lake Indian Reserve, saw my mother, who was then fifteen, wanted her and took her. He was a very good-looking man with black curly hair and blue-grey eyes, strong, rowdy and wild. He loved to dance and was dancing when Mom first saw him, his moccasined feet flashing in a Red River jig. Dad first saw Mom cooking bannock over a fire outside her parents' tent. She flipped the bannock over just like his mother did. When she looked up he nearly fell off the wagon she was so pretty. He told me that he asked some people about her and learned she was Pierre Dubuque's only daughter and he'd best leave her alone or the old man would shoot him. Daddy said Mom had many admirers, the most ardent of these a Swede from a nearby community who had a large farm and lots of money. Dad said he made up his mind he was going to marry Mom, and that night he noticed Mom liked to dance, so he danced as hard as he could, hoping she would notice him. Mom said she saw him and knew she belonged with him. I remember Dad being the same when I was a little girl—warm, happy, always laughing and singing, but I saw him change over the years.

My Mom was very beautiful, tiny, blue-eyed and auburn-haired. She was quiet and gentle, never outgoing and noisy like the other women around us. She was always busy cooking or sewing. She loved books and music and spent many hours reading to us from a collection of books her father gave her. I grew up on Shakespeare, Dickens, Sir Walter Scott, and Longfellow.

My imagination was stirred by the stories in Mom's books. In good weather my brothers and sisters and I gathered our cousins behind the house and organized plays. The house was our Roman Empire, the two pine trees were the gates of Rome. I was Julius Caesar and would be wrapped in a long sheet with a willow branch on my head. My brother Jamie was Mark Anthony, and shouts of "Hail Caesar!" would ring throughout our settlement. Other times we would build a raft with logs and put a bright patchwork quilt canopy over it, with Mom's bright scarves flying from the four corners. An old bearskin rug was laid down and Cleopatra would go aboard. She was our white-skinned, red-haired cousin.

Oh, how I wanted to be Cleopatra, but my brother Jamie said, "Maria, you're too black and your hair is like a nigger's." So, I'd have to be Caesar instead. Cleopatra's slaves would all climb aboard and we'd push the raft into the slough and I as Caesar would meet it on the other side and welcome Cleopatra to Rome. Many times poor Cleo and her slaves came to a bad end for the logs would come apart and they would fall into the water. Then the Senators (our mothers) would fish everyone out and we would have to do something else. Many of our white neighbours who saw us would ask what we were playing and would shake their heads and laugh. I guess it was funny—Caesar, Rome, and Cleopatra among Halfbreeds in the backwoods of northern Saskatchewan.

The New Jerusalem?

In the following pages I may from time to time allow myself
to look very hard at modern society, not with any wish to be unkind,
but rather to show how, with our wealth, our power and our pride,
we have lost much which made life thoroughly satisfactory and full
to our forebears in spite of their lack of modern conveniences;
all for the very simple reason
that man does not live by bread alone.

R.D. SYMONS
Silton Seasons

Saskatchewan is known, among other things, for the fierceness and intelligence of its politics. The postwar period was dominated by Tommy Douglas and John Diefenbaker, both populists whose political views were formed in Depression-ravaged Saskatchewan. The province's voters were quite capable of sending CCFers to Regina and Conservatives to Ottawa.

·····························

One Canada

JOHN G. DIEFENBAKER

On 10 June 1957 Diefenbaker realized his life's dream. He won a narrow upset victory over the Liberals and was later appointed prime minister. A prairie populist, Diefenbaker believed he spoke for ordinary Canadians. He was fiercely partisan and had a tumultuous relationship with the Canadian media establishment.

THE LIBERAL HIGH COMMAND may have been staggered, even stunned, by the election results, but I suspect that no one had cause to view them with greater dismay than Blair Fraser, Ottawa editor of *Maclean's* magazine, whose magazine had been put to press before the election results were in, assuming that the universe would unfold as it always had. He had written, with supreme Liberal confidence, on the return of the St. Laurent government to power: "For better or for worse, we Canadians have once more elected one of the most powerful governments ever created by the free will of a free electorate. We have given that government an almost unexampled vote of confidence, considering the length of its term in office."

I can only imagine how trying the world was for all these mainstays of the Liberal Party those first few days following the election. For me, there were no ringing telephones, no hurried consultations, no meetings with the press. I was

·······

fishing on Lac La Ronge. And, for a trout fisherman, the northern and eastern portions of the lake are in a class by themselves. Those too-few halcyon days were interrupted by a message from Mr. St. Laurent asking me to meet him in Ottawa as quickly as convenient, a reminder that the events of 10 June were indeed reality.

The limitations of this reality, however, were demonstrated one day as I was fishing out of sight of and some distance from my companions. One of the local game wardens approached me and demanded to see my fishing licence. His only concern was whether or not I had a valid fishing licence, and properly so. I might say that he looked at me with unveiled suspicion while I fumbled through my pockets in search of it. Finally I found it. He examined it. Satisfied, he left. Had I not had one, and I might easily have forgotten to get one the morning after the election, I am sure he would have proceeded to do his duty. It would have given my prime-ministership a rather unusual beginning.

Olive and I arrived at Uplands airport, Ottawa, at 7.35 a.m. on Friday, 14 June 1957, having paid our own way on a regular commercial flight. Later that morning, I saw Mr. St. Laurent in his East Block office on Parliament Hill. He told me that the Right Honourable James G. Gardiner and one or two others in the Cabinet considered that he should stay on until the House met, and that their ability to continue as the government should be determined on a confidence motion. Mr. St. Laurent, however, felt that the people had spoken. He said that unless the soldiers' vote brought about a substantial change in the election result, he would resign.

As I left our meeting, the press judged from the expression on my face that Mr. St. Laurent was going to continue in office. Blair Fraser joined me as I walked towards my office in the Centre Block. I referred to his editorial: "Blair, you must feel very much like a lawyer who, knowing he has a good case, argues it with enthusiasm. Concluding that his position is impregnable, he then to his amazement finds that the lawyer on the other side has produced an authority binding the reverse of his argument on the court." Although he laughed, I detected a certain lack of enthusiasm for my analogy. I might have reminded him of an earlier article in *Maclean's* on 1 December 1953, in which he suggested that I lacked the stamina ever to become a party leader.

The soldiers' vote changed only one seat, and Mr. St. Laurent announced his decision to resign on 17 June. I am unable to recall my reaction when I was sworn in as a member of the Privy Council of Canada and Secretary of State for External Affairs. (There is no oath of office for the Prime Minister.) Naturally, it meant for me the opportunity to achieve some of those things I had advocated over the years. From my earliest days I wanted to become one of the leaders of my country. I wanted to bring about the realization of an ideal that went back to my collegiate days: one Canada, one Nation. I wanted to end discrimination within this country. I wanted to do something for the poor and the afflicted. I saw the difficulties of the farmer. I knew what it was to be a common labourer. I knew what it was to have lived in a home in which every dollar had to be carefully spent. I had always believed that some day I would have the opportunity now presented. This was one of the reasons why, while often rejected, I was never dejected by defeat. June 21, 1957, was the culmination of a long, long trail to the mountain peaks. If I may adapt Lincoln's reply to the Congressional Committee on 9 February 1865 as a description of my feelings, it was with deep gratitude to my countrymen for this mark of their confidence; with a distrust of my own ability to perform the duty required; yet with a firm reliance on the strength of our free government, and the loyalty of the people to the just principles upon which it is founded; and above all with an unshaken faith in the Supreme Ruler of nations, that I began the tasks of government.

The Doctors' Strike

ROBIN F. BADGELY & SAMUEL WOLFE

The introduction of medicare in Saskatchewan in July 1962 precipitated an epic battle that pitted the CCF and its supporters against most doctors, the private insurance industry, and the opposition Liberals. Dr. Samuel Wolfe was directly involved in these events, leaving his position at the University of Saskatchewan shortly after the strike began to practise medicine in a community clinic supporting the medicare plan. At the time of the strike Robin Badgely was teaching health and preventive medicine at the University of Saskatchewan.

THE HOLIDAY WEEKEND at the start of the strike was generally a quiet one for the emergency service. But on Tuesday, July 3, the province's emergency service co-ordinator warned that 'the real crisis . . . would come when surgery could no longer be performed in some of the province's hospitals because of shortage of personnel.'

On the same day a Canadian Medical Association executive said that sixty doctors had been helped to relocate in other places. On July 4, headlines announced, 'Estimate 100 doctors have left province.' On July 5, headlines declared, 'Volunteer doctor force cut sharply.' The emergency force had dropped from 240 to 204 doctors.

In Montreal twenty-four prominent citizens, including Eric Kierans, at the time president of the Stock Exchange and later Quebec's health minister, Hugh MacLennan, the novelist, and Gérard Pelletier, editor of *La Presse*, sent a telegram to Dr. Dalgleish:

> ... the undersigned deplore the attempt by an organized group to stand above the law ... irresponsible action of Saskatchewan doctors ... will seriously undermine public trust in the profession. In the name of humanity and of respect for democratic government the undersigned urge the immediate resumption of normal practice and peaceful negotiations with the government.

In Toronto the president of the Canadian Council of Churches said that there were faults on both sides but these 'do not justify the doctors' action.' The *Daily Mail* of London said that 'when doctors strike and neglect patients, the voice of humanity protests.'

Other persons, from the United States, thought otherwise. The third-ranking official of North America's 850,000 Shriners, the Imperial Chief Rabban from Zem Zem Temple, condemned the C.C.F. government before the Toronto Kiwanis Club. He charged that the Saskatchewan government was the unwitting accomplice in a Communist plot to overthrow the West.

Meanwhile, in Saskatchewan, funeral directors reassured the public that doctors were willing to sign death certificates. In Weyburn, the Keep Our Doctors Committee wired U Thant at the United Nations for help, concluding their telegram with 'Our freedom is at stake. Urgent.' The co-ordinator for the emergency service for the southern half of the province had warned that 'I don't know if we will have enough men to carry on for another week.'

The Keep Our Doctors Committees were holding public rallies and organizing TV panels across the province. In a CBC radio broadcast at 9:00 p.m. on July 9, Premier Lloyd expressed his concern about these meetings.

> Highly charged mass meetings ... cannot contribute to a solution of the problem ... I suggest tonight that Saskatchewan citizens carefully examine the activities of ... the Keep Our Doctors Committee. At a meeting in Prince Albert on Friday, this group

sponsored the appearance of Father Athol Murray of Wilcox. According to the *Prince Albert Herald*, Father Murray told the meeting, and I quote: 'We must get off the fence and make our views known. This thing may break out into violence and bloodshed any day now, and God help us if it doesn't.' . . .

These statements came strangely indeed from a man of the cloth . . .

. . . Does he speak for the Keep Our Doctors leadership? After his outburst which I quoted earlier, he has continued to appear at meetings under the auspices of this Committee . . . I call on them to publicly repudiate . . . Father Murray and his statements . . . .

THE BEGINNING OF THE END. The most important rally of the K.O.D. was planned for the afternoon of Wednesday, July 11, on the grounds of the Parliament Buildings in Regina. By July 6, the newspapers were carrying announcements about the mass march on the capital city.

Dentists announced that their offices would be closed so that they, their employees, and their patients could march to Regina. Drug stores as well were to close. The retail merchants planned a blitz in support of the mass rally to Regina. Mr. Thatcher called a Liberal Party caucus for the day of the K.O.D. rally, demanded a special session of the legislature, and told the Premier that the opposition would be in their seats in the legislature to await the special session.

On July 9, in the Birch Hills district of the province, where the medical care plan had been announced during the by-election campaign three years earlier, fifty women picketed a private meeting held by the C.C.F. member of the legislature, Arthur Thibault. Their signs read: 'We Want Freedom for Our Doctors' and 'We Don't Want Foreign Scabs.'

On the Monday and Tuesday before the rally, radio, TV, and newspapers were flooded with K.O.D. releases. Donations of 'Dollars for Freedom' were requested. Full-page advertisements set out the K.O.D.'s 'Protest and Petition':

. . . Assembled upon these grounds upon which stand the Legislative Buildings of Saskatchewan, consecrated to the ideal of self government by free men and women associated in a democratic society;

Dedicated to the concept that no ruler in a free society may in conscience coerce a minority group of citizens in their way of life or in the conduct of their affairs, nor may a ruler under the law discriminate against them in their profession, work or calling, however humane or beneficient the motives of the state may be thought to be;

> ... compulsion and coercion are subversive ... the government ... alone is responsible ... has caused irreparable damage ... [it should] suspend the operation of the Act ...
> ... citizens ... protest the callous disregard ... shown to the expressed will and sentiments of the citizens ... [we] protest the dictatorial and arbitrary provisions of the ... Act ... [the government] enlists the aid of paid mercenary doctors from abroad ...

The full-page advertisement asked the Queen's representative, the Lieutenant-Governor, to dissolve the parliament and issue the writs for an election if the government did not suspend the Act.

History was repeating itself. Fifty years earlier, in 1912, the same kinds of petitions were circulated in Britain, when medicare was being introduced in that country.

> ... amid cries of 'Scab!' ... were laid the foundations of the welfare state ... A circular thrust through letter boxes read: ' ... Shall free-born Britons have their doctor thrust upon them ... by a petty, tyrannous, bureaucratic method—made in Germany? Insist upon your right ... as freeborn Britons, instead of slaves ... How much longer shall Englishmen be dragooned? ...

During this period of time, the trade-union movement, the farmer's union, and most co-operative organizations reacted quietly, encouraging the government to stand firm, by and large heeding the Premier's plea to use restraint.

The government, of course, awaited July 11 with apprehension. If 30,000 or 40,000 marchers converged on Regina, the anti-medicare campaign would succeed.

July 11 was bright and clear—a typical warm, sunny summer's day in Saskatchewan.

> Hundreds of cars ... converged on the provincial capital ... to present a petition ... sincere attempts were made by [the K.O.D.] to keep order ... But at one point the ugly temper showed through ... Two students ... walked ... with pro-medicare placards ... Angry demonstrators moved in on them ...
> A watching U.S. television network correspondent said: 'This is just like covering the anti-integration movement in the Southern

United States. They're the same kind of people! . . . '
A knot of demonstrators hemmed in Smith . . . pushed him . . .
told him to drop dead, or go to Russia . . . the group taunting Smith
and Brown also railed at reporters who interviewed the youths . . .

Fearing violence, the police scanned the crowd, which was sprinkled with
anti-government banners. Two girls carried effigies of Premier Lloyd and T. C.
Douglas with the caption: 'Down with dictators.' Police intervened to protect
a handful of government supporters who were cursed off the grounds with 'they
are Communists. They are going back to the Kremlin.' Pennants bore the
names of each community represented. Nurses in uniform and medical
students were also dotted throughout the crowd.

Mr. Thatcher and his Liberal group tried to force their way into the
legislature. When Mr. Thatcher discovered the door of the legislative chamber
was locked, he attempted to kick the door down, for the benefit of photographers. '"We feel these were tactics one would expect to find in Russia or Cuba,"
Mr. Thatcher told reporters . . . "It's just another indication that freedom is
being extinguished in Saskatchewan."'

The Premier, Mr. Lloyd, rejected Mr. Thatcher's 'theatrics': 'The Opposition members had ample space to meet elsewhere. I see no point in making a
farce of the legislative chamber.'

The K.O.D. leaders presented their petition to the government. The march
was a failure. According to Canadian Press, only 4,000 people attended. The
momentum of the doctors and the K.O.D. was never regained . . .

Negotiations were resumed with the help of a visitor from Britain's House
of Lords. Lord Taylor's advice had been sought in London on June 7 by the
Commissioner who had flown there to arrange to recruit doctors. Following
these meetings he had agreed to write to Premier Lloyd. An invitation for him
to come to Saskatchewan as a consultant to the government was extended
through the offices of the government's representative in London in early July.

The histrionic, colourful, hyperactive, tall, and shaggy-browed Lord Taylor
arrived in Regina on July 16. By July 18 he was meeting with the Saskatchewan
profession's negotiators, as well as with its advisers from the Canadian Medical
Association. Taylor became accepted as an effective mediator. Striding back and
forth between the two sides, alternately cursing and extolling, pleading and
demanding, speaking softly and pounding tables, the colourful peer, advised
primarily by lawyers for the two sides, forced them to sign the Saskatoon
Agreement, which ended the strike . . .

The settlement was signed in the picturesque hotel in Saskatoon on the
banks of the Saskatchewan River on July 23.

Rumours of Glory

ᗞALE ᗴISLER

Ross Thatcher was a gruff and capable businessman from Moose Jaw. He spent ten years in the House of Commons as a CCF member but later quit the party to sit as an independent, then became leader of the Saskatchewan Liberals in 1957. He lost to Tommy Douglas and the CCF in 1960 but rebuilt the Liberals around his own leadership. By 1964 Douglas had left to head the federal NDP and Thatcher led the Liberals in an intense election campaign against Woodrow Lloyd.

W HILE EVERYONE WHO KNEW THATCHER realized how obsessed he was by his aim to unseat the CCF-NDP, few people understood the almost religious fervour he had attached to his political task. One day during the campaign, Thatcher and Bill Towriss were driving in Thatcher's car west of Morse, with the campaign nearing the midway mark and the Liberals picking up momentum.

Thatcher unexpectedly broke the silence. "Everyone has a place in this world, and I believe I've been chosen by God to get rid of these socialists." The comment perfectly summarized his political attitude. The end justified the means, which meant that whatever overtures had to be made to people who normally supported the Progressive Conservative or Social Credit parties, would be . . .

"Many people who cast a vote Wednesday will have searched their souls to find the courage and reasoning to support Liberal candidates. We will have the endorsement of many Conservatives, old CCFers and Social Crediters. These citizens deserve great respect, for the decision they have made is not an easy one. Their vote is for the good of Saskatchewan, more than for the good of the Liberal party, and we will make every effort to justify their decision," Thatcher said.

"There is nothing wrong with socialism, except it doesn't work," he told virtually every audience he addressed from the time he was elected leader. He said it as often as he did because he fervently believed it.

This was Thatcher's straightforward, unrelenting, and unchanging strategy for more than five years. The key to making it work, Thatcher believed, was to make sure that the Liberal party accommodated Saskatchewan people who considered themselves Progressive Conservatives. The labels of political parties—at least those of the Liberals, Progressive Conservatives, and Social Credit—had to be dissolved so that people who wanted to vote out the CCF-NDP could feel comfortable doing it by supporting the Liberals.

If this union of political forces was to succeed, Thatcher knew it wouldn't happen quickly. All candidates recruited for the 1960 election were told that they would be expected to build a broad enough base so that the party could win the province in 1964. It was a long-range strategy Thatcher wanted to permeate the ranks because he knew it would take at least four years to build the organization and find the candidates capable of attracting the support of those whose basic political priority was to defeat the CCF.

By the time Lloyd called the 1964 election, momentum was with the Liberals. The party was in the final phase of Thatcher's five-year plan, the organization was in place, money for the campaign was in the bank, and all the candidates were in the field. The strength of the Liberal machine was evident in the party's 26,143 memberships, which had brought $136,573 into party coffers. All along, Thatcher had adopted the strategy Douglas had used to build and maintain the CCF. If the Liberals could sell 25,000 memberships, which was always the target set for the CCF by Douglas, Thatcher believed victory was possible . . .

There could be no denying that a political metamorphosis was happening. It was as if when Douglas left to lead the NDP, the dam broke politically in Saskatchewan. There no longer was the personal attachment to the CCF that had been built over the years with Douglas at the helm. In the vast spaces and extreme climate of the prairie, Saskatchewan people had managed not only to survive, but in some cases to flourish. Individual initiative and pride in achievement might have been the backbone of life on the farm, but Douglas had seen beyond that. He harnessed the strength of character that came with living on the prairie with the spirit of co-operation. Fearing a return to the drought and economic collapse of the 1930s, Douglas and the CCF had become a political party that allowed people collectively to do things they could not do individually.

The CCF believed the economic system had failed during the Great Depression and sought to build security into the future. The CCF promised to form a government that would put the basic concerns of people first, and as a result developed a health care system that provided for all, allowed working people to form unions, and used the government as a tool for economic development through Crown corporations.

But with the passage of time, Saskatchewan's political consciousness changed. The scars of the Depression had gradually healed, and a new generation had emerged that had not directly experienced the 1930s. For them, the 1950s had become a decade of economic and social progress and socialism was no longer as relevant. The attitude was something Thatcher wanted to capitalize on. He talked often about how the Liberal party had a history as the party of reform in Canada and promised progress under free enterprise. It was a balance that was to make the transition back to the Liberals, after 20 years of CCF rule, as painless as possible. Still, there had to be a basic level of discontent with the CCF in order for the Liberals to defeat the government. While on the surface there were no glaring signs that Saskatchewan had fared poorly under the CCF, the idea that the government had become insensitive and too large for a province with fewer than 1 million people had taken root in many people's minds. It was a discontent increased by the medicare crisis. While most people by 1964 supported medicare, the confrontation and deep divisions it created made people politically uneasy.

A less explosive issue than medicare but one that fuelled the belief that the CCF-NDP government had become insensitive was the proposal that rural Saskatchewan be reorganized into county units. The idea came from a Royal Commission on Agriculture and Rural Life formed in 1952. In 1955, the Commission had recommended formation of larger county units from the existing rural municipal structure.

While reorganization of rural governing units had been discussed intermittently since 1932, across-the-board restructuring had been consistently opposed by the Saskatchewan Association of Rural Municipalities (SARM). There was similar resistance to the concept of county units, which strengthened as the government formed a Local Government Continuing Committee to explore changes in rural municipal government. When Meyer Brownstone was named deputy minister of municipal affairs, after he had been research director for the Royal Commission and then a member of the Local Government Continuing Committee, Thatcher argued that it was proof the government intended to proceed with rural reorganization despite the wishes of rural municipalities . . .

What Thatcher ultimately did was create the idea that the CCF-NDP government had lost touch with the people. Medicare was never used as an example of the CCF's autocracy because by the time of the election it had been accepted by the people, but in the midst of the election there were other examples the Liberals used to argue that the CCF-NDP had become insensitive to the people. One was an announcement that the government planned to hold a vote among hog producers on a compulsory hog marketing board, with anyone who marketed as few as five hogs a year eligible to vote in the plebiscite on whether to institute the board. The fact the government was allowing producers with only five hogs an equal say was, for Thatcher, an example of how the government was ignoring the interests of large-scale hog farmers.

The issue of funding for separate schools also came up before the election and provided a religious focus against the Lloyd government. Amendments to the Secondary Schools Education Act exempted separate school supporters from paying taxes to the public school system. Instead, Roman Catholics could direct their school taxes to the separate school system, which in effect created a private school system paid for from the public funds.

While the Liberals supported the move, realizing that they held most of the Roman Catholic vote, Thatcher also promised that his government would support other private religious schools. Although he was never specific on what support his government would give such schools, his promise was enough to put the Liberals on the right political side of the secondary schools issue.

In the meantime, the issue created dissension within the CCF-NDP because some felt there had been insufficient discussion before the amendments were put forward. Some members of the legislative advisory committee, such as Walter Smishek, urged the caucus to appoint a committee to study the issue so that, if nothing else, it could be delayed until after the election. But after the turbulent experience of the Thompson Committee on medicare, most government members believed they should deal directly and immediately with the issue. Finally, Education Minister Ole Turnbull announced that changes to the legislation would be made although the caucus never voted on the issue.

Meanwhile, Thatcher's public courting of Tories and Socreds in the election undermined Thatcher in his own party. His strategy contradicted what the federal Liberal party stood for under Lester Pearson, who had come to dislike Thatcher, whom he saw as a brash, uncompromising right-wing ideologue. The Liberals had come to power in Ottawa a year before the Saskatchewan election and did so by espousing moderate and sometimes left-wing policies. For Pearson the enemy was not the NDP but the Tories, and for that reason he did not approve of Thatcher's courtship of the Tories in Saskatchewan.

Thatcher didn't care what Pearson thought. He had established himself as the unquestioned Liberal power in Saskatchewan, federally and provincially. As a result, the federal Liberals did little to assist the provincial campaign, and Thatcher did not ask them for help.

On with the New

NORMAN WARD

Although he was best known as one of Canada's preeminent political scientists, Norman Ward was also a gifted writer of humour. This selection is taken from Mice in the Beer, *which won the Leacock Medal in 1960.*

O N SASKATOON, the pearl of the prairies, it was my pleasure several houses ago to acquire a dwelling whose windows on one wall commanded an almost uninterrupted view of the plains. I have to say "almost," because the first day we were in the house, as I was steadying myself for a long look at one of those tidy green sunsets that nature has reserved for the city and district, I noticed that in the middle distance the skyline was broken by the roof of a familiar fabrication that, like the grain elevator and the Chinese restaurant, is a far truer symbol of the Canadian West than that overrated farm-hand, the cowboy. I refer to a common type of outbuilding that Roget, with his customary tendency towards needless repetition, would doubtless describe as a latrine, privy, jakes, john, sump, or biffy.

Subsequent research established that the edifice was not, as I had feared, on a public right of way across my property; that it had been built in compliance with city ordinances pertaining to the subject, and as a further proof of its integrity bore the hallmark of the International Union of Carpenters, Joiners and Platelayers of America, Local 792. Its owner, with whom I shortly entered into negotiations with the idea of having it towed away, had an impressive fund of knowledge relevant to the building and others like it, having indeed in days gone by been a pioneer architect in several parts of Canada. By his own account, he had turned the first sod for more of them than he could conveniently remember. (I am happy to add that his record—presumably in other connections—in due course led to his being chosen to play the role of a Harbinger of Happiness in a pageant written to celebrate the jubilee of the founding of Regina, an obscure town situated on a railway siding south of Saskatoon.)

"In my experience," he told me during our first back-yard interview, "there are more of these per head in the West than anywhere else north of the American border."

The use of the head as a yardstick struck me as statistically unsound, but before I could go into the matter he swept on. "I'd be glad to get rid of this one," he went on, "but I can't. At least not yet. The city wouldn't let us, not without water in the house."

"No water?"

"Nope. This is an old farm-house, and what the real-estate agents call unmodern."

Instantly several words and phrases, most of which had mildly puzzled us as we coursed through the bazaars seeking a house, fell into place. I had not paid much attention to them at the time, since all the realtors had assumed for some reason or other that we were interested only in what is technically known as a modern house. When I thought of it, I recalled that I had lost some sleep over a statement made by one aggressive salesman. When we had said, in answer to a query, that we wanted a reasonably modern house, but preferred an older one to what was being glued together today, he had observed tartly that all good houses were completely modern, no matter how old they were.

Now I learned that in the real-estate advertisements words like "modern" (three-piece bathroom), "un-modern" (none at all), "semi-modern" (one or two utensils), "on modern street" (you can get water from the neighbours), "summer tap" (you and the neighbours can both get water when the pipes aren't frozen), and "older type of house" (no water nearer than the city-hall fountain), had subtle meanings whose consequences we had escaped only by the intervention of a kindly Providence. So far as I can recall, my faith in the soundness of Canadian house-builders and their houses is such that I have never, when occupying various premises, first gone to the trouble of turning on the taps to see if they actually worked. It is a moot point whether I would notice their total absence.

"You also want to watch 'suburban' when you're buying a house, Jack," my neighbour advised me. "On this side of the Great Lakes it can have a dimension I never struck down East." I barely heard him, for by then my mind was playing around with a pretty conceit to the effect that much modern art was, in the best and fullest sense of the word, essentially un-modern.

"Tell you what," said the pioneer, apparently misunderstanding my intent. "I hope to modernize this place in a few weeks, and I'll give you first crack at this one."

I shook my head. "I'll give you a good price," he added.

This fraternal offer raised a question. "Suppose I don't buy it, how will you get rid of it?"

"Advertise it in the papers, like everybody else."

"You mean to say there is commercial traffic in these things?"

"Only retail. No wholesale."

"Any dealers or agents? Street peddlers?"

"Never heard of any."

"What is the asking price on this sort of job?"

He scratched his chin. "They're rather like used cars, I guess. A buyer wants to know the mileage, and the number and temperament of the previous owners. Except, of course, that you don't see corner lots covered with them."

On this philosophical note we parted, he to his affairs and I to make a scholarly analysis of the classified advertisements in a pile of newspapers. Sure enough, there was a regular trickle of wee houses available to local investors. The ads were marked by a striking similarity, for when you have an article like that to sell, it is not easy to pretend that you are trying to unload something else. The ads thus sounded a bold, manly note unusual in modern merchandising. "Outdoor toilet" was the standard insertion, normally followed by a box or telephone number, though rarely by an address.

Some of the ads, however, achieved an almost cosmic level of irrelevance. One, after identifying the centrepiece, threw in "fifty feet of hose." Another included, as part of a package deal, a child's tricycle and a fur coat, conjuring up a wild picture of activity in a back yard on a bitter night. "Will trade for anything of value," a third bafflingly added. Sundry citizens felt obliged to explain why they were offering so quaint a commodity for sale. "Leaving city," the owner of one item wrote, clearly anxious to allay any apprehensions that he planned to take it with him. One had a social aspect; the huckster had spent an extra nine cents to boast, "house recently modernized," at once making me think of some domestic behemoth lording it over less solvent neighbours. Though I looked hopefully, none of the ads resorted to testimonials.

As for my own neighbour, in time he brought running water into his house, and duly reported that despite frequent trips to the newspaper office to spread the news that he had a surplus of a certain staple, the market for same had remained sluggish. Solely to improve the shape of the horizon, I took it off his hands. For several months thereafter I was probably the only taxpayer in Canada whose garage was merely the outer husk of an even more down-to-earth structure, and certainly the only one who had ever accumulated such an article for aesthetic reasons.

When we sold the house, I left it there for the new owner, who had rather carelessly inspected the garage only from the outside. From time to time I bump into him downtown, and he invariably looks as if there were something he'd like to talk to me about. Once or twice I have caught him pointing me out unobtrusively to a companion, whispering the while.

But I don't mind. One of the many advantages of a formal education is that it keeps your mind alive to the fact that there are people who are unwilling to believe that there may be a rational explanation of everything.

Silton Seasons

R.D. SYMONS

After a varied career as a cowboy, game warden, homesteader, successful writer and illustrator, R.D. Symons and his wife, Hope, moved to a cottage on Pelican Point, which juts into Last Mountain Lake north of Regina.

IF YOU DRIVE NORTH FROM REGINA, Saskatchewan, on highway No. 20, you will, shortly after crossing the Qu'Appelle Valley, see a gravel road leading to the west.

There is a signpost here which reads: "Silton 2 miles." All you can see to explain that sign is a quick glimpse of the top of a grain elevator, for this is a rolling, almost hilly country, dotted with bluffs and sloughs to tell you that you are in the parkland prairies.

Hope and I live up that road.

Our summer cottage is eight miles west of the village, overlooking the sixty-mile stretch of water called Last Mountain Lake. You might wonder at that name, for you see no mountain. But the map will show to the northeast an area called the Touchwood Hills. These used to be called mountains, and in a generally level plains country that was forgivable. The last outpost of these hills, separated from the main body by over twenty miles, lies about that distance north of Silton and perhaps twelve miles east of the lake. It dominates much of the landscape, even though it is only a low hill. The quite heavily wooded crest adds both deeper colour and a further illusion of height as you get your first view of it seven miles north of Silton. Early travellers from the East quite naturally called it the last mountain, for from its height they could look westward across the water to the vast expanse of translake prairies and see only a level horizon.

Silton, Saskatchewan, was named for Silton in the county of Dorsetshire, England, by Charles Benjafield, who came to the district in the early eighties. He died in 1912 and was buried in the little cemetery just west of the village. This enclosed piece of ground occupies the crest of a high hill overlooking the lake.

Silton is not a town, only a very small village. An old village in terms of the settlement of our province, yet a very new and callow one when we compare it to the wattle-house villages of Celtic Britain, for less than a hundred years ago it was a buffalo pasture under the hand of the red man.

The anthropologists like to tell us that man was once a wanderer, migrating as the needs of game or water dictated.

The first step towards a more settled life—the taming of wild sheep and cattle—was followed by a much greater one, the sowing of seeds. Man saw, in the new art of agriculture, the possibility of settling down in a chosen spot, and from this came the permanent village.

Now, the man who excelled in making hoes or baskets, or in tanning leather, could follow his chosen bent and live by trading his artifacts for his farmer neighbour's grain.

Crafts and trade were born together, but back of both was always the husbandman. This triple interdependence is still the basis of our economy. In spite of centralisation, internationalised firms, and changed concepts, many small communities exist as tiny worlds within the greater—limited, it is true, in many ways and more and more dependent on the larger centres.

But community ties, community activities, are still strong, and this is what makes a village as opposed to a mere trade depot.

Village life was the beginning of civilisation; and it may constitute, someday, the last vestige—for we are in danger of losing the arts which are civilising, by a blind adherence to "progress."

Village life dominated the ancient civilisations of the East. Jesus was a village man. He spoke in the simple terms of village language and thought. He told us of lost pennies, of barren fig trees, of bushel measures, and of the flowers of the field which put to shame the glory of kings.

The commercial jargon of every age dies out—as will the stilted, soulless language of technology. Village speech remains.

"Father is late." "The hens are laying." "It looks like rain." We said these things in Chaldea, in Egypt, by the Ganges, on the Sussex downs, and on the shores of Nova Scotia. We shall be saying them when automobiles are obsolete and petroleum oil forgotten.

Silton village itself consists of one grain elevator, a store, a telephone exchange, a garage, and a post office—the latter being one room of a private house. These establishments, together with a number of dwelling houses, are scattered over perhaps eighty acres.

As we shall see, the village was once considerably larger, as evidenced by certain old foundations and by the groups of planted trees which originally sheltered these sites. Silton has not been immune from the shrinking effects which have left their marks all through the rural scene on these prairies.

The population does not exceed twenty families, of which nearly half are retired farmers whose children have grown up and left.

The surrounding countryside, which can be properly accredited to Silton by way of trade, comprises the area lying within seven to ten miles, but includes several small summer resorts on the lake. The rolling farmlands are occupied mainly with grain culture, but every farm has some cattle, and there are several good-sized herds of pure-bred Herefords and Angus of excellent quality.

Not much of the native grassland remains—perhaps 15 per cent—but what there is shows us how this land must have appeared to the first settlers. Throughout we see small bluffs or groves of white poplars, together with clumps of silvery wolf willows, saskatoons, and rose bushes.

Many other small towns and villages are within easy distance—Earl Grey and Southey to the east, Craven (in the Qu'Appelle Valley) to the south, and Strasbourg (a market town) twenty miles north in the shadow of Last Mountain.

There is nothing unique about Silton. It is no more than a tiny dot in the parkland prairies which stretch northwest to Edmonton and southeast into Manitoba, yet Silton represents a cross section of prairie life, prairie ways, and prairie people.

For all the shiny new cars and up-to-date machinery, it is still essentially rural, with a less rapid pulse than is seen in the cities and with a little more time to consider thoughts instead of being entirely preoccupied with things. The rural scene, too, with its natural environment, its animals, and its wider horizons, gives a little more understanding of fundamental principles of life and happiness in a day when facts are shot at us like bullets. We may see that it is better to understand the implications of one fact than to memorize a hundred . . .

This locality never considered itself the "Wild West." These early settlers had been reared in an atmosphere of orderly living, nurtured in thrift and honesty and religion. They transplanted their savoury herbs in their new gardens, and they fed them to their young families. For they found these flowery fields, very garden-like, where the shimmering poplars alternated with grassy sloughs, where cool waters gleamed and rolling grasslands vibrated with the songs of meadow larks and pipits. Here was rich soil for the ploughshare, water for the stock, wood for the cookstoves, stones for building, and limestone rocks to burn for mortar.

They built well, these people from Downpatrick, from Simcoe, from Peggy's Cove, from Lancashire, Dorset, Durham, and Kent; they built a new England, a new Ontario, under the Red Ensign which would forever insure that they were building Canada. Flavel, Swanston, Wright, Dale, Metcalf, Burrows, Robinson—these are just some of the names.

From here they sent their sons and grandsons to fight tyranny, their daughters and granddaughters to nurse the wounded, to drive trucks, and to build ships, in those desperate years when there was so little to cling to and we lived by faith.

From here young men and women have gone to positions of trust and responsibility far beyond the dim horizons guessed at by their forebears.

Times changed.

The branch-line railway came. Wagons gave way to cars. Horses, the so recent successors of the patient oxen, were discarded for tractors.

But, as Thoreau says, most inventions are simply another way of doing the same thing; and farming, trading, and raising a family do not change essentially. Fields must be cultivated, men must be fed, babies must be put to bed, and young people must fall in love.

Neither do the fields and groves change essentially, for the birds are still here. Even the buffalo birds, which Kelsey saw on the shaggy humps of the bison, have only changed their name. They are cowbirds now, and they perch on the humpless, swaying shoulders of the homeward-bound milk cows. The bright warblers still flash and twitter among the wild roses, and the flowers themselves still have the same fragrance which inspired many an Indian mother to name her baby daughter Sweet Prairie Rose.

The lake, in spite of the clusters of summer homes, still bears on her breast the handsome ducks and stately swans of yesterday, still holds within its depths the silvery whitefish and the savage, jewelled pike.

Meadowlark Cottage, our summer home, squats high on the bank overlooking the blue water of that lake at a spot called Pelican Point. The first time we climbed that hill we were greeted by the fluting of one of these yellow-breasted birds, and the name came naturally to us. Nor has it proved a misnomer, for each spring a pair nests close by, and the male salutes us daily at sunrise.

From here, between the sparkling waters and the upland grain fields, I see a world untouched (except for the cottage area) by the plough; I see all I have just mentioned—the groves, the birds, the flowers. I smell the perfume of wolf willow in June, I hear the thrill of the vesper sparrow stealing across the greening grass of May.

But for the muffled sound of a far-off tractor, we might be—except at weekends—the first pioneers.

Here I wander, sketchbook in hand, in an earthly paradise, while Hope— more practical—bakes her brown bread and writes long letters to our daughter in England. Often she joins me, nonetheless, and when she sings the birds stop to listen.

Just as the métis buffalo hunters of long ago left the open prairies for the shelter of the Red River Valley, seeking the company of their kind at the approach of winter, so do we—Hope and I—move into Silton at that season, and once again become members of the village family till the April sun thaws the ice of Last Mountain Lake . . .

If an apology is required for offering these observations of a small world, may I suggest that the large world is made up of communities like this? And the life force of any community is found in the image of family life. Each such small ecological community, where man and beast and plant are all affected by rainfall, soil, and topography—no less than by inheritance, culture, and tradition—is a family of God, surviving cycle after cycle by virtue of the life force which activates it.

This is the pattern from which man stepped forth to occupy the earth. This is the underpainting of the canvas which is Canada. It is also, I believe, the underlying strength of this nation. We might well ask ourselves, as Canadians, has the weakening of these community ties and loyalties affected the ties and loyalties of our people as a whole? Is this why we must examine our Confederation anew? Was it the lack of a proper understanding of this which has divided urban and rural societies into two solitudes more real and more dangerous than those which divide French and English Canada?

Man is still one-half animal. The process of evolution did not destroy the animal desires, but simply substituted free will for innocent instinctual motivation.

For too long this free will has been directed to the point not of contentment, but of power and wealth and so-called progress.

I may be criticized by some for mentioning such a thing as biological evolution. To those who say this is an ungodly idea, I can only reply most humbly that in denying this very natural theory we put great limitations on the very Creator we say is omnipotent.

We are all dust of the earth—man and beast and tree. We come from dust and to dust we shall return, and to suggest that the Creator could take one kind of dust and not another to perfect his Creation in the image of man is hardly logical.

We need, I feel, to allow once more for this instinctual wisdom, which shows us values and beauty and good taste in living. Primitive man was not a fool, by any means. He knew better than to put all the eggs of the spirit in the basket of materialism. So in the following pages I may from time to time allow myself to look very hard at modern society, not with any wish to be unkind, but rather to show how, with our wealth, our power, and our pride, we have lost much which made life thoroughly satisfactory and full to our forebears in spite of their lack of modern conveniences; all for the very simple reason that man does not live by bread alone.

Rocks, Ice, and Heartbreak

MURRAY CAMPBELL

> The winter sport of curling, in which opposing players send granite
> stones over an ice surface toward a target circle in an attempt to place
> them nearest the centre, might possibly have been born in prehis-
> toric times when cavemen heaved rocks at each other from oppos-
> ing ends of glaciers. It is just remotely possible. Curling is a sport
> that produces strange stories.
>
> *The Black Bonspiel of Willie MacCrimmon*
> W.O. Mitchell

HAROLD WORTH KNOWS about strange stories. Well, sad ones at
any rate.

Nearly 30 years ago, he and his rink put together an amazing
winter of matches and ended up playing in the Brier, the national curling
championship. The hometown fans in Saskatoon, a half-hour's drive from
Delisle, spun the turnstiles in record numbers looking for a showdown
between the local foursome and a Winnipeg powerhouse.

Saskatchewan had owned the Brier for a decade and the pressure was on.
The rinks were 7-1 going into the final days of the contest when Mr. Worth
and his mates went against a hapless team from Nova Scotia.

The result, alas, added another page to the catalogue of disappointments
that Saskatchewan residents carry with them like a well-thumbed reference
book.

"I can remember it like it was yesterday," Mr. Worth says as he recounts
how his last shot lost the game. And, indeed, the way he launches into a tale
of guards, full houses and hog lines leaves little doubt that those few seconds
in the spring of 1965 are burned into his brain.

"It didn't draw," he says about the unfathomable mystery of the rock that
didn't do what it was supposed to do. "It just didn't draw. I lost a few nights'
sleep over that."

If it were football or even hockey, it might not have mattered so much. But
this was curling, a sport owned lock, stock and barrel by the Prairies ever since
Easterners—never mind Maritimers—showed they didn't have the stomach for it.

There are a few eternal verities in Saskatchewan. "Things will always be better next year" is one of them. Another deals with curling. The population of Delisle may have shrunk in recent years but the lure of thwacking rocks is as strong here as it is in dozens of other communities across the province.

Sure, curling was invented by the Scots. But what do rain-soaked Scots know about weather so harsh that tires freeze into squares?

No, the home of curling is in Canada and its warm hearth is on the Prairies. There are as many curlers in Saskatchewan as there are in Ontario—making it the highest per-capita concentration in the country.

If there's a sound that defines winter nights in the province's small, isolated hamlets, it's the rhythmic slap of corn brooms, the clack of the granite rocks against each other and the urgent, unintelligible commands of the team skip.

"It's the northern-climate thing," W.O. Mitchell tells me. "It's the brutality of winter and the fact that there's no shortage of ice."

It's not a tough game to figure out. Two rinks (teams) of four people take turns tossing 40-pound granite rocks down a 46-yard length of ice. The team with more stones closer to the centre of a 12-foot circle wins the end and then they repeat the procedure nine more times. At its best, it's got a bit of chess to it. But at its most fundamental, it's a brutal succession of knockout blows.

In that way, it is ideally suited to the obstructive Canadian character. If you can't put a rock in the centre of the circle, it's just as good to block everyone else or knock them out of the house.

By the turn of this century, almost every town in the West had its own curling rink where farmers would sit around a Quebec heater to second-guess the players and, uh, socialize.

The rinks were mostly rough-hewn affairs with natural ice—the climate not being much of a problem on the Prairies—but they always had a bar. Indeed, the large amounts of whisky consumed at curling games delayed the participation of women for a century.

Mr. Mitchell grew up throwing concrete-filled lard cans down the Little Souris River in Weyburn, Sask. Later, he managed the curling rink that his mother inherited when the town could not repay his father's loan. Curling is in his blood, no surprise to anyone who has read his recently published novella about a curler who makes a pact with the devil, *The Black Bonspiel of Willie MacCrimmon*.

"You know what it is?" he says after noting his sad fate of having spent several childhood winters in snowless Florida. "It's a kind of winter golf. It's the same thing of swing, and watching that rock travel the same way as a golfer does. It's extremely, extremely mental."

Not too long ago, the spectators' area of almost any curling club in Saskatchewan would have been filled with men wearing heavy topcoats, smoking cigars and drinking rye-and-ginger. The presence of children was tolerated, for short periods, but not encouraged.

There's still a time-honoured rule that for every hour curlers spend on the ice, they spend a couple in the bar. (Mr. Worth can pass his time in the Delisle bar gazing at a huge photograph of himself at the height of his fame.)

But these days, all comers are accepted. The notion that it's a man's game has died. More than half the curlers playing in leagues in Saskatchewan are women and there are 240 high schools in the province entered in competition. And in Delisle, at least, there's no smoking in the spectators' area.

There are more than 600 teams competing this winter for the right to represent the province at the Brier next spring and the best of them consider themselves to be athletes and not just curlers. The sport achieved demonstration status at the 1988 and 1992 Winter Olympics and while it will be passed by in Lillehammer, Norway, this winter, it will return as a full-fledged event in Japan in 1998.

These days, curlers wear the sort of garb a baseball-team trainer might—the woollen sweater is long gone—and they've adopted an ergonomically correct janitor-style push broom to replace the elegant corn brooms. The more up-to-date, chasing the serious money offered by made-for-television bonspiels, can even buy $200, polished-chrome, stainless-steel sliding shoes.

But all that's really required to be a curler is a willingness to turn off the television, hop into the truck and spend a few hours talking about the weather and politics with neighbours.

"It's popular because anybody can do it," says Warren Dodds, a coordinator with the Saskatchewan Curling Association. "You don't have to be big, you don't have to be strong, you don't have to be fast. You can just do it for your own satisfaction."

Mr. Worth, now 62, gave up competing more than a decade ago, when the years of hoisting rocks took their toll on his back. But he still gets out with his friends and family once in a while. "It's a social thing," he says, not surprisingly.

On this night, sitting in the stands of the Delisle Curling Club and watching leisurely mixed games, it all seems quite benign. Only two of the three sheets of ice are in play this night and Mr. Worth seems to be related to about half the people out there.

He still farms four sections of land (2,560 acres) and, like a lot of farmers dealing with outsiders, he is genial but spends words as if they were hard currency. Unless he's discussing curling, that is.

He talks about how he learned the long slide from the hack from the skip who took him to his first Brier in 1953, about how his biggest pay day was $2,500 and about how his hotel room turned into a "hospitality suite" in the 1965 Brier.

"I kind of miss the fellowship," he says. "They're a great bunch of guys."

But it's clear, amid all this easy talk, that he has no trouble recalling the passions the game can arouse in the land where the winters are long.

A couple of years after his fateful 1965 game, Mr. Worth and his wife were in Hawaii at the same time as another Brier was being played back home. A Canadian tourist asked him why he wasn't there and then reproached him for that errant rock.

"A lot of people don't let you forget about it," he says.

Rider Pride

ᏏᏏ𝓑OB 𝓒ALDER & 𝓖ARRY 𝓐NDREWS

The Saskatchewan Roughriders were created in 1910 and have an illustrious history. Fans drive hundreds of kilometres in all manner of weather from across the province to attend games, and the team's numerous financial crises have been overcome by the provincial community rallying around it. Throughout the 1960s and 1970s, the team made five Grey Cup appearances, led by canny quarterback Ron Lancaster and indomitable runningback George Reed.

A T FIVE FOOT, ELEVEN INCHES, and about 208 pounds, Reed was not big, even by CFL standards, but he was the complete running back. His twenty-nine-inch thighs, which meant that he had to buy size 40 pants and have the waist taken in six inches, gave him enormous power going into the line, not only in breaking the initial tackles but in gaining the extra couple of yards which became his trademark. A series of great middle linebackers—BC's Tom Brown, Edmonton's Dan Kepley, and Calgary's

Wayne Harris among others—waged monumental battles with Reed over the years, and some paid a heavy price. Winnipeg's Brian Palmer once broke a bone in three places trying to arm tackle him, and the Bombers' Jack Delveaux had the nerves in his shoulder so badly damaged in one collision with the fullback that he never played another game. As Reed calmly explained, "I have to earn my living by running over anyone who gets in my way. I want the ground you're standing on."

Reed also possessed great quickness which let him shift outside to open territory, and he could read defenses superbly. Winnipeg's Mickey Doyle once expressed the frustration of a multitude of linebackers when he said: "Reed picks his holes so well, it's unbelievable. A lot of times, I'm sure he runs to daylight. He reads so well. Most times, most teams run the plays where they are supposed to be run. Not George. He runs where the opening is. You have to adjust. It's tough."

The CFL record book tells a great deal about Reed's greatness, but it does not explain that he was an excellent faking back or that his superb blocking was an essential part of the Roughrider passing attack. Neither do they properly reflect the leadership he gave to the team. Al Ford, a dedicated athlete himself, speaks with awe of Reed's condition:

> When Reed stepped on the football field he mentally could just give more than anybody else could. Condition wise, I know I was in better condition than George ever was but in training camp or whenever, he was the first guy in line. I'd try to hustle and beat him to being the first one in line but he was always there. He always did the drills 110 percent, always gave so much in games.
>
> I always marveled that Lancaster and Reed used to sprint to the locker room at half time during games so that they'd have enough time to get their two cigarettes in. They'd walk out on the field during training camp putting their cigarettes out. Of course I'd quit smoking back in February and ran miles and miles and was in great shape yet I'd just be sucking air during practice and George would be O.K. (Ron was a "puffer.")

The other remarkable attribute of Reed was durability, and his thirteen seasons of top-flight play are nearly three times the average effective careers of running backs. To miss only a half dozen games in that time, to get the tough yards and take the incessant pounding of defenses keyed to him, took more than mere physical conditioning. It took the courage to play with pain, something which Sandy Archer estimates that Reed did seventy percent of the time. John Payne once confessed that he never knew when his fullback was hurt—"He won't tell you. He gets upset if you take him out of a game"—and Calgary's Frank Andruski complained that you could not knock him out: "There's nothing you can do that's going to get Reed out of the game or get him upset. You can hit George, step on his face and spit in his eye . . . he just keeps ploughing over top of you." Eagle Keys argued that "George doesn't really start playing until he's hurting a little."

Reed once explained that he had "a high pain threshold." Only he really knows what that means, but we do know that he once played half a season on a fractured leg, that he scored a touchdown against Calgary wearing an eyepatch after getting a Wayne Harris finger in the eye, and that he always went onto the field with a multitude of aches and bruises. Sandy Archer still recalls with amazement the year that he played seven games on a dislocated toe. Before each contest, the club physician would inject the toe with a hypodermic, working the point of the needle slowly and deeply into the first joint where there is virtually no muscle. This was repeated at half-time for each of the seven games. "That's fourteen times," says Sandy, "that he had to take the needle and thirteen times he knew how much it was going to hurt."

Over the years people marveled at Reed's ability to play with injuries, but he was a consummate professional for whom pain was part of the job. He once explained to a reporter: "Look, if you have a headache, you still go to work, right? If you're out at night, and you get a hangover the next day, you still go to work. You suffer, but you go to work, right? Well, this is my profession. If I'm hurt, I still have to play." Maybe—just maybe—some of us go to work hurt or hungover, but we do not have to meet Dan Kepley or Angelo Mosca charging across the desk at us every thirty seconds.

It is doubtful that any other Roughrider player has ever earned the respect of people in the province or the country that Reed has done. As president of the Player's Association, he spearheaded a number of significant improvements such as raising the Grey Cup prize money, the pay for exhibition games, and the team pension contributions. Outside football, he put his mark on the province of Saskatchewan, in part through his coordination of the special Olympics for the mentally handicapped and the formation in 1975 of the George Reed Foundation for the Handicapped. Employed at more than a figurehead position with Molson's in Regina, Reed summed up his career in Canada when he told 850 people who honored him at a dinner in 1976: "I came, I played, I stayed." That has to be the understatement of the century.

Premier Administrator

ⅅENNIS ꞬRUENDING

*Allan Blakeney presided over the last real boom that Saskatchewan
has known. During his eleven-year tenure as premier, international
grain prices improved, markets for Saskatchewan potash picked up,
and the Arab oil embargo inflated prices for the province's oil and
uranium. The windfall set off a round of federal-provincial battles
over control of the resource industries, and whether Ottawa or the
province should benefit most from the improved prices.*

ⅬLAN BLAKENEY was sworn in as Saskatchewan's tenth Premier by
Lieutenant-Governor Stephen Worobetz on June 30, 1971. He took the
oath of office just after 10 A.M. in the red-carpeted, oak-paneled
Legislative Chamber. The galleries were filled with invited guests, including
Woodrow Lloyd and Robert Walker. Anne Blakeney received a surprise when
she arrived in the gallery above the house with the three oldest Blakeney
children. The commissionaire didn't know who she was, and refused them
entry until she produced their invitations. Immediately after Blakeney took his
oaths, eight other cabinet ministers were sworn in. The entire ceremony took
45 minutes . . .

Allan Blakeney carried with him in 1971 a detailed model of the governing
structures he intended to put into place. Many of them harkened back to his
experience as a civil servant, and later a cabinet minister. Cabinet was central.
Blakeney did not, in his own words, "want to be the minister of everything,"
as he thought Ross Thatcher had been. He was a delegator, and placed great
emphasis on process.

The ministers regularly met on Tuesdays in the large cabinet room off
Blakeney's offices. They gathered at about 9:30 A.M., with Romanow always
seated to Blakeney's right at the oval table. The meetings continued through a
sandwich lunch into at least mid-afternoon. Wes Bolstad, the Cabinet Secretary, sat in a corner away from the table and took notes. "Blakeney really
expected ministers to be there," says Bolstad. He wanted cabinet to deal with
policy, not administrative detail, with recommendations and not with prob-

lems. Blakeney, recalling his experience as Legal Secretary, insisted on a streamlined paper flow. The procedures became increasingly refined: "The cabinet agenda had to be on paper. I wanted an outline of the problems, but with some recommendations. If it wasn't worth someone's time to figure out what the answer was, or at least recommend an answer, then why was it worth ours? Back to the Fines kind of approach."

Roy Romanow says Blakeney was a stickler for process, rules, procedures, and thoroughness. "Bring in the Kentucky Fried Chicken, and we would sit there until one or two in the morning, with ministers half asleep, and Al stuck on the stray animals act amendments. But there were occasions when this held us in good stead."

The Premier gave short shrift to any civil servant who came with problems rather than recommendations. Stories are legion about the devastating Blakeney cross-examinations. His staccato questions, delivered in an icy and impersonal manner, would bring an unstructured presentation tumbling down on its unfortunate presenter—again, much in the manner of his mentor, Clarence Fines. If the Premier was at times curt with his staff, he was gentler, although no less effective, with his ministers. If a minister was carrying a proposal prepared by a deputy, but was not knowledgeable about it, a few penetrating questions by Blakeney could prove embarrassing. "He could cut your idea up quickly," Elwood Cowley says. "Three sentences. He quit, and so did you."

The meetings, although serious, had their lighter moments. Cowley, particularly, was known for his cynical sense of humour, and his quick rejoinders. He was also the minister who lived the hardest. A colleague says: "He would come into cabinet, unshaven, after a hard night of poker playing and beer drinking, and you'd think that he was dead or asleep, or both. Then he would contribute most creatively to the agenda item before them. Blakeney appreciated him because he was more ingenious and creative than Blakeney himself in some areas." Blakeney had no appetite for the high stakes, all night poker games, but he did like Cowley's mind. He would sometimes repeat Cowley's witticisms at home to Anne.

Blakeney insisted that ministers leave their departmental hats at the door. They were the Executive Council, and expected to consider the needs of the whole government. If departments were having turf wars, he wanted them worked out in advance, often by having Bolstad sit down with the Deputy Ministers. He wanted everyone to participate in cabinet discussion. He did not want ministers "lying in the reeds." He chaired the meetings and led the discussions. Several of his ministers describe him as school masterish, always wanting to be sure that everyone understood the issues. He worked on the basis of consensus. "If there was something he was uneasy about or that cabinet was divided about," says Cowley, "he'd worry the damn thing to death."

In the House, Blakeney obviously relied on certain ministers, particularly Romanow, Messer, and Cowley. He showed no similar need around the cabinet table. He had his own categories for ministers and tended to look to them for help in those areas. He relied on Kramer and MacMurchy to tell him what people were thinking in the country. Cowley provided political advice, Romanow tactical advice. Ed Tchorzewski gave guidance on how the party might react to certain issues. Once in cabinet, the political categories of left and right became less important. Blakeney looked to ministers for the specific skills they brought to the table to advance the government's program.

Blakeney did not have an obvious lieutenant, as Tommy Douglas had in the tough-minded administrator Clarence Fines. Romanow says Blakeney would have liked a Douglas-Fines model: "I would be the bean counter, on top of the nuts and bolts of cabinet, the financial side, the civil service side." Blakeney may have been disappointed when it became obvious that those weren't Romanow's interests. "As it turns out," Romanow says, "we might have changed roles a little bit. I think Al channeled me into the area of being the politician. I became one of the chief political operators of the government."

Blakeney also had a clear idea of the administrative relationship his ministers should maintain with senior civil servants. His description was formalized in a lecture he gave around the oval table shortly after the election, one he repeated every time a new minister was added. It came complete with a chart. "It would have cabinet and ministers on top," says Wes Bolstad, "then there'd be a very hard line drawn, with Deputy Ministers below that line. He was telling ministers they were not to get involved in the administration of their departments. And he would tell the deputies, 'Don't delegate problems up to ministers. Your responsibility as public servants is to look at policy options, weigh them, make a recommendation as to what you think best.' His favourite expression was, 'Well, what do you recommend?'"

That was the Blakeney Lesson in Public Administration. When, in later years, he pulled out the chart, veteran ministers like Jack Messer would moan, "The Speech," and reach for a newspaper. "The Speech" passed into literature when Blakeney gave it as an address to a national conference of the Institute of Public Administration of Canada. It is central to his view of how to govern. The emphasis is on public servants to create policy options. The role of the cabinet minister is to add a political component, testing those ideas out on the public, and also informing the planners how supportive people will be of a policy, whether it's medicare or a new park. The politician also explains policy to the public in a way that will build support. In Blakeney's view, any policy which falls outside the "range of public acceptability" cannot be pursued, no matter how good it might be from a technocratic point of view. The contradiction in this approach was that it placed great emphasis on planners to provide ideas, but did less to encourage people, in the NDP or the public at large, to engage in the same exhilarating process. This emphasis on central planning, rather than on a broader community, caused the dynamic agrarianism of the earlier CCF to wane during Blakeney's years. Some argue that the trend would have occurred in any event . . .

The work was constant and demanding. Weekdays it was the office, night events, and frequent travel. On weekends there were often party meetings. He wanted at least one Sunday free every two weeks. He would nap and watch sports on television, and perhaps go to church. On the Friday afternoons preceding such weekends he might be found in the stacks of the Legislative Library, searching for a mystery novel. His idea of relaxing was to be cocooned at home. The Blakeneys rarely went to movies, the theatre, or the symphony, because he knew he would have to respond to people, which he did not consider relaxation. For the same reason, his idea of a vacation was to be out of the province. The annual summer Premiers' conference was usually an opportunity for a long driving trip. Beginning in 1975 Blakeney and Anne took an annual winter holiday in Hawaii. For two or three weeks they would book into a light housekeeping suite on the west island of Kauai, where they would relax in the sun.

He admits that during his years as Premier, Anne was virtually a "single parent." He was less available to his younger children, David and Margaret, than he had been for Hugh and Barbara. When Margaret, the youngest, was in grade school, she wrote a brief portrait of her father for a class composition, describing him as short, with a scar on his forehead and always sleeping. Barbara recalls visits with him when she was a university student in Saskatoon. "I'd be booked in—you know, 'fifteen minutes to see your daughter'—usually at his hotel room. I'd sit there and talk to him while he shaved. There was absolutely no way to see him if you weren't part of the itinerary."

Close social contacts for the Blakeneys waned in direct proportion to his succession through the political ranks. Many of their closest friends in the bureaucracy had left after Thatcher's victory in 1964. The Blakeneys maintained an easy and open contact with them, but did not see them often. The Lloyds left in 1971 when Woodrow went to work for the United Nations in Korea. He died there, suddenly, in 1972. The Smisheks, Walter and Ruth, remained friends throughout, and had a cottage near the Blakeneys on Last Mountain Lake. The list of close cabinet and caucus friendships ended there, although there were Christmas parties and the odd sing-song. The latter would include the families of politicians such as Gordon Snyder, and civil servants like Grant Mitchell or John Burton. Occasionally, Blakeney would invite an out-of-town MLA home for supper during the Legislative Session.

Blakeney believed that for a Premier isolation is part of the job: "The more senior your political office, the fewer friends you have." He was aware of the dangers of being on better social terms with some members of the cabinet and caucus than others, and the potential accusation that he played favourites. Like Tommy Douglas before him, he chose to isolate himself. At the Premier's level, friendship cannot always survive politics.

Holy Crow

*D*ENNIS *G*RUENDING

For decades farmers relied on the Crow's Nest Pass freight rate when shipping their grain to market. The subsidy, regulated by the federal government, was in return for earlier land grants and subsidies made to the railroads. But by the 1970s Ottawa, which paid the freight subsidy, wanted to do away with it, and to tear up thousands of kilometres of branch rail lines as well. Western farmers considered the Crow Rate untouchable, and attempts to dismantle it aggravated the sense of western grievance. Emmett Hall, a retired Supreme Court judge from Saskatchewan, was appointed to lead a royal commission investigating the future of Western railways. Hall recommended that the Crow Rate be maintained, but the federal government has now done away with it.

SUPPORT FOR THE HOLY CROW has always been an article of faith, and survival, for politicians representing the west. In the 1970s Liberal cabinet minister Otto Lang learned the hard way. A Rhodes scholar and dean of law at the University of Saskatchewan, he was first elected in 1968. He quickly became the west's most powerful member in the Trudeau governments. In 1974, he orchestrated a plan intended to change the Crow before the next election. He also began to talk about closing some of the thousands of kilometres of smaller rail branch lines which fan out, like capillaries, across the prairie map . . .

Lang had toyed with the idea of unilaterally changing the rate, but that was considered politically unwise. So in 1975 he moved on two fronts. He appointed an American economist, Carl Snavely, to investigate railway costs. Lang believed they were losing money on grain and thought proof would be an added argument for change. That left the thorny question of branch lines. What Lang wanted was an impressive campaign of public education to convince people that some of the lines would have to go. He wanted to prevent the political furor which would result from the federal government's arbitrarily making those decisions. He decided to use a royal commission as his instrument.

Emmett Hall was an obvious person to lead it. He was revered as the father of medicare, and a man who could always get the grain moving again when it was tied up by railway or dock strikes. There was no one else to match his stature in the west. "I knew his posture with people was very good," says Lang. "He liked the image of himself as a listener, one who took all people's opinions into account." Lang believed, correctly, that no one would attack Hall in the way that western governments and farm groups frequently pounced upon Lang, a man they loved to hate. Hall, an old Tory, had two years earlier interrupted his work for an NDP provincial government to settle a national rail strike at the invitation of a Liberal minister of labor. He had allies in all camps.

Lang also had some doubts. He knew Hall well, for he had been a student in his class in criminal law procedure at the University of Saskatchewan. They had been colleagues of a sort when Lang became dean of the law school. Hall had been at his wedding. Lang saw him as a populist above all else. "The risk I was taking was that he had a strong political sense, a consciousness of his own image in relation to what he was doing, so he might not want to offend people by deciding that some lines had to go." Nevertheless Lang made the call and Hall accepted his offer . . .

The Hall commission became to people of the rural west what the Berger commission, occurring simultaneously, was to the Native people of the north—an opportunity in the face of change to make their case to someone they trusted. When the commission came to town it was an important community event. The halls were filled with farmers sitting on metal chairs which scraped when they moved. When it came time to break for lunch, women would serve up hot soup and heaping plates of turkey and mashed potatoes.

In Wishart, Saskatchewan, a hamlet southeast of Regina, a crowd of two hundred packed the hall. Every local person presenting a brief, from an eleven-year-old school child to senior citizens, called for retention of the community's rail line. An old woman said, "The CPR brought me here and now they are going to abandon me here." In Edburg, Alberta, nineteen social studies students presented the commission with the results of a survey taken among local farmers. Ninety-nine per cent of them were opposed to abandonment of the local rail line. Everywhere people pleaded with Hall to save the lines. Without them, they said, a way of life would die. Once farmers began hauling their grain long distances, the economics would favor big trucks and larger farms. Smaller farmers would be chased from the land and into the cities. With the farmers gone, the small towns would disappear. In Waldheim, Saskatchewan, a man told Hall, "These communities were built by our grandfathers and great-grandfathers. We want to continue this tradition and pass it on to our descendants" . . .

Hall maintained a populist stance. He was patient and affable with farmers and small-town people, but he was capable of becoming an inquisitor when the railway and grain company representatives appeared in the big city hearings. Commissioner [Reg] Forbes says, "You could almost feel Emmett's tenseness as soon as a corporate president or solicitor walked in. He was immediately a different person from when he met with local people." In fact, Hall was finding it difficult to get information from the railways and private grain companies about future plans for closing elevators and building new ones. The information was important to him in deciding which lines should be kept, since there was no point in keeping a rail line if the elevators it served were going to be closed. The companies argued that such information might be useful to their competitors. Eventually Hall demanded that they "put their cards on the table" . . .

Hall had been asked to report on some rail branch lines. He did that, but also transcended his technical mandate to produce an economic manifesto attempting to use transportation policy to keep wealth, people and jobs in the west. The report, Grain and Rail in Western Canada, was strong with a sense of western grievance. "Feelings exist that Western Canadians are the source of someone else's affluence," wrote Hall, "and to a degree they blame the transportation system for their frustration."

It was a national royal commission, but Hall and the others saw themselves representing a regional cause. They made recommendations which they believed would benefit grain producers and western Canadians in general. They assumed throughout that public subsidies to transport western grain were synonymous with the national interest, although the value of grain as a total of all exports had been declining for some years.

Hall was cautious on the question of branch lines. He had studied ten thousand kilometres of track in three provinces. Only one-third of it would be abandoned. Another third would be kept and added to the nineteen thousand kilometres protected against abandonment. A decision on the final third should be made only after further study by the new Prairie Rail Authority, a government body based in western Canada. It would assume ownership of those lines from the railroads for a nominal fee and ensure that they were kept in usable condition. The authority would hire the railroads to haul grain from the branch lines at profitable rates. No longer would the railroads be able to accept subsidies and still allow lines to fall into disrepair. The authority would become a new institutional presence located in western Canada and would replace the Ottawa-based Canadian Transport Commission, which Hall accused of "indecision and procrastination" in its regulation of western railway performance and safety.

Hall obviously rejected completely the call from the railroads and agri-business for deregulation. The government, not the railways, must continue to set the freight rate on grain. The rate must remain protected by legislation which only the House of Commons could change. He did agree that the railways might be able to make a case for rates higher than the Crow. In the body of his report Hall left open the possibility that farmers could be asked to pay more for shipping their grain. However, in the recommendations section at the end, he sent a different message, hinting strongly that any additional payments should be made by the federal treasury to the railroads. Hall went even further, suggesting that the Crow rate be extended to all processed agricultural products leaving the prairies by rail. He recognized that critics had a point when they argued that lower rates on grain than meat or processed products meant the loss of industry and jobs in western Canada. In the name of equity, the cattlemen and others wanted the Crow rate abolished. Hall said the equity should be achieved not by abandoning the subsidy, but by extending it. He provided no detail about the costs of such a move, and none of the studies prepared for the commission dealt with the issue.

Love and Hate

MAGGIE SIGGINS

Following his father's death in 1971, Colin Thatcher became involved in provincial politics with the Liberals, then the Conservatives, for whom he served as energy minister. He fought bitter divorce, custody, and property battles with his ex-wife, JoAnn. When she was brutally murdered in 1983 Thatcher became a prime suspect and was later convicted of the crime.

MAY 1, 1984

TO AVOID ALARMING THE NEIGHBOURING FARMERS, the four members of Regina's crack SWAT (Special Weapons and Tactics) squad arrived under cover of darkness at 3 a.m. Constables Jim McKee, Ray Golemba, and Ron Seiferling and Sergeant Ron Strassburger wore bush-green battle fatigues, and each carried a survival knife and a .38 revolver; the two group leaders were armed with M16-A1 rifles, the others, the snipers, with Remington .243 rifles. Their faces and hands blackened with camouflage paint, the four huddled together in the dark for a last-minute conference. It was chilly and wet—it had snowed only yesterday—and they had to speak above the whine of the wind sweeping across the abandoned farm. Quickly they laid their plans. Two of the men would take up position on the cold soggy ground at the hedges near the front of the property, the other two would dig in at the rear of the farmhouse . . .

Five hours later, exactly as planned, Garry Anderson drove up in his half-ton truck. With his neatly trimmed jet-black beard and his hawk nose, he might have been considered handsome, except for the shifty look that always made a local teacher think of Iago whenever she saw him. At six-foot-two and 235 pounds, Garry was a hefty, macho-looking man, and in recent years he had developed a paunch. This was somewhat exaggerated today; for this morning beneath his shirt Garry Anderson was wearing a bullet-proof vest.

Under the vest was a body pack, a portable tape recorder placed there to preserve the conversation he hoped to have with his neighbour Colin Thatcher. The tape had already been running for some fifteen minutes, and it testified to the fact that Garry Anderson was a very nervous man. A Crown prosecutor would later say that the sharp intake of Anderson's breath was so exaggerated that he was close to hyperventilating.

While the four SWAT team members waited anxiously, Anderson paced up and down outside the ramshackle barn. The sun was bright, but spring had yet to grace the province of Saskatchewan, and only the odd touch of green could be seen here and there. This gave the old Bergren homestead a forsaken, sullen façade. Built in 1904, this had once been a prosperous place, and the rambling farmhouse retained remnants of pride and grandeur even in its present ruin. In summer when the fields were golden, grasshoppers swarmed around the barn in great clouds, and hawks perched in nearby trees, screaming and swooping low at human approach. Surrounded by the vast sweep of prairie, the deserted homestead stood as a symbol of man's determination to cultivate these plains, and indeed the rich land produced some of the finest grain grown anywhere in the world. Colin Thatcher had bought this farm for his sons, Gregory and Regan, in the hope that, whatever happened to him, his children would uphold the Thatcher reputation as prosperous and successful farmers.

The five men tensed as they heard the sound of an approaching car. A small grey Mayfair (owned by Sandra Sparks, the secretary of the nearby Caron Rural Municipality and one of the future organizers of the Colin Thatcher Defence Fund) turned off the grid road and halted in the yard. Colin Thatcher got out, explaining that the battery in his three-quarter-ton truck was dead. As he and Anderson stood talking, all four SWAT members trained their rifles on Thatcher. The cops felt that if he discovered the stakeout, or Anderson's body pack, Colin Thatcher could turn ugly very fast. Constable McKee was listening to every word of the conversation on an FM receiver so that he could give a signal to the others the instant something went wrong.

Thatcher asked Anderson if he wanted to go for a ride, but Garry prudently replied no, he preferred to stick around. "Have to be awfully cautious. One never knows," urged Thatcher. It was the first of many times during the conversation that he would warn Anderson about the danger of being overheard, revealing his terrible fear of police bugging. The two men chatted about everyday topics—farming, their travels—until Thatcher suddenly asked, "Have you been hassled?" Anderson understood right away that he meant hassled by the police. "Well, they came once and talked to me and just asked me about the Chev car, and that was about it. Other than that, nothing at all. How about you?"

"Just the once, the day after . . . there's been some attempts to put us together and we should not be seen together."

The two men continued to talk intensely, walking about the yard as they did so. They discussed the "cheap stunts" pulled by the police to entrap Thatcher; the whereabouts of two men with whom Anderson and Thatcher had carried on shady business dealings a couple of years ago; and Thatcher's desire to get even with certain individuals who had crossed him. They also discussed the interesting matter of a car that Anderson had disposed of for Thatcher. "I had a bitch of a time getting the blood and stuff off," Anderson complained.

"Yeah. Is there no chance that it can ever surface? There is a chance it can surface?" asked Thatcher. "No," responded Anderson. "The car was cleaned."

At one point Thatcher asked, "Do you need some bread?" "Yeah, I can use some," Anderson replied. "I can use some for that car." Thatcher admitted he was strapped for cash at the moment, but he promised to round up some money. The two men agreed he would put it in a white envelope, which would be placed in a green garbage bag and then stuck under a weathered board near the abandoned farm's red Quonset hut. The date agreed upon for this drop-off was the following Friday, two days later.

After twenty minutes the conversation wound down. "Next time I see you, just give me that same sign," said Thatcher. "And there is no problem unless you do something stupid." "Okay," replied Anderson. "I'm glad you got her," he called out. "Okay," said Thatcher. The two men then got into their vehicles and went their separate ways.

As the sounds of the car and truck died away, Constable Jim McKee got up and walked over to the exact spot where Thatcher had been standing. He then turned and looked back at his hiding place; he could see the impression that his body had left on the ground. Colin had come within fifty feet of the policeman—so close that McKee feared Thatcher might step on him. "I was scared shitless," he told his colleagues, as they stood around shaking the stiffness and tension out of their limbs . . .

MAY 7, 1984

As he left home at about 7:45 a.m. and set out once again for the Caron area, life must have seemed brighter for Colin Thatcher than it had for a year: the weather was a little warmer, seeding operations on his farm were under way, and, most important, a lawsuit that had nagged at him for fifteen months had been decided mostly in his favour. He drove his pick-up through the old Moose Jaw neighbourhood where he had grown up, and out to the main street, which would lead to the Trans-Canada Highway. As he neared the major intersection, he saw a Royal Canadian Mounted Police cruiser, lights flashing, waving him down. Assuming he was being stopped for not having his seat belt buckled, Thatcher screeched to a halt. Almost immediately a second unmarked police car pulled up alongside the first. Sergeant Street of the Regina city police jumped out, strode quickly to Thatcher's truck, opened the door and told him to get out. Meanwhile two of Regina's most experienced and wily policemen, Inspector Ed Swayze and Detective Wally Beaton, had arrived. As the two unflappable cops walked slowly towards him, Thatcher glanced around in a manner that seemed to Swayze like "an animal trapped in a cage." Out of nowhere police cars had materialized to block the three other streets at the intersection. Other police in the vicinity had cordoned off the area to keep motorists away. There were even some Moose Jaw cops who had nothing whatsoever to do with the operation; they had come to watch history being made.

"Wilbert Colin Thatcher, I have an information here charging you with the first-degree murder of JoAnn Kay Wilson," barked Swayze. "Do you wish to say anything in answer to the charge? You need not say anything. Anything you do say may be used against you as evidence. You are entitled to consult counsel without delay. You will be transported back to Regina in the company of Detective Beaton." Swayze noticed that Thatcher's tongue had turned white and he kept swallowing as though the saliva had dried in his mouth. "He's in a state of shock," thought the policeman. Sergeant Street then snapped handcuffs on Thatcher. As he was being led to the police car, Thatcher whined, "Jeez, can't I even take my coffee?"

This was a man with a vivid, exaggerated reputation: a tough and wealthy rancher, a powerful, intimidating politician, a debonair man-about-town, and the cops arresting him were just a little awed by their prize catch. They were also extremely curious. For the last eighteen months they had listened to his telephone conversations which had been legally wire-tapped, and they had talked to anybody who had the remotest connection to him, including many beautiful and fascinating past and present lovers. They knew that this was a man who played entirely by his own rules.

The police had been informed that Thatcher had a loaded gun in his house and they were determined to avoid a shootout where he, a member of his family, or one of them might be killed. So they had put off his arrest for three days, waiting for the moment when he left his house alone and headed for his farm. They wanted to approach him at the edge of town, so that he would be out in the open but not in a place so secluded that he would prematurely catch sight of police officers approaching. And it had worked; they now had Thatcher under arrest and were taking him to the provincial capital, Regina, seventy kilometres to the east along the almost arrow-straight, four-lane Trans-Canada Highway. On the way, Thatcher chatted for a few moments with Sergeants Street and Beaton about his seeding operation . . .

By 6:45 a.m., on a mild June day, sixty people were lined up outside Regina's modern, utilitarian courtroom on Victoria Avenue. Ten minutes after the doors opened at 9 a.m. all eighty of the seats reserved for the public were filled. This public presence only hinted at the widespread interest in Colin Thatcher. The saga of his downfall and the horrible deed he was accused of committing had gripped the entire province, and millions beyond its borders. The fascination would continue unabated.

Thatcher himself would arrive each day in the back seat of a cruiser. At first he shied away from the media, attempting to hide his handcuffs from the cameramen and photographers gathered in a large intimidating knot at the courtroom entrance. But when this proved impossible he grew more defiant, shouting out retorts in answer to reporters' questions. For the next four days he would be forced to listen to twenty-five witnesses testifying against him, without the opportunity to tell his side of the story. It would be an excruciating test of strength for anybody; not once did Colin Thatcher lose his composure. Indeed hardly an emotion flickered across his set, grey face as each of the Crown's witnesses appeared and told his or her mournful but compelling story, each symbolizing a different aspect of Colin Thatcher's turbulent life.

There was Tony Wilson, JoAnn's dapper and coldly intelligent second husband. In the courtroom he would represent the violent matrimonial battle fought between JoAnn and Colin Thatcher. Wilson could barely contain his contempt for the accused, a man he considered a phoney, a bully, and a liar. "As long as I have known JoAnn," he told the court, "she has been, or she was, subject to a constant terrorization by her ex-husband . . . Any relations, any transactions that took place between JoAnn and Mr. Thatcher were the subject of extreme duress, constant pressure, constant harassment." Wilson had been called to provide a motive for the murder: he testified that as a result of JoAnn's death, Thatcher was able to postpone the payment of debt to his ex-wife. That, said Wilson, was the prime reason he killed her.

After he stepped down from the witness stand, Wilson stopped for a few moments in front of Thatcher's seat. There, for endless seconds, he glared at the accused with such ferocious hatred that time seemed to halt and everybody in the court froze in horror.

Glamorous Lynne Mendell, petite, blonde, and as thoroughly tanned as only a permanent resident of a southern clime could be, would symbolize Thatcher's taste for the fast-lane life of Palm Springs, California, where streets are named after Bob Hope, Gene Autry, and Frank Sinatra. Thatcher's lover for two years, Mendell had lived in his Cathedral Canyon condominium, had travelled with him on government business to Europe, and had provided him an opportunity for catharsis. Now here she was, nervously revealing all she knew about Colin Thatcher. She testified that when she asked him about his ex-wife's murder, he replied, "Well, it's a very strange feeling to blow your wife away." Every pair of eyes in the courtroom was riveted on her at that moment, as everyone wondered if she could possibly be telling the truth. Gregory and fifteen-year-old Regan, both in attendance, looked particularly aghast.

Garry Anderson lived with his mother on a farm near the town of Caron, and his very poverty highlighted the vast wealth of the nearby Thatcher farm. Anderson had always been in awe of his big-shot neighbour, and he was surprised when Colin suddenly had become so friendly. And now here he was, the prime police informer, slowly, methodically, revealing the plot concocted by Thatcher to kill JoAnn and describing, in his own unimaginative way, the criminals and punks involved.

But there was one witness who, although called by the Crown, might prove that Colin Thatcher could not personally have murdered his wife. Craig Dotson, a slender, moustached civil servant, was the only person to spot the killer coming out of the Wilsons' garage. Although it was 6 p.m. and quite dark, and although he saw the suspect only for a moment, he had been able to give a description to the police. Now he testified that the individual he had described looked nothing like Thatcher. This helpful testimony was ironic because Craig Dotson was director of research for Saskatchewan's New Democratic Party. If there was one type of political animal that Colin Thatcher had despised with a passion—indeed he had built his political career around this hatred—it was the wretched socialist. And yet the testimony of this truthful NDPer might prove to be his only hope.

On the fourth and last day of the preliminary hearing Thatcher abandoned his businesslike apparel and dressed in his version of country—plaid shirt, designer jeans, expensive suede jacket, cowboy boots—almost as if this persona would bolster his spirits the most. Once the evidence of the twenty-five witnesses had been concluded, the lawyers made their final arguments. [Serge] Kujawa's, typically, was so short as to seem non-existent, and Allbright's, also typically, was a lattice-work of sentences, which formed a final attempt to have his client discharged. Marion Wedge, an elegant and effective provincial court judge, did not even adjourn to consider the evidence. She simply said to the accused man standing before her, "I find that there is sufficient evidence to commit you for trial."

As he was led away, a policeman on each arm, Colin Thatcher yelled at the gathered media, "Eventually I'll be exonerated."

When Fact Meets Fantasy

CAROLINE HEATH

Saskatchewan, since the 1970s, has become a creative hotbed, known well beyond its borders for the number and quality of its writers. Caroline Heath, a perceptive editor and critic, was for many years the editor of Saskatchewan-based Grain *magazine and the first owner of Fifth House Publishers.*

IS PRAIRIE WRITING IDENTIFIABLE AS SUCH? Does it matter if it is? And is Prairie writing changing? It always puzzled me that *Grain* was considered a regional magazine, since only about a third of the writing in the magazine was by Prairie writers and many of them came from such places as Poland, India and New Zealand. Was it the name *Grain* (which never ceased to stimulate people's worst punning compulsions and invite misconceptions about the nature of the magazine) that made people jump to the conclusion that it was a regional magazine? Or was it simply the fact that it was published in Saskatoon?

When preparing submissions for circulation to my associate editors at *Grain*, I always put the editors' critique sheet at the end of the ms. and then tucked the covering letter under that. We wanted to approach the writing with as little extraneous information as possible. But as I read the submissions later I couldn't help trying to guess the geographical origin of the author and it was amazing how often one could tell.

It's obvious that Canada is comprised of regions and that they are quite distinct. It wasn't just reference to Niagara Falls or oil rigs that gave away the geographical identity of those *Grain* submissions. It was there in the obsessions, the stance, the tone, the language of the writer. Ontario became the easiest to spot. Always wordy, always taking a moral position.

Prairie writing most closely resembled Maritime writing—sparse, understated, ironic, flecked with black humour.

Certain things about Prairie writing have not changed in the last fifteen years. It is impossible to talk about Prairie writing (or Prairie art) without talking about landscape. It may be possible for a Torontonian, but not for a Prairie person, to be unaffected by sky and land and the elements, so this awareness continues to permeate our writing.

There may be, however, some change in the way landscape appears in the writing. We probably have fewer poems about gophers and grain elevators, generally less writing *about* the landscape, more internalization of the landscape and use of Prairie images as metaphor. But some of the best of this kind of writing was already being done ten years ago by Anne Szumigalski and Lorna Crozier, whose first book suggested this internalization with its title: *Inside is the Sky*.

Prairie writing continues to display an awesome reverence for historical fact. People are always asking the author: Is that a true story? And they don't mean true in an ontological sense, they mean *did it happen* and they don't care about the subtleties of fact being filtered through perception, etc.

Canada has earned an international reputation for documentary film. Documentary has become a Canadian fetish. It serves as a substitute for myth. I suspect this is the result of never having had a revolution, never having rejected our European antecedents.

Because Prairie society is so young, it only recently felt the need to document its history. The realization that its pioneers were dying set off a race to record the settlement of the West before they were all gone. This impulse to record and preserve, as seen in the rash of local histories that have been written in the last few years, has also motivated much of the creative writing done on the Prairies. The common form it took in the 70s was a quest for "roots." The *Best of Grain* anthology, published in 1980, opens with a spoof on this pursuit:

Roots

(This poem is not about Rudy Wiebe)
Rudy Wiebe, wiping the sweat from his brow,
calls a spade a spade.
He has a spade in his hands.
He is digging a hole near Winnipeg,
in the middle of a potato field.
He has blisters in his hands.
He has roots on the brain.
He is looking for his roots.

David Waltner-Toews

We're hearing a variation on the documentary theme now from women writers. "We need to tell our story," they say. These are often the stories of ordinary lives. Sandra Birdsell and Lois Simmie are both good writers, but I think they have been particularly warmly welcomed because they write with honesty and compassion about the ordinary lives of ordinary people, most frequently women. Sharon Butala and Merna Summers have been able to elevate ordinary, rural characters, despite their stark, routine existence, to heroic status.

The more traditional means of creating such larger-than-life characters has been to rely on historical figures, as Ken Mitchell has done with his plays on Davin and Bethune. The need for heroes, symbols and a mythology is legitimate; the danger lies in creating them artificially, either by borrowing the content from Native or European sources, or by forcing indigenous material into classical structures.

Eli Mandel's interest in mythology has provided an antidote to the documentary fixation, and Rudy Wiebe has tried to blend the two. But we are still working toward a true Prairie voice.

The man who has been talking most about voice in these last few years, of course, is Robert Kroetsch. Returning from New York, Kroetsch introduced young Prairie writers to structuralism and other stimulating ideas, and his influence as a teacher, like Rudy Wiebe's, has been profound.

It is in Kroetsch's poetry, however, that we can hear the Prairie voice most clearly. Kroetsch's poetry rings true because stone hammers and seed catalogues are powerful metaphors for the Prairies—of mythic proportion/significance. But the structure of his poetry also rings true. His use of silence/space within the poem recreates a key characteristic of Prairie speech. The loquacious storyteller is less typical here (at least among non-Natives) than the person who speaks quickly, in bits and phrases, often omitting the main point or not saying what he really thinks.

Some of our most recent writing seems less concerned with the search for an authentic Prairie language and form. Geoffrey Ursell's novel, *Perdue: Or How the West Was Lost*, bears resemblance to the writing of Gabriel Garcia Marquez. Bizarre occurrences are not unknown on the Prairies; it is the way this story is told that is foreign. *Perdue* is a clumsy, wooden construct, but it won the 1984 *Books in Canada* Best First Novel Award and I think that tells us something. It is a novel which retains the Canadian/Prairie preoccupation with history and fact, but breaks out of the documentary frame and allows fantasy to play with the facts. There must have been a collective catching of breath among the judges at this daring. (Never mind if it worked or not.)

Two short stories that have particularly delighted readers in recent years are Gloria Sawai's "The Day I Sat with Jesus on the Sun Deck and a Wind

Came Up and Blew My Kimono Open and He Saw My Breasts" and Carol Shields' "Various Miracles: A Roundup." Both these stories, like Geoff Ursell's novel, remind one of South American literature in their seriously playful rearrangement of our notions of historical event.

It is too early to tell what permanent effect this infusion of fantasy will have on Prairie writing. I don't like to see the link with reality severed in fiction, but we certainly needed to be shaken loose from a slavish devotion to fact, and Prairie writers in the future may have more freedom as a result of this infusion of fantasy.

Prairie poetry has been strong for a long time. Now fiction is catching up. In 1984, four out of five finalists for the Books in Canada Best First Novel Award were from the Prairies. In 1982 Guy Vanderhaeghe startled and pleased people by winning the Governor General's Award with his first book of short stories.

This is not to suggest that fiction blossomed overnight on the Prairies. Guy Vanderhaeghe's first story was published in Grain in 1974. He had been working in isolation for eight years, determined to develop his craft slowly and surely, when Macmillan accepted that first manuscript. But to the outsider it may look as if Prairie fiction has blossomed suddenly.

It's also noticeable that many of the new fiction writers are women and that most of them are writing short stories. For that reason, I responded to the suggestion that Fifth House should publish an anthology of Prairie women's fiction.

As I read the more than one hundred submissions for that collection, I noticed that most of the stories were about relationships (man/woman, mother/daughter, father/daughter, even the relationships between the laws of physics and human behaviour). Hence the title, Double Bond. It occurred to me then that women do tend to be obsessed with relationships, while men are more interested in action and its extension in time, namely history.

This would suggest that women write short stories not only for the practical reason that they don't have time to write novels when they're looking after children, but also because the short story lends itself more naturally to this often deep but narrow focus. Men, on the other hand, in order to show their characters' actions/effect on the world, need the scope of a novel. (I had thought of exceptions to this generalization before even finishing the sentence, but it may, nonetheless, provide a part of an explanation for the current explosion of short fiction by women.)

From my perspective, then, the most noticeable changes in Prairie writing in the last fifteen years (apart from the proliferation of writers, publishers, organizations and related activities) have been the coming to the fore of fiction, women writers and fantasy. Most Prairie writers are content to live and work here, and they continue to invite outsiders to teach and give workshops here. It is a healthy writing climate. The challenge for each writer, I think, will continue to be finding the voice and the form correct for him/herself and for this time and place.

Home

SHARON BUTALA

In 1976 Sharon Butala married a rancher and moved from Saskatoon to Eastend. As she struggled to integrate into a new and strange environment she began to write. Her fiction has given the people and the landscape of the rugged Cypress Hills area to world literature. The following selection is taken from The Perfection of the Morning, *her first book of nonfiction, a reflection on the spirituality of the land and environment, and on the crisis facing the rural community.*

AS I WRITE THIS WE ARE CALVING. In the past two weeks I've been present at the births of five or six calves, running to get equipment, helping get the heifer into the barn or corral, on one occasion narrowly escaping being flattened by a cow who'd decided to leave through a gate I was standing at, not yet having made up my mind whether to go in or stay out. Peter teased me about it, saying he didn't know I could still move that fast. I never get over the excitement of seeing that calf emerge, at that moment when it opens its eyes and blinks and its sides tremble with its first breaths of air. "It's alive!" I always catch myself saying in astonishment and joy, and "Welcome to the world!" to the little creature. If the grim inevitability of death is always present in rural life, so is the never-ending surprise and joy at the birth of new life.

I don't go out every day with Peter to help him anymore. We agree that my writing is more important. I am no longer as curious as I once was, nor am I as young. He has responded to this, as most people in the business have to the lack of help, by mechanizing as far as possible. I sometimes regret this, but I know now that I would never be as content, even as happy, as some of my friends and neighbors seem to be checking pregnant heifers with a flashlight in the middle of the night, pulling calves, driving tractors, balers or combines, pickling and canning and freezing food and in the evening playing cards or making quilts or crocheting or knitting or just visiting. I envy those who find contentment in these things, because in them, it seems to me, there is a calm, a sense of peace and of the simple rightness of existence from which, for whatever reason, I have been forever barred. Nonetheless, through working with Peter all these years and sharing in the joys and the trials of this ranching life, I had been gathering another, deeper kind of understanding about rural life.

The circumstances of our neighbors and acquaintances grew more and more critical and the talk everywhere—on the streets, on coffee row, at dances and family gatherings—grew more and more despairing. Loss was everywhere around me, fear, anger and an omnipresent, inexorable sadness at the destruction of a way of life several generations old and of the dream of the future that had proven to be unattainable. In the midst of the confusion and chaos and contradictory ideas going on around me, I tried to make sense out of the desperation of farm families to stay on their farms no matter what the price. I tried to see beyond the reasons they gave when asked: because they were too old to start a new life somewhere else, or because they knew how to do nothing else, or because they knew the virtual impossibility of finding work in towns or cities in the midst of a general recession, even beyond those who called on a moral right—this was my father's and my grandfather's place and nobody is putting me off it.

Clearly there was more to this need to stay on the farm than what was being said, no matter how true these reasons were. The more I thought about it, the more I lived the life myself, the more it seemed to me that the roots of the profound sorrow and genuine desperation of farm people lay in something deeper than these things. Because I had finally come to know a life lived in Nature myself, I began to believe that, at root, the basic loss to farm people was greater even than a loss of livelihood or a familiar way of life, as hard as these things would be to endure. The greatest loss, it seemed to me, was the loss of constant contact with Nature and of all that implied.

I didn't believe the hopeful prophecies that salvation was just around the corner and that soon everything would go back to the way it had been in the late seventies. When I heard experts prophesy about even bigger and better technologies which would save us, I shuddered, since it seemed to me that it was technology run rampant that had brought on the disaster in the first place. When I heard about corporate farms I saw only a modern-day feudal system where people would work the land for the profit of landowners whose faces they would never even see. When I heard about any ideas for saving the place which involved moving people off their farms, I saw only unlivable, dangerous megalopolis full of the poor and homeless—and an empty landscape.

North America, obsessed with the notion of progress and the technological means to achieve it, and increasingly urbanized, has failed to make a place for people on the land. Thousands of people, rural for generations, have been driven off it. We have raped our natural resources and despoiled them, overused pesticides, insecticides, chemical fertilizers and huge machinery to subdue Nature, and devalued the rural person and his/her way of life along with rural culture.

It seems to me unavoidably true that the plight of the farmers is directly related to the question of our need as a species to come back to Nature. If we abandon farms and farmers as we have known them for the last ten thousand years, we abandon our best hope for redefining ourselves as children of Nature and for reclaiming our lost souls, for what other sizable body of people exists in North America with their knowledge? There are only Native people left who have been speaking to deaf ears since their conquest from five hundred to a hundred years ago. We may at last be ready to listen to them, but the cultural differences—in particular, religion—make it difficult for many non-Natives to hear what Natives are saying. Increasingly we know in our hearts they are right, have been right all along, but we can't seem to find a way of implementing their knowledge, of blending it with our own beliefs into a workable salvation both for the land and for all of us as a species.

At the simplest level is the fact that all the values we cherish and that we consider to be the basis of our culture as a whole, and that provide for its continuity but that are difficult to keep alive in cities, live on in the country: tightly knit extended families and small communities, where the loss of any one member leaves a gap but where deviance is tolerated and doesn't mean a life on the streets, where interdependence is clear and cooperation thus a way of life, but without destroying self-reliance essential for survival in a sparsely populated countryside and in a harsh climate.

Country people understand how the world was built; it didn't appear whole and shiny the morning they were born; their fathers and mothers built it step-by-step each day. With only the most fragile and minimal of support systems rural people have learned to do everything for themselves: to build roads and houses and machinery and to grow crops to feed thousands as well as their own families. Even more precisely, each individual farmer knows his acres of land intimately, knows the weather patterns over it, knows what grows best where and why, and he knows intimately what the minute variations in the color of his crop or the way it stands mean and what he must do to rectify problems. No society can afford to wipe out the whole class of people in whom the practical knowledge laboriously passed down by generations remains alive.

Though we can't all live on the land, we have to keep a substantial proportion of us on it in order to reestablish and maintain our connection with Nature. Further, these people have to live on the land for a long time, they need a lot of time to come into tune with it, and to do so it is vital that they not be driven only by the need to feed their families and themselves, which always results in their disregarding what they know very well about the needs of the land, and to overwork it or overstock it with animals, or to plow up marginal land—that is, to exploit Nature instead of nurturing her.

It is unbelievable to me that futurists and experts at universities and in government don't see how important it is to all of us that a stable body of people remain in intimate touch with the land, and include it in their equations about the future. So far there has been no concerted effort that I know of by governments at any level to address the issue of rural depopulation in a creative way. Any efforts have so far been based on the unexamined belief that rural life and farming or ranching must be synonymous. As long as we pursue reasoning from this narrow foundation, given current market conditions and the prospect of more and more countries becoming self-sufficient or exporters of food, we are unlikely ever to find a solution that allows for a considerable, stable body of rural people.

Years ago an old man who had farmed and raised cattle on this land all his life, when we were speculating about the future for people out here given financial disaster and rapid depopulation, remarked that he thought one day there would be people on every quarter again as it had been during his childhood. I asked him how he thought this would come about. He had no answer, not conceiving of a mechanism that would produce this result, but when I asked he looked not at me but into the distance and repeated his belief. I couldn't forget what he'd said, because it seemed so clearly a visionary moment to me, beyond reason, beyond the facts. I thought he had seen something that was more than a dream, even if he had no logic with which to defend it.

Ideas for a new life out here are beginning to be heard: small, highly specific farms, medium-sized farms with a high rate of diversification, a buffalo commons with no farms at all, advanced, amazing new technology doing what we can't imagine, on enormous tracts of land, partnerships between urban families and farm families to produce food for a specific, small population, and numerous other vague and mostly unsatisfactory notions.

Much of this land, that which should never have been broken because of its marginal agricultural value, needs to be put back into grass and to do so will require money, time and a love of grasslands for themselves. Because of the extreme fragility of this landscape, any such project would require many years, probably more than one lifetime. I have no doubt that there are many people, from former farmers driven off their land to people aching to get out of the city, who would be overjoyed, if given a salary, good advice and equipment, to move onto quarter or half sections in need of reseeding and/or nurturing and to devote their lives to this project as stewards of the land.

I don't think the repopulation of the Great Plains will be easy, nor do I claim to have a clear notion of how to do it. But any such repopulation has to be based on a belief in what I have been saying, that in a renewed relationship with Nature as a people, and in a flourishing rural life, lies the salvation and the foundation of our nation. First we have to begin with the vision and with the desire; we do not lack the wit to bring it about; what we require is leadership.

Most environmentalists tend to be urban, and as Neil Evernden has shown in *The Natural Alien*, the only way they have known how to fight the corporate world and governments has been to put Nature in their terms, as manageable, sustainable resources, withholding the designation of value of another kind—its innate value—as the primary issue. This seems to me the same kind of mistake farmers made when they asked to be taken seriously by urban people by saying that farming was a business like any other business and that farm life was just like city life, except that it took place outside of cities. Those who genuinely saw it (as distinct from those who merely paid lip service to the idea) as such destroyed it. Farm life is overwhelmingly unlike city life in most ways, despite the presence of microwave ovens, dishwashers, and even the occasional swimming pool by farmhouses. True family farming has never been a business like any other business and ought never to be seen as such. What is best in farming and farm life is that it takes place, day in and day out, in the bosom of Nature.

I think of that old man's vision of a countryside dotted with houses and houses filled with families, children in small country schools, churches filled again on Sundays, weekend dances and entertainments, well-traveled roads, a vibrant, living culture flourishing far from cities. In his vision he sees this place as it was sixty or seventy years ago; I see it too, but I see a people with a different ethic than those of his childhood had.

I see them less poverty-stricken, less driven by the simple need for survival. I see them as aware of themselves as vital to the human community in providing the direct link to Nature our species must maintain. I see them as the preservers of a body of knowledge thousands of years old, as caretakers, stewards of the land, and maybe even, in a much better world than this one, as the wise men and women to whom others will turn for guidance and healing.

Notes on Contributors

MARIA ADAMOWSKA (1890-1961) was born in Western Ukraine and emigrated with her parents to a farm near Canora, Saskatchewan, when she was nine years old. As a young woman she began to publish poetry and articles in Ukrainian-language publications. She lived the last twenty years of her life in Melville and was active in local Ukrainian organizations.

EDWARD AHENAKEW (1885-1961) was born on the Sandy Lake Indian Reserve. He attended mission and boarding schools and was later ordained an Anglican priest. He lived for a time on Thunderchild's Reserve, and it is there that he and others crowded into the house of the old chief to hear his accounts of the past. After Ahenakew's death, Ruth Matheson Buck, a writer and family friend, found his notes, assembled them, and had them published under Ahenakew's name in *Voices of the Plains Cree*.

GARRY ANDREWS (1945) was born in Moose Jaw. He played football for the Regina Rams and the University of Saskatchewan Huskies. He signed with the Montreal Alouettes but suffered a career-ending injury in his first pre-season. He has graduate degrees from universities in Minnesota and Ohio and is director of education for the Prince Albert Roman Catholic Separate School Division.

ROBIN F. BADGLEY (1931) was born in Montreal and holds postgraduate degrees from McGill and Yale Universities. From 1959 to 1963 he taught at the University of Saskatchewan. He has been a visiting lecturer at Yale and Columbia Universities, and a consultant on health services to many organizations in North America and abroad. He is now at the University of Toronto as chair of the faculty of medicine's graduate department of community health.

ARCHIBALD BELANEY (see Grey Owl).

SHARON BUTALA (1940) lives with her husband Peter on a ranch near Eastend, Saskatchewan, a region that she has described in her fiction. Her first short story collection, *Queen of the Headaches*, was short-listed for the Governor General's literary award in 1986. *Fever*, another of her collections, was nominated for a Commonwealth Award in 1991 and won the 1992 Authors Award for Paperback Fiction.

WILLIAM FRANCIS BUTLER (1838-1910) was born in Ireland. As a British soldier he became an intelligence officer for the Red River Expedition against the Metis in 1870. He was appointed in the same year to make a fact-finding tour of the western interior. In his report he described the region as lawless, violent, and ungoverned, and he recommended a police force and treaties with the Indians. Butler's poetic travelogue, *The Great Lone Land*, made for even more interesting reading than his report. He wrote a sequel called *The Wild North Land*.

ROBERT CALDER (1941) was born in Moose Jaw and grew up in Saskatoon. After studying English literature at the Universities of Saskatchewan and Leeds, he joined the English department at the U of S. He won the Governor General's literary award for nonfiction in 1989 for his biography *Willie: The Life of W. Somerset Maugham*.

WILLIAM BLEASDELL CAMERON (1862-1951) was born in Trenton, Ontario. He was a young HBC clerk in Frog Lake on the fateful day in 1885 when young men from Big Bear's band killed whites at the trading post. Cameron was spared and later became a writer, serving as the editor of *Field and Stream* and contributing to *Harper's Weekly* and *Colliers*. He recounted the Frog Lake events in *The War Trail of Big Bear*, a book later reissued as *Blood Red the Sun*. Cameron returned to the North-West in the 1940s and lived the last years of his life in Meadow Lake.

MARIA CAMPBELL (1940) was born in a Saskatchewan Metis community located on a road allowance. She left home at fifteen and went to live in Vancouver, but later returned to the Prairies to work as an activist and organizer. She became a writer as well, and her autobiography *Halfbreed* was a bestseller. She has continued to write, but has also turned her attention to making films and remains an activist and spokesperson in the Metis community. She has been writer-in-residence at the University of Saskatchewan and has taught Native literature and creative writing in the university's department of English. She now lives in Regina.

MARJORIE WILKINS CAMPBELL (1902-86) was born in London but emigrated to Saskatchewan as a child with her parents, who filed on a homestead near Leross, north of Fort Qu'Appelle. She became an accomplished writer, winning the Governor General's literary award for two of her books, *The Saskatchewan* (1950) and *The Nor'Westers* (1954).

MURRAY CAMPBELL (1950) was born in Saskatoon and edited the student newspaper *The Sheaf* while attending the University of Saskatchewan. He has a degree in journalism from Carleton University in Ottawa and has been with *The Globe and Mail* since 1977. He has served as a general reporter and foreign correspondent and is currently a national correspondent.

GEORGINA BINNIE-CLARK (1871–1947) was born in Sussex, England. She was well educated and became a magazine writer. In 1905 she came to Fort Qu'Appelle to visit her brother, who had arrived the year before as a homesteader. She believed passionately that women could farm just as successfully as men. She purchased land, buildings, and machinery and operated her farm well into the 1930s, making frequent trips to England to speak and write. She lived in England during both world wars and died there in 1947.

ROBERT COLLINS (1924) was born on a farm near Shamrock, Saskatchewan, and served in the RCAF during the Second World War. He later attended journalism school and became a newspaper reporter and magazine writer. He has written more than a dozen books. His *Butter Down the Well* is a prairie classic.

FRANK CREAN (1875–1932) was born in Ireland and served in the Boer War. He emigrated to Canada in the early 1900s and in 1908 was recruited to lead an exploratory expedition to assess the suitability of northern Saskatchewan and Alberta for farming. He travelled throughout the region by canoe, horseback, and wagon in 1908 and again in 1909, and wrote enthusiastic reports both years. He left government work in 1913 and served briefly in the armed forces during the First World War, but he was discharged, allegedly for drunkenness. Following the war he lived in Ontario.

LES CROSSMAN (1913) was born on a farm near Rosetown. He studied at the Saskatoon Normal School and became a rural teacher. He has graduate degrees from the Universities of Saskatchewan and Washington. During the Second World War he served in the RCAF as a navigator in Halifax and Lancaster bombers. He taught English at Regina College and the University of Regina. He has had a story in every issue of the *Saskatchewan Historical Baseball Review* since 1984. He now lives in retirement in Victoria but spends part of each year in Saskatchewan.

HUGH DEMPSEY (1929) was born in Alberta and began his career as a newspaper reporter with the Edmonton *Bulletin*. He worked for the Alberta government and in 1956 became the first archivist at the Glenbow Museum. He retired from the Glenbow, as Chief Curator Emeritus, in 1991. He has written many articles and monographs as well as books on chiefs Crowfoot, Red Crow, and Big Bear.

JOHN G. DIEFENBAKER (1895-1979) was born in Ontario but as a child arrived with his family on a homestead near Borden, Saskatchewan. They later moved to Saskatoon, where Diefenbaker studied law and became well known as a defence lawyer, practising first in Wakaw, Saskatchewan, then in Prince Albert. He attempted to win elected office but failed repeatedly, until he was elected as an MP in 1940. He was chosen leader of the Progressive Conservative party in 1956, then led the party to a minority government in 1957, and to a landslide majority in 1958. He won another minority government in 1962 but lost in the election of 1963. He was replaced as leader during an acrimonious convention in 1967, but continued to represent Prince Albert, winning his thirteenth election to the House of Commons in 1979. He died the same year.

FATHER BRUNO DOERFLER (1866-1919) was born in Richfield, Minnesota, and worked on his family's farm until becoming a Benedictine monk in 1892. In 1902 he led a reconnaissance mission of German-American Catholics seeking farmland in western Canada. The Germans settled what is now the Humboldt area. The settlers were accompanied by a group of Benedictine monks who established St. Peter's Abbey, a monastery at Muenster, Saskatchewan. Father Doerfler was elected abbot in 1906 and presided over the monastery until his death in 1919.

EARL G. DRAKE (1928) attended elementary and highschool in Regina and later studied at the Universities of Saskatchewan and Toronto. He was Saskatchewan's assistant provincial archivist from 1952 to 1955, when he left to join the Department of External Affairs. He served in Karachi, Kuala Lumpur, and Washington, prior to being named Canadian ambassador to Indonesia, and from 1987 to 1990 was Canada's ambassador to The People's Republic of China. He is now adjunct professor at Simon Fraser University's David Lam Centre for International Communication.

DALE EISLER (1950) is a veteran Saskatchewan political journalist. He is currently editor of the Leader-Star News Service. He is a frequent contributor to Maclean's magazine, a columnist for Saskatchewan weekly newspapers, and a guest analyst on radio and television news programs.

GARRY FAIRBAIRN (1947) was born in Arcola, Saskatchewan, and raised in Winnipeg. He studied history and political science at Manitoba and Carleton Universities. He spent twelve years with Canadian Press in Ottawa, Montreal, Toronto, Regina, Calgary, and Washington, D.C. He is now the editor and deputy publisher of The Western Producer in Saskatoon.

JAMES GRAY (1906) was born in rural Manitoba and grew up in Winnipeg. He left school to support his family and for a time during the Depression he lived on relief. He worked for the *Winnipeg Free Press* from 1935 to 1947 and later moved to Alberta. He is best known for his vivid and popular social histories, all written after his retirement. They include *Booze*, *The Winter Years*, and *Red Lights on the Prairies*. He is the recipient of the 1995 Pierre Berton Award.

GREY OWL (1888-1938). Archibald Belaney was born in Hastings, England. As a child he became fascinated by stories he had read about Canada, and at seventeen he left England and lived with the Ojibwa in northern Ontario, with later stops in Quebec, Manitoba, and Saskatchewan. He presented himself as the son of a Scot and an Apache and began to call himself Grey Owl. His Iroquois wife, Anahareo, convinced him to give up trapping and become a conservationist. When he published his first book in 1931 his message of conservation led to international fame, especially in Britain. Shortly after his death in 1938 it was discovered that he had fabricated his identity.

DENNIS GRUENDING (1948) was raised in St. Benedict, Saskatchewan, a small farming village in the parklands near Humboldt. He has been a reporter for three Canadian newspapers, a television reporter, and the host of CBC Radio current affairs programs. He has written four books, including biographies of Emmett Hall and Allan Blakeney. He now lives in Ottawa.

STAN HANSON (1942) studied English and history at the Universities of Saskatchewan and Regina. He has worked as an archivist with the Saskatchewan Legislative Library and the Saskatchewan Archives Board and is currently university archivist at the University of Saskatchewan. He has been a director of the Rt. Hon. J.G. Diefenbaker Centre and is the author of many historical articles.

CAROLINE HEATH (1941-89) was born in Oregon and studied journalism and German at the state university. She arrived in Saskatoon in 1964. She became a founding editor of *Grain* magazine, and its senior editor between 1973 and 1979. She founded Fifth House Publishers in 1982, but sold it in 1988 after being diagnosed with cancer. Although Heath is best remembered as an editor and publisher, in the last two years of her life she began to write poetry of her own.

ANTHONY HENDAY was born on the Isle of Wight and at a young age became a labourer for the HBC at York Factory. In 1754 he volunteered for a mission to encourage distant Indian tribes to bring their trade goods to the British fort. His travels took him farther into the western interior than any white person before him, and his journal contains invaluable glimpses into aboriginal life at the time. Henday left the employ of the HBC in 1762 and probably returned to England.

A.L. (ART) KARRAS (1914) was born near Rosthern and moved to Yellow Grass, Saskatchewan, as a child. He spent much of the Depression living and working as a trapper in northern Saskatchewan. He left the trapline in 1939 and became a grain buyer. He served in the Canadian army during the Second World War and later became town administrator at Indian Head, then secretary-treasurer for the Cumberland Community College in Nipawin, where he lives in retirement.

DAN KENNEDY (1875-1973) was born in the Cypress Hills and given the name "Ochankugahe," which means Pathfinder in the Assiniboine language. The band later moved near Montmarte, Saskatchewan, and he was sent to the Indian Industrial School at Lebret. Kennedy later attended business college in St-Boniface, Manitoba. He worked for Indian Affairs, but later gave it up to farm. He served as chief at Carry-the-Kettle Indian Reserve in southern Saskatchewan.

DON KERR (1936) was born and raised in Saskatoon and teaches English at the University of Saskatchewan. In addition to being a playwright, he has written five books and edited seven others. He has been an editor of *Grain* magazine, co-editor of *NeWest Review*, a member of the board for Coteau Books, and a film and theatre critic. He was founding president of the Saskatoon Heritage Society.

RONALD LIVERSEDGE was born in Yorkshire. He came to Canada in 1926, following service in the First World War. Much of his time during the Depression was spent travelling the country looking for work. He helped organize the BC relief camp strike and participated in the On-to-Ottawa Trek. In 1936 he volunteered to fight with the International Brigades in the Spanish Civil War. Following his return to Canada, he lived and worked in British Columbia.

ROY MACSKIMMING (1944) is an Ottawa-based book and magazine writer and arts consultant. He is a former books columnist for the *Toronto Star*, and has also written two novels.

FREDELLE BRUSER MAYNARD (1922-89) was born in Foam Lake, Saskatch-ewan. Her parents were merchants who lived in several small towns and later in Winnipeg. She studied at the Universities of Manitoba, Toronto, and Harvard, and taught at the Universities of New Hampshire and Durham. She contributed to literary journals and popular magazines including *Reader's Digest* and *New Republic*. She later returned to Canada and lived in Toronto. Her book, *Raisins and Almonds*, tells of growing up as a Jewish child in small-town Saskatchewan.

EDWARD MCCOURT (1907-72) was born in Ireland and grew up on an Alberta homestead. He later studied at the University of Alberta and at Oxford as a Rhodes Scholar. After teaching at several Canadian universities, he arrived in Saskatoon in 1944 and began a distinguished career as a professor of English at the University of Saskatchewan. He was also a prolific writer of fiction, travel literature, literary criticism, biography, and radio plays.

JOHN MCDOUGALL (1842-1917) was born in Owen Sound, Ontario, and was ordained a Methodist minister in 1874. He was a missionary to aboriginal people in western Canada for many years, but worked on behalf of the federal government during both the 1869-70 and the 1885 Metis revolts. After retiring in 1906, he wrote several books, including *Parsons on the Plains*, based on his experiences accompanying his father, Rev. George McDougall, on missionary forays in the West.

IAN MCLEOD (1953) was born in Saskatoon and is a graduate of Queen's and Carleton Universities. He worked as a radio reporter with private stations and the CBC, covering federal and provincial politics and energy. He has also worked as a communications consultant for the federal New Democratic Party. He lives in Ottawa.

THOMAS MCLEOD (1918) was born in Weyburn, Saskatchewan and became a supporter of Tommy Douglas at an early age. In 1944 he worked as an economic advisor to Douglas and later occupied various posts, including that of deputy treasurer of Saskatchewan. He has a doctorate in economics and government from Harvard University. McLeod left Saskatchewan in 1952 for a varied career in Canadian universities, overseas development, and the federal civil service. He lives in Ottawa.

J.R. (JIM) MILLER (1943) is professor of Canadian history at the University of Saskatchewan, with an emphasis on the history of relations between Natives and non-Natives. In addition to *Skyscrapers Hide the Heavens*, he has also published *Sweet Promises: A Reader on Indian-White Relations* and *Shingwuak's Vision: A History of Native Residential Schools*.

JAMES M. MINIFIE (1900-74) was born in England, but at age twelve emigrated with his family to a homestead near Vanguard, Saskatchewan. After serving with the Canadian Expeditionary Force in the First World War,

Minifie entered Regina College and later became a Rhodes scholar. In 1929 he began working for the *New York Herald Tribune* and launched a distinguished career as a journalist. He served as CBC correspondent in Washington from 1953 to 1968.

ALEXANDER MORRIS (1826-89) was born in Perth, Ontario, and was a law clerk for Sir John A. Macdonald before serving in his cabinet. He was appointed chief justice of Manitoba in 1872 and lieutenant-governor of the North-West Territories in 1873. He negotiated four treaties with the Indian nations. *The Treaties of Canada*, first published in 1880, is his account of those events.

FARLEY MOWAT (1912) was born in Belleville, Ontario. He began writing as a child and has never stopped. He is a naturalist, an environmentalist, and a Canadian nationalist whose books and views are often controversial. He has written more than two dozen books and been published in forty countries.

RITA SCHILLING was born in Lac du Bonnet, Manitoba, and later lived in Winnipeg and The Pas before moving to Saskatoon in 1969. She has worked extensively as a freelance writer, columnist, researcher, radio interviewer, documentarist, and short story writer.

MAGGIE SIGGINS (1942) was born in Toronto and now lives in Regina. She has been a magazine writer, political columnist, television producer, and journalism professor. She has written five books and received the Governor-General's literary award for nonfiction in 1992. In 1995-96 she served as chair of The Writers' Union of Canada.

SIR GEORGE SIMPSON (1787-1860) was born in Scotland, an illegitimate child who eventually became governor of the HBC in North America. Simpson was a brilliant and hard-nosed businessman who travelled constantly, usually by canoe. He frequently had female travelling companions, usually young Metis women, whom he disparagingly described as "bits of brown." He had at least five children from these liaisons before marrying his cousin while on a trip to England. They lived first at Red River and later at Lachine, where Simpson entertained lavishly and invested shrewdly in banks and transportation companies.

DONALD B. SMITH (1946) was born in Toronto and is a professor of history at the University of Calgary, where he has taught since 1974. He became fascinated by the story of Grey Owl and spent more than twenty years documenting material for his biography, *From the Land of Shadows: The Making of Grey Owl*.

IRENE M. SPRY (1907) was born in South Africa and later studied in England at Cambridge and the London School of Economics. She taught economics at the Universities of Toronto and Saskatchewan and is now professor emeritus at the University of Ottawa. A humanist and activist, she was a member of the League for Social Reconstruction, the precursor to the CCF. She served as executive chair and later deputy president of the Associated Country Women of the World between 1954 and 1964.

SAM STEELE (1849-1919) was born in Upper Canada and joined the militia during the Fenian raids. He enlisted in the Red River expedition against Riel, and when the North-West Mounted Police was established in 1872 he joined the force, serving as a commissioned officer throughout the West. He fought a battle against the Cree during the 1885 Metis revolt. He later served in the Boer war, and was a commander of Canadian forces in the First World War.

WALLACE STEGNER (1909-93) was born in Iowa. His parents moved often, always in search of new frontiers. When their homestead near Eastend, Saskatchewan, failed the Stegners returned to the U.S., where Wallace became a professor of English and creative writing at Standford University in California. He wrote and edited dozens of books, novels, short stories, essays, and articles. His 1972 novel *Angel of Repose* won the Pulitzer prize.

R.D. SYMONS (1898-1973) was born into a well-off family in Sussex, England. He emigrated to Canada in 1914, arriving at Maple Creek, Saskatchewan, where he took a job on a ranch. He served in the Canadian army during the First World War but spent most of his life in the Prairies and British Columbia. He worked as a ranch hand, game warden, and homesteader but was also a painter and successful writer.

DAVID THOMPSON (1770-1857) was born in England and apprenticed to the HBC in 1784. While recovering from a broken leg in 1790, he studied surveying, and devoted much of the rest of his life to siting and mapping the western interior. He explored every major river system in the West, as well as the mountain passes into what is now British Columbia. Thompson left the West in 1812 to live in eastern Canada. When business failures left him in penury he turned to writing about his life and explorations in western Canada. His diary is considered a classic of travel literature.

SYLVIA VAN KIRK was born in Edmonton and studied at the Universities of Alberta and London. She is a professor of history at the University of Toronto.

NORMAN WARD (1918-90) was born in Hamilton but is most closely associated with the University of Saskatchewan, where he was a distinguished political scientist. He specialized in writing about the Canadian parliamentary system. He was also a humorist, and won the Leacock Award in 1960 for his book *Mice in the Beer*.

MARY WEEKES (1884-1980) was born in Nova Scotia and trained as a nurse in Boston. She moved to Regina in 1914 with her husband, a civil servant. She began to write short stories, then history, and after encountering the blind old Metis trader Norbert Welsh in 1931 she was determined to recount the events that he had described to her. Her book, *The Last Buffalo Hunter*, was eventually published in 1939.

SAMUEL WOLFE (1923-93) was born in Poland but grew up in Toronto, where he studied medicine. He interned in Regina and practised in several small Saskatchewan towns before continuing his education at the University of Saskatchewan and Columbia University in New York. He returned to Saskatchewan in 1961 and soon became involved in the medical-care dispute. When doctors went on strike in 1962, he helped organize an airlift of physicians from Great Britain to Saskatchewan. He left the province in 1968 and later served as chair of the department of health administration in Columbia University's school of public health.

J.F.C. WRIGHT (1900-70) was born in England but moved with his parents to Manitoba, where they established a homestead. He worked as a farmhand, bank clerk, and oilfields roughneck, but made his lasting contribution as a writer. He worked for several newspapers and wrote scripts for the National Film Board and served as editor of *Union Farmer*, a publication of the Saskatchewan Farmers Union. In 1940 he won the Governor-General's literary award for *Slava Bohu*, a history of the Doukobors. In 1955 he published a history of Saskatchewan commemorating the province's Golden Jubilee.

Permissions

The editor and publisher are grateful for permission to include the following copyright material in this anthology.

"The Saskatchewan" by Marjorie Wilkins Campbell, from *The Saskatchewan* (Toronto: Clarke, Irwin & Company Ltd., 1982). Reprinted by permission of Stoddart Publishing Company Ltd., Don Mills, ON.

"Henday's Journal" by Anthony Henday, from *York Factory to the Blackfeet Country: The Journal of Anthony Henday 1754-55*, Lawrence J. Burpee, ed. (Ottawa: The Royal Society of Canada, 1908).

"The Nahathaway and Chipewyan" by David Thompson, from *David Thompson: Travels in Western North America 1784-1812*, Victor G. Hopwood, ed. (Toronto: Macmillan of Canada, 1971).

"Fur Trade and Empire" by Sir George Simpson, from *Fur Trade and Empire: George Simpson's Journal 1824-1825*, Frederick Merk, ed. (Cambridge: The Belknap Press of Harvard University Press, © 1931, 1968 by the President and Fellows of Harvard College). Reprinted by permission of the publishers.

"Many Tender Ties" by Sylvia Van Kirk, from *Many Tender Ties: Women in Fur-Trade Society in Western Canada, 1670-1870* (Winnipeg: Watson & Dwyer Publishing Ltd., 1980).

"Recollections of an Assiniboine Chief" by Dan Kennedy (Ochankugahe), from *Recollections of an Assiniboine Chief*, James R. Stevens, ed. (Toronto: McClelland & Stewart, 1972). Reprinted by permission of the Canadian Publishers, McClelland & Stewart, Toronto.

"A Winter of Hardship" by Edward Ahenakew, from *Voices of the Plains Cree*, edited and with an introduction by Ruth M. Buck (Toronto: McClelland & Stewart, 1973).

"The Last Buffalo Hunter" by Mary Weekes, from *The Last Buffalo Hunter* (Saskatoon: Fifth House Publishers, 1994).

"The Palliser Expedition" by Irene M. Spry, from *The Palliser Expedition: The Dramatic Story of Western Canadian Exploration 1857-1860* (Saskatoon: Fifth House Publishers, 1994).

"The Great Lone Land" by William Francis Butler, from *The Great Lone Land: A*

225

Narrative of Travel and Adventure in the North-West of America (London: Sampson Low, Marston & Company, 1891).

"March to the Wilderness" by Colonel S.B. Steele, from *Forty Years in Canada* (Toronto: McClelland, Goodchild, Stewart, Ltd., 1918).

"Big Bear" by Hugh Dempsey, from *Big Bear: The End of Freedom* (Vancouver: Greystone Books, an imprint of Douglas & McIntyre, 1984). © 1984 by Hugh Dempsey. Reprinted by permission.

"Parsons on the Plains" by John McDougall, from *Parsons on the Plains*, Thomas Bredin, ed. (Don Mills: Longman Canada Ltd., 1971).

"Treaty Six" by Alexander Morris, from *The Treaties of Canada* (Saskatoon: Fifth House Publishers, 1991).

"Thunderchild's Conclusion" by Edward Ahenakew, from *Voices of the Plains Cree*, edited and with an introduction by Ruth M. Buck (Toronto: McClelland & Stewart, 1973).

"The Queen City" by Earl G. Drake, from *Regina: The Queen City* (Toronto: McClelland & Stewart, 1955).

"Riel" by Maggie Siggins, from *Riel: A Life of Revolution* (Toronto: HarperCollins Publishers Ltd., 1994). © 1994 by Maggie Siggins.

"Blood Red the Sun" by William Bleasdell Cameron, from *Blood Red the Sun* (Edmonton: Hurtig Publishers, 1977).

"Skyscrapers Hide the Heavens" by J.R. Miller, from *Skyscrapers Hide the Heavens: A History of Indian-White Relations in Canada* (Toronto: University of Toronto Press, 1989).

"Beginnings in Canada" by Maria Adamowska, from *Land of Pain, Land of Promise: First Person Accounts by Ukrainian Pioneers, 1891–1914*, research and translation by Harry Piniuta (Saskatoon: Western Producer Prairie Books, 1978).

"Quest for a New Homeland" by Father Bruno Doerfler, OSB, from *Quest for a new homeland: the founding of St. Peter's Colony in Saskatchewan* (Muenster: St. Peter's Press, 1988).

"Homesteader" by James M. Minifie, from *Homesteader: A Prairie Boyhood Recalled* (Toronto: Macmillan of Canada, 1972).

"Greenhorn" by R.D. Symons, from *Where the Wagon Led: One Man's Memories of the Cowboy's Life in the Old West* (Toronto: Doubleday Canada, 1973).

"Wheat and Woman" by Georgina Binnie-Clark, from *Wheat and Woman* (Toronto: University of Toronto Press, 1979).

"Exploring the North" by Frank Crean, from *New Northwest Exploration* (Ottawa: Government Printing Bureau, 1910).

"Boom and Bust" by Don Kerr and Stan Hanson, from *Saskatoon: The First Half-Century* (Edmonton: NeWest Publishers Ltd., 1982).

"Coyotes and Grain Elevators" by Fredelle Bruser Maynard, from *Raisins and Almonds* (Toronto: Doubleday Canada, 1972).

"Booze" by James Gray, from *Booze: When Whisky Ruled the West* (Saskatoon: Fifth House Publishers, 1995).

"Sapiro and the Pool" by Garry Lawrence Fairbairn, from *From Prairie Roots: The Remarkable Story of the Saskatchewan Wheat Pool* (Saskatoon: Western Producer Prairie Books, 1984). Reprinted by permission of the Saskatchewan Wheat Pool.

"Desolation" by Edward McCourt, from *Saskatchewan* (Toronto: Macmillan of Canada, 1968). Reprinted by permission of Michael McCourt.

"The Winter Years" by James Gray, from *The Winter Years* (Toronto: Macmillan of Canada, 1966). © 1966 by James Gray. Reprinted by permission of Macmillan of Canada.

"Dustbowl Baseball" by Les Crossman, from "Of Lost Balls, Booze, and Brothers," in *Saskatchewan Baseball Association Digest* (Battleford: Saskatchewan Baseball Association, 1985).

"Nature Conquers All" by Farley Mowat, from *Born Naked* (Toronto: Key Porter Books Ltd., 1993). © 1993 by Farley Mowat. Reprinted with permission.

"The Trek" by Ronald Liversedge, from *Recollections of the On-to-Ottawa Trek*, Victor Hoar, ed. (Toronto: McClelland & Stewart, 1973).

"North to Cree Lake" by A.L. Karras, from *North to Cree Lake* (New York: Trident Press, 1970). © 1970 by A.L. Karras. Reprinted by permission of Simon & Shuster, Inc.

"Tales of an Empty Cabin" by Wa-sha-quon-asin (Grey Owl), from *Tales of an Empty Cabin* (London: Peter Davies, 1936).

"End of a Legend" by Donald Smith, from *The Globe and Mail*, 12 April 1988.

"Sudeten in Saskatchewan" by Rita Schilling, from *Sudeten in Saskatchewan: A Way to Be Free* (St. Walburg: St. Walburg Sudeten German Club and Saskatchewan German Council Inc., 1989).

"Last Days" by Robert Collins, from *Butter Down the Well* (Vancouver: Greystone Books, an imprint of Douglas & McIntyre, 1980). © 1980 by Robert Collins. Reprinted by permission.

"A Hockey Legend" by Roy MacSkimming, from *Gordie: A Hockey Legend* (Vancouver: Greystone Books, an imprint of Douglas & McIntyre, 1994). © 1994 by Roy MacSkimming. Reprinted by permission.

"Tommy Douglas and the New Jerusalem" by Thomas H. McLeod and Ian McLeod, from *Tommy Douglas: The Road to Jerusalem* (Edmonton: Hurtig Publishers, 1987).

"Mother of the CCF" by J.F.C. Wright, from *This Time Tomorrow: The Louise Lucas Story* (Montreal: Harvest House, 1965). © 1965 by Harvest House.

"Wolf Willow" by Wallace Stegner, from *Wolf Willow* (Toronto: Macmillan of Canada, 1977). ©1955, 1957, 1958, 1959, 1962 by Wallace Stegner. Copyright renewed